Beth Chatto's
Woodland Garden

Beth Chatto's Woodland Garden

SHADE-LOVING PLANTS FOR YEAR-ROUND INTEREST

PHOTOGRAPHS BY STEVEN WOOSTER

EDITED BY ERICA HUNNINGHER

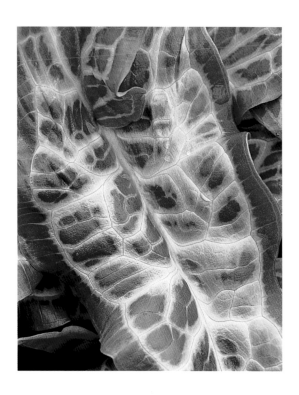

To MY STAFF

First published in the United Kingdom by Cassell Illustrated
The Octopus Publishing Group
2-4 Heron Quays, London E14 4JP

Text copyright © Beth Chatto 2002
Photographs copyright © Steven Wooster 2002
   except for those by David Ward on pages 16 & 17
   and by Howard Rice on page 35
Garden plan by Chrissy McDonald
   copyright © Beth Chatto 2002
Design and layout © Cassell Illustrated 2002
The right of Beth Chatto to be identified as the author of this
work has been asserted by her in accordance with the
Copyright, Designs and Patent Act 1988 (UK)

British Library Cataloguing in Publication Data
A CIP catalogue record for this book is available from the
British Library

ISBN 0 304 36366 9

10 9 8 7 6 5 4 3 2 1

Conceived and edited by Erica Hunningher
Designed by Nigel Soper
Horticultural consultant Tony Lord
Copyedited by Ruth Baldwin
Index by Hilary Bird

Typeset in Bembo
Printed and bound in China by Toppan

Above: In winter *Hydrangea anomala* subsp. *petiolaris* makes a pattern of bronze stems embracing the lichen-green bark of an oak.
Page 1: Primroses nestling at the base of protective oaks.
Page 2: The glossy, hollow stems of *Dicentra spectabilis*, bowed by horizontal fringes of deep-rose and white lockets.
Page 3: A favourite foliage plant, *Arum italicum* 'Marmoratum', with dark, glossy-green, spear-shaped leaves, veined with ivory.

Contents

Introduction

MOST PEOPLE HAVE SOME SHADE in their garden; it may be dry and dusty, or dark and damp; often it is a problem. Whether it is a bed shaded by a wall or fence or an area beneath trees or shrubs, somehow it tends to look dull. Plants grow tall and lanky, or disappoint by failing to flower, generally because the gardener is keen to fill every space with colour – with flowers, of course – and uses plants that thrive in open, sunnier parts of the garden. But plants are like people and do not take kindly to being thrust into any situation, any more than we can tolerate being pushed into any kind of job.

Fortunately there are plants adapted by Nature to a vast range of conditions and, by choosing suitable plants, we can transform almost any problem site into something beautiful. In shade it is possible to create interest in every season and such a feeling of peace and serenity that the area becomes a favourite part of the garden. Infinite possibilities are open to us: there are as many plant associations as there are melodies in music and ideas for pictures to paint. This is brought home to me from meeting and talking to many visitors who come to enjoy a quiet time in my garden and to learn more

Left: With ever-fresh moss, autumn's fallen leaves epitomize the cycle of life coming and going in woodland.

about plants – by observing them as individuals and enjoying the effect of harmonious associations.

This book is by no means a comprehensive account of plants suitable for shade. I write about those I know and am able to grow in my own garden, very much aware of the limitations imposed by our particular situation. As gardeners, the older we grow, the more we realize how limited is our knowledge, and our experience, and how we each have to discover what is aesthetically pleasing in our contrived associations, without losing sight altogether of the simple harmonies of Nature. In one lifetime I have touched only a small part of the plant world. Whenever I open Hillier's *Manual of Trees and Shrubs*, I marvel at the vast choice of plants available, of which we know so few. Fifty years ago my late husband, Andrew Chatto, and I sometimes spent a day or two at Kew Gardens, fascinated to look for unknown relations among familiar families, like holly (*Ilex*), Mountain Ash (*Sorbus*), Silver Birch (*Betula*) and rhododendrons.

Conditions vary so much according to the site, aspect, soil and climate that each of us has to discover, by trial and error, which plants will grow best in our individual situations. Here, in dry and windy Essex, average annual rainfall is generally around 51cm/20½in, divided equally between winter and summer, making us possibly the driest part of Britain. During the mid-1970s one year's total was 35cm/14in, and in several years in the 1980s the annual total was less than 48cm/19in. Between October 1999 and March 2000, we measured just over 23cm/9in of rain, very little compared with many parts of Britain. Generally, rain falls in light showers, rather than steady downpours, rarely reaching the lower strata, and in most summers, after weeks without rain in July and August, I am obliged to irrigate the Wood Garden, especially areas that contain 'mother' plants needed for propagation. In winter even small amounts can give a false impression, with mud and puddles everywhere and the soil surface soggy; but deep digging to, say, 1m/40in for trenches or fence posts reveals the ground beneath dust dry.

Global warming is disturbing weather patterns all round the world, and during the mid-1990s we had exceptionally high temperatures in July and August, reaching 33C/92°F, with winds from the Sahara leaving a coating of red dust over the cars in our car park. The rainfall remained the same, worryingly low. Since 1998 summers have returned to normal average temperatures, 18–24C/65–75°F, comfortable for living and gardening, and winters have become milder and wetter. In 2000 and 2001, however, we had exceptionally high rainfall. We did not experience the distress, as did other parts of Britain, of having our homes and farmland under feet of water, but none of us can remember seeing our land at saturation point, as it was in the autumn of 2000 when the rainfall for October alone was 16cm/6½in. As a result, bulbous plants were busy underground throughout the winter and many flowered early, whereas in past years snowdrops and daffodils were often late, and we prayed for snow to melt and trickle down through dust-dry soil to plump up their bulbs. In 2001 we recorded an unheard-of annual total of 95cm/38in of rain, so trees and shrubs, provided they had not been waterlogged (unlikely in gravel soil), benefited, and bulbs too. In low-lying areas, where water cannot escape freely, some herbaceous plants were lost from root rot. It has been a strange experience writing much of this book during a period when there has been no call to voice my concern over the effects of drought, normally a reliable occurrence, as our rainfall figures on page 215 show.

I try to follow Nature (not to copy her; we cannot do that in a garden), putting together plants which have similar needs in a situation for which they are adapted. Small variations in climate over the years have enabled us to extend the range of plants we grow. We have done much to provide shelter from drying winds in the Wood Garden, but because the soil is light and our normal rainfall is low, it is unfair to try to grow plants which need constant moisture, especially those which require cool air and high humidity. I am thinking of the lovely range of Blue Poppies, including *Meconopsis betonicifolia*, *M. grandis*, and *M. quintuplinervia*, which come from woods and shrubby places in the Himalayas, shrouded in mist, high up in the cloud layers. I have tried them all, loved and lost them. I have no wish to destroy any more!

Much of my north Essex garden is too dry and windswept for ericaceous plants but *Rhododendron* 'Sappho' has flourished in a sheltered corner.

Similarly, in this area of desiccating winds, I could scarcely consider exotic-looking rhododendrons, the mainstay of many woodland gardens. However, when we began the gardens more than forty years ago, I was a novice and excited by the possibility of growing some, especially in damp places near to underground springs. Most of these have survived and made large shrubs. *Rhododendron* 'Sappho', an old hybrid I first fell in love with at Kew Gardens, has done so well that we have had to cut it back to reveal its handsome framework of intertwining trunks and branches. Within a few years it refurbished itself, its branches reaching down to the ground, with every tip shoot holding trusses of wide, funnel-shaped flowers, mauve in bud, opening pure-white, wavy-edged petals, with a heavily speckled, dark-purple flare, almost black where the colour is dense.

When I began writing, I confined myself to describing the Wood Garden, perhaps because woodland gardening is a romantic subject (and title). However, the transformation of the derelict wood, which is on lime-free, gravelly sand, was by no means my first experience of learning how and what to grow in various types of shade – as well as what I cannot grow! Therefore I decided to include plants I grow on shady walls, in beds and borders in dappled shade, and in particular, to include the Long Shady Walk, the north-facing clay bank and the Little Grassy Wood. These areas are shown on the garden plan on pages 12–13.

For forty years we have been adding to the collection of shade-tolerant plants in the Long Shady Walk on the garden's west boundary, where the soil is mainly fine, black silt, and terminates in a north-facing clay bank. This gently meandering walkway, about 125m/400ft long and 2m/6½ft wide, has become a cool refuge for people and shade-loving plants. It lies beneath the canopy formed by a row of ancient oaks that grow at the top of a sloping bank and have formed part of a natural boundary between two farms for centuries. Rain falling on the gravel-based farmland finds its way underground to a spring-fed ditch and into the lowest, clay-based levels of the garden, where we excavated three ponds. Beyond the oaks lies arable farmland, virtually devoid of trees and hedges, where both east and west winds scour the land uninterrupted.

One of the first decisions, forty years ago, was to plant an efficient windbreak and, I have to admit, something to exclude schoolboys as well as rabbits, who enjoyed the peace and freedom of this wild patch. The soil being too poor and dry on the gravelly slopes and too waterlogged in the hollow to be worth farming, this area between my husband's orchards and the neighbouring farm had lain untouched for years. After we had removed the native scrub, elder, blackthorn, hazel and blackberries growing on the bank between and beneath the trees, our next job was to erect a rabbit-netting fence, buried several centimetres deep, with the base turned outwards into the field to foil determined scrappers. Impatiently I began to plant inside the netting, but soon found my young shrubs battered by the west wind which almost blew me over as it tore across the empty fields. For immediate shelter I bought many yards of Netlon, usually used for shading, and draped it over the wire fence, where it lasted for several years, long enough to help the young shrubs to become established as a windbreak. I planted evergreens to create a screen, both in winter and summer; among them is a Golden Yew (*Taxus baccata* 'Elegantissima'), laurustinus (*Viburnum tinus*), various cotoneasters, Common Laurel (*Prunus laurocerasus*) and a few upright conifers for contrast.

A few years further on, with more help available, I decided to pipe the ditch at the base of the shallow bank to carry surplus spring water beneath the new grass we had sown to make a broad walk. With the ditch filled in, I had room to plant a mixture of herbaceous plants and shrubs tolerant of dry shade on either side of the Long Shady Walk. Being fine, black silt, the soil is better than the raw sand and gravel I have elsewhere, but it needs plenty of compost to feed and help retain moisture. We add a crushed-bark mulch, but even so, in times of real stress in high summer, we are sometimes obliged to irrigate.

Many of the plants chosen to create the Wood Garden began life in the Long Shady Walk where, on a smaller scale, we have studied their needs and habits in the shade of trees, and discovered the problems they might make for us. Spreaders, such as *Symphytum ibericum*, *Pachyphragma macrophyllum* and *Euphorbia amygdaloides* var. *robbiae*, had begun to be invasive but, when it came to planting the Wood Garden, many of these throw-outs helped to clothe yards of bare soil. All gardeners at times have to be ruthless, to despatch some over-vigorous plants which threaten choice neighbours.

The Little Grassy Wood is a partially shaded patch of rough grass on poor, hungry soil beneath trees which covers an area of about 0.24 hectares/½ acre alongside the Wood Garden. Here I have experimented with bulbs and spring woodlanders which naturalize in grass that is neither lush nor vigorous, thinking it might teach us something and, perhaps, help visitors who have such an area, possibly a run-down orchard.

The Long Shady Walk and north-facing clay bank, the Little Grassy Wood and other smaller areas of shade appear as threads in the story as I write about the Wood Garden through the year. First I describe how we set about transforming the derelict wood into a favourite area of my garden – tranquil and yet full of life and interest in every season.

Beth Chatto

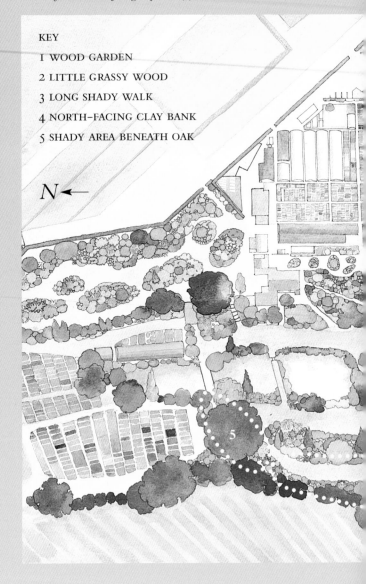

The Beth Chatto Gardens

THE PLAN SHOWS THE WHOLE GARDEN. The main areas of shade about which I write are the Wood Garden, the Little Grassy Wood and the Long Shady Walk, which at one end curves round to a north-facing clay bank and at the other is shaded by an ancient oak which keeps the sun off a mixed planting of shrubs.

Above: The area beneath the Great Oak (5)

Below left: The north-facing clay bank (3)

KEY

1 WOOD GARDEN

2 LITTLE GRASSY WOOD

3 LONG SHADY WALK

4 NORTH–FACING CLAY BANK

5 SHADY AREA BENEATH OAK

N←

Above: The Wood Garden (1)

Above: The Little Grassy Wood (2), *below: The Long Shady Walk* (4)

1 | Starting the Wood Garden

IN WINTER, MY MIND AND EYE ARE ENGAGED in observing the endless permutations of three living forms: the oak, the holly and the ivy. Familiarity sometimes breeds indifference, but in East Anglia, where only small patches of woodland have escaped the plough, these survivors of long-gone woods and forests, together with russet heaps of tumbled bracken, prickly cages of blackberry, a rope or two of wild honeysuckle and various grasses, form a small eco-system – limited, but harmonious. Apart from the grasses, all these were growing naturally in the small area, about 1 hectare/ 2 acres, that is now my Wood Garden.

When my husband arrived here seventy years ago to start a fruit farm, the area consisted mainly of young oaks rising above a scrub of blackthorn, blackberry and elder. Because the trees were never thinned, they grew long, straight trunks with few lower branches. Gradually the overhead canopy shaded out the lower storey of brushwood. The floor was mostly moss-covered; there was no grass. We called it Badgers' Wood since a family of badgers had lived there for many years, creating large mounds of sandy soil as they excavated warm chambers deep down beneath the tree roots. To our

Left: The Wood Garden boundary looking south to the neighbouring farm beyond the gate, where Booster hunts for his supper in long grass and Queen Anne's Lace. Four cats earn their keep by controlling mice and rabbits.

On a wintry afternoon in 1989 sparks and flames flare up from the bonfire as work begins preparing the site for the Wood Garden.

sorrow, suddenly the badgers vanished – perhaps they objected to us as neighbours as we developed the garden nearer their home. Next we knew, a family of foxes had taken over the sett and we had the thrill of watching young cubs tumbling among carpets of copper-coloured oak leaves.

We had always intended to preserve this area as a natural feature, to allow it to develop as it would, as a home for native flora and fauna, but then came the hurricane of October 1987. In one wild night Nature made decisions I would not have dared contemplate, twisting trees out of the ground like corkscrews, whipping off heads and limbs indiscriminately. It was a shocking scene of destruction.

Once we had stopped mourning the loss, I decided to make a new garden where, beneath green-lichened tree trunks, shade-loving plants would carpet the floor and groups of shrubs would create microclimates and backgrounds for herbaceous plants and bulbs that provide a long season of interest. I would not limit my choice of plants to English natives, since I felt the area was too small, and my life span too short. I would plant predominantly species plants from countries around the temperate world. Neither would I try to keep any country's associations together, but would combine, for example, American and Japanese shade-loving plants if they would set one another off, or would

prolong the season of interest. I would try to avoid anything which would look incongruous in this setting, or which needed plentiful rainfall.

With a mass of other work on the nursery and main garden to be done, it was a couple of years before our technical man, Gerard Page, who is also trained in tree surgery, went in to tackle the mess. He cleared the undergrowth and felled spindly or ill-shaped trees. We selected suitable oaks to save, so that only the best were left standing like pillars, their broken limbs pruned and tidied. Next, small tree stumps were dug out. Gerard used a tractor to haul out the bigger ones and to level the badgers' mounds and fill in their underground caverns. (The fox family had already fled.)

Once the site was cleared of everything but the columns of tree trunks, the area looked as clean and bare as an empty church, yet there was more than enough to provide the framework for a garden of shade-loving plants. The late John Bond, who spent many years as Keeper of the Royal Windsor Gardens, gave me *Quercus rubra* 'Aurea' whose young leaves are lemon-coloured in spring, hoping it would be protected from scorch by my tall, spindly oaks. He also told us to take out more young oaks, as from experience he knew how the overhead canopies would develop now that the remaining trees had less competition. (In later chapters you will see how much more

In spring 1990, cleared of debris and with a network of paths delineating planting areas, the wood looked as bare as an empty church. The wind whistled between the tree trunks, blowing leaves into the next village. We loosened up the earth, removed surface roots and spread barrowloads of compost and well-rotted manure over the sandy soil in preparation for planting.

What a transformation! But it was not difficult to establish ground-covering plants during the first few years, while waiting for the understorey shrubs to grow up and provide background and shelter. This photograph, taken in 1999, shows hostas, hardy geraniums, ferns and pools of blue forget-me-nots carpeting the floor of my once empty church.

thinning we have been obliged to do to maintain the balance between light and shade.)

I formed paths through the new garden by walking in front of Gerard, who used the tractor to push a wide scoop that we use for levelling nursery paths or collecting heavy materials. In this simple way we made the network of curving paths that delineate the planting areas. Little single tracks I made just by shuffling my feet. Since many of the ground-cover plants we hoped to grow in the Wood Garden would become stock plants for the nursery, we could not risk losing them in prolonged periods of drought, so we dug trenches along the two main paths to lay underground irrigation pipes. The 'soil' we dug out looked like the sand piles on the beach at nearby Frinton-on-Sea – just yellow sand and gravel.

When the earth paths had been rolled, we loosened up the ground around the trees, removed fine surface roots and added barrowloads of compost and well-rotted manure, as much as we could lay hands on. Because oaks tend to put down a deep taproot to reach moisture and their side roots make strong guys, we had to cut through more roots when digging generous holes for new plants.

The area was open to all the winds of heaven, and the leaf litter beloved of low-growing woodlanders was being hoovered into oblivion, so I planted tough shrubs on the boundaries to form windbreaks and both evergreen and deciduous shrubs between the straight boles of oak to create a protective understorey. As well as planting invasive spreaders from the Long Shady Walk to clothe bare soil, I used vigorous ground cover, such as epimediums, ivies and periwinkles, to trap leaves and create a suitable microclimate for a wide range of shade-loving perennials and bulbs.

TREES AND SHRUBS FOR SHELTER

The east-facing boundary of the Wood Garden divides the wood from our stock beds of drought-tolerant plants, which are exposed to full sun. Here, where a ditch forms part of the boundary, we have somewhat damper soil. I planted the evergreen privet, *Ligustrum* 'Vicaryi', which is possibly a hybrid between *L. ovalifolium* and *L. vulgare*, but with larger leaves, suffused with yellow in early summer, slowly fading to pale green. Attractive, lilac-like panicles of creamy-white flowers appear in spring, while in November the arched branches are wreathed with clusters of purple-black berries. It needs enough light to perform well, but that we have given it, fully exposed to the sun-drenched nursery beds opposite.

The privet's evergreen foliage provides shelter, and makes a good background for the intensely scarlet stems of *Cornus alba* 'Sibirica', known as the Westonbirt Dogwood. I also planted several other forms of *Cornus alba*, including the lovely yellow-leaved *C. a.* 'Aurea', and *C. a.* 'Elegantissima' with white variegation, and one of my favourite willows, *Salix × stipularis*, a native of Japan, introduced in about 1895. One would not immediately think of planting willows in dry woodland conditions, but once again, when studying the genus, I have been astonished at the variations in shape, size and soil tolerance. *S. × stipularis* forms a delicate-looking, medium-sized shrub, composed of graceful, olive-green branches. Soft-grey catkins appear in pairs before the leaves, quickly becoming suffused with red before the anthers burst open to show bright yellow pollen. This reddish tinge picks up the exact shade of some of the plum-coloured hellebores. The young leaves are narrow, like the catkins, a pale, tender green, tinted with bronze on first appearance, giving the shrub a light and delicate overall effect.

For the boundaries overlooking neighbouring farmland I chose tough evergreens, such as *Lonicera pileata* and cotoneasters, together with holly and ivy, Common Laurel (*Prunus laurocerasus*), Silver Birch, bamboos and a few *Rhododendron ponticum*. Among yellowy spring-greens I love the soft-lavender shade of these rhododendrons which I grew from seed, preferring it to the more typical mauve colour. *Lonicera pileata* is one of the toughest evergreens. I have learnt to value this underrated shrub since I discovered it will grow in the poorest of dry soils, both in sun and shade, always providing a healthy-looking, tidy background. Totally weed smothering, it spreads horizontally, gradually building up dense layers of branches, the lowest ones rooting as they extend. The neat, narrow, evergreen leaves are similar to those of *L. nitida* but larger and, although it is not suitable for hedging, I think *L. pileata* has a better presence. In spring I enjoy the effect of the new pale-green leaves contrasting with the background of mature foliage; while in sunnier situations, you sometimes find small, purple berries, translucent like glass beads.

Cotoneaster lacteus is a native of north-west China, where it grows in scrub. This handsome, strong-growing shrub tolerates my dry conditions, making a graceful, spreading shape, laden in winter with clusters of red berries. It needs adequate light to flower and fruit well. If left unpruned, its natural span is up to 5m/16½ft (not in my soil, however!), but it tolerates regular cutting where space is limited. We have planted it along a short stretch at the entrance to our drive, where it forms an impenetrable hedge, about 2.4m/8ft tall, kept trim by annual clipping in mid-summer, when the new growth is about 30cm/1ft. The shape of *C. conspicuus* 'Red Alert' fascinates me. It has made a wide-spreading framework carrying long, wand-like branches that are closely set with tiny, shining, dark-green leaves, studded with little white flowers in early summer. The resulting trails of red berries should 'look as if they were simmering like red-hot lava', according to the plant hunter Kingdon-Ward, who saw these shrubs growing over rocks in south-east Tibet. There is the rub, I have no rocks for my bush to clamber over, and it does not have enough light to encourage such good fruiting. (This is a good example of my disregard for the plant's natural environment.) We must find a site where we, too, stand a chance of seeing 'simmering flows of red-hot lava', but I still value it as an evergreen feature.

One of the first hollies I planted when we began the garden more than forty years ago was grown as a cutting, taken from a friend's garden, once part of a large estate, which had become sadly neglected when the means to care for it were no longer there. For my young daughters and me it became a tradition to go there to collect evergreens for Christmas. Cuttings from some of those decorations survive in my present garden, including two hollies and the Golden Yew. The first holly is *Ilex aquifolium* 'Myrtifolia', well-named 'myrtle-leaved', since it has the prettiest miniature holly leaves, glossy, dark-green, evenly edged with small spines. They were in perfect scale for decorating the Christmas cake. Although slow-growing, this tree, with judicious pruning, has made a tall, elegant shape that is ideal for small gardens. Incidentally, we have cut hollies to the ground, intending to remove them. Some escaped the mattock, strong shoots springing from ground level. We reprieved them and now keep them lightly pruned, continuing to appreciate controlled shapes and bright, new foliage.

I have already touched on the sensitive subject of unnatural-looking cultivars in my Wood Garden. It was a point on which Andrew and I were not always as one! I understood and sympathized with his opinion that they were aberrant. In the case of strong variegation, even if it had occurred naturally, in all probability it would not have continued to survive or increase in the wild. In the same way, among animals, any departure from the normal, in colouring for instance, can result in the poor creature being driven away, forbidden to breed. In making a garden we need to combine our limited understanding of what occurs in Nature with our desire to show plants to their best advantage, and to create pleasing pictures for as much of the year as possible. Again and again I write of the effect of contrast, both of colour and form, especially in shady places where we rely for much of the year on foliage. Sometimes there is a need for one or two really large, bold plants to offset a mishmash of small plants, which can look fussy. Such a place is beneath the vast, pollarded oak at the entrance to our water gardens. This noble tree, over three hundred years old, has a magnificent, umbrella-like head. Beneath it now the main feature is *Ilex* × *altaclerensis* 'Golden King'. It has made a wide-spreading bush in suffused shades of cream and green, beautiful all the year round. Its large, oval leaves are spineless, each with a different pattern, with irregular, cream margins and the centres looking as if washed in shades of light- and dark-green paint. A floor covering of ivy, contrasting with the largest-leaved of bergenias, *Bergenia* 'Ballawley', completes a satisfying picture.

I have planted in the Wood Garden *Ilex aquifolium* 'Handsworth New Silver'. It has more defined variegation, with glossy, dark-green leaves, narrowly margined with cream and prickle-edged. It makes a light, elegant shape in shadowy places. The other survivor from our Christmases of long ago is *I. a.* 'Bacciflava', the yellow-fruited holly. This will not be for you if tomatoes must be red, beetroots purple (there are yellow and white forms of both!), but I enjoy seeing the pendulous branches wreathed in clusters of bright yellow berries – unless the pigeons have found them before me.

Hedera helix f. *poetarum* 'Poetica Arborea', from Greece and Turkey, makes an interesting winter shrub propagated from mature arborescent growth. It makes a large, rather loose mound, but can be kept in good shape by pruning in spring. Unlike our common ivy with black fruits, it is smothered in late winter with clusters of green fruits slowly turning yellow, before being stripped by birds. We also grow beneath one of our ancient oaks the fruiting (or mature form) *H. canariensis* 'Gloire de Marengo' as a shrub. Normally seen as a colourful, evergreen climber, this ivy has large leaves marbled in shades of dark green and silvery grey, margined with white. Neither of these ivies produces long, climbing shoots, but each slowly makes a bulky, rounded shape.

EVERGREEN SHRUBS FOR THE UNDERSTOREY

Faced with a lime-free sand-and-gravel soil, but low rainfall and drying winds, I avoided the temptation to plant large-flowering, exotic-looking shrubs, particularly hybrid rhododendrons and other ericaceous plants that are normally associated with woodland gardens. I had no drawn plan but I knew I wanted to mix deciduous and evergreen shrubs to make the understorey, since leaf-losing shrubs by themselves can appear formless in winter, like dead brushwood, while evergreens remain full of life and energy, as well as making good accents. Harmonious combinations would, in time, not only create a comfortable microclimate for plants and people, but also have the effect of making the area seem bigger, more mysterious, by interrupting the wide, drafty aisles between tall trees.

Left: *Ilex aquifolium* 'Handsworth New Silver' is a feature all year round with its clean, cream-and-green variegation and is especially valuable in winter when it makes a lively vertical above evergreen carpets of epimediums and periwinkles.

For bold effect all the year round I planted three hybrid mahonias. I think they may have been selected from crossing *Mahonia lomariifolia* and *M. japonica*, and therefore have partially inherited the spectacular foliage of the former (which is none too hardy) combined with the toughness of *M. japonica*. So far, *M. × media* 'Winter Sun' has made the biggest, boldest shrub. Its elegant leaves, up to 60cm/2ft long consist of a central stalk furnished with pairs of spiny, glossy, evergreen leaflets arranged in whorls around stout stems. From the centre, usually in December, appear large trusses of small, yellow flowers, 25–30cm/10–12in long, reminiscent of Lily-of-the-Valley in their powerful scent and shape. *M. × media* 'Lionel Fortescue' is one of the first to open stiffly upright racemes of bright flowers, sometimes in November, its leathery, pinnate leaves 38–45cm/15–18in long. *M. × m.* 'Charity' has gracefully drooping leaf-stems, with lax racemes of flower, the latest opening to greet the first winter aconites, which make sheets of yellow beneath. When the magnolias are in flower there are already long strings of jade-green berries on *M. × m.* 'Winter Sun'. *M. × m.* 'Lionel Fortescue' has shorter strings of plum-shaped, plum-coloured fruits covered with a grey bloom.

The common mahonia, *Mahonia aquifolium* from north-west America, is certainly not considered among the choicest of shrubs, yet any fault lies largely with those of us who plant it in out-of-the-way-places where it produces leggy, suckering stems topped with clusters of leathery leaves, not nearly so remarkable as those cousins I have described from the Far East. Yet, wait a bit while I go outside on this bright, cold day in mid-winter to check. Despite having grown it for years, how well do I know it? Why do we so often take for granted too-familiar plants, rushing past on our way to see something else? The suckering habit does, I admit, make for a loose, open effect, but many carpeting plants grow comfortably among the wandering stems. Now the polished, pinnate leaves are simply beautiful burnished by frost, the dark-green background overlaid with reddish tones, brightest in the tip leaves. Overall this glossy, darkly ruddy effect takes me by surprise, as do the bunches of jade-and-purple, bloom-coated berries which follow spring's bright clusters of tiny, yellow flowers. When the prickle-edged leaves hold crystals of frost, the effect takes my breath away.

I was tempted by eucryphias when I saw them growing in my friend Pippa Rakusen's garden, near York. To my surprise and delight two have grown well and now flower regularly in the Wood Garden. *Eucryphia × nymansensis* 'Nymansay' makes a tall, columnar shape of glossy, dark-green leaves with finely serrated edges. In August and September it is smothered with pure-white, four-petalled flowers 5cm/2in across, alive with bees foraging among the red-tipped anthers. *E. cordifolia × lucida* has rounder, saucer-shaped, white flowers, each centred with the most delicate boss of reddish-brown stamens. While appreciating semi-shelter from both icy winds and scorching sunlight, these eucryphias need an open aspect to promote free flowering. We have gradually lifted or removed neighbouring trees as they have grown to demand more space and light.

Skimmias I enjoy all the year round. They need little attention, maintaining well-behaved, evergreen shapes, but will respond to trimming back when required. There are various cultivated forms of *Skimmia japonica* that grow in sun or shade. Among the many variants (some have white berries), we have *S. j.* 'Bowles' Dwarf Male' and *S. j.* 'Bowles' Dwarf Female' in the Wood Garden and the Long Shady Walk. They make small, compact bushes which are useful in smaller spaces. On the edge of our sitting area, beneath a tall *Magnolia × soulangeana*, I have planted both male and female plants to form a low screen where we can enjoy perfume in spring and berries later. The male has large, glossy, evergreen leaves and large trusses of creamy-white flowers whose perfume drifts on a still spring evening. The female has smaller leaves, crowded with red, holly-like berries all winter, still hanging on to them beneath the previous year's new growth when just about to flower. I particularly enjoy watching the development of the new berries. They form conspicuous clusters, green at first, paling before they flush pink, finally turning scarlet. Unlike holly berries, they are not attractive to birds until the weather becomes severe. Although they make relatively neat bushes, we keep them from becoming blowsy and unwieldy by pruning when necessary in March. We remove to the base old or shabby pieces and reduce the tops, not too hard but enough to leave a presentable feature while letting in light to encourage replacement branches.

Skimmia japonica 'Rubella' has smaller, darker leaves, with every tip shoot bearing conical clusters of mahogany-red buds accented by mahogany-tinted stems and petioles. A mature specimen crowded with flower buds to the ground is a heart-warming sight on a chill February day. Younger plants already look handsome in the Wood Garden, in open situations which encourage flower production. Surrounded by plum-coloured *Helleborus × hybridus*, this skimmia is at its best in bud, yet attractive still when it opens cream flowers.

Skimmia × confusa 'Kew Green' is a recent, popular cultivar, good-looking all the year round, forming dense bushes. I love it for its low, compact habit and glossy evergreen leaves, smothered with clusters of pale-green buds opening cream flowers and good, as is *S. japonica* 'Rubella', for winter vases.

Above: *Skimmia × confusa* 'Kew Green' is a delight for weeks in spring when it is crowded with dense clusters of pale green buds opening cream flowers.

Left: *Skimmia japonica* 'Bowles' Dwarf Female' provides colourful berries in autumn. Skimmias form compact bushes with leaves that are richly aromatic when crushed in the hand.

In April *Magnolia × loebneri* 'Leonard Messel' catches my breath when it flaunts delicate flowers against a background of leafless trees.

LEAF–LOSING UNDERSTOREY SHRUBS

I selected deciduous trees and shrubs for their garden-worthy qualities and long season of interest. These include magnolias, dogwoods, flowering currants, deciduous viburnums, a collection of lacecap hydrangeas, which I write about in high summer (Chapter 5), when they are so valuable in a woodland setting, and sorbus (see page 157).

Magnolia stellata, from mountain woods in Honshu, Japan, is slow-growing with me, making a twiggy shrub, flowering on the bare wood in April. Each flower is composed of a double row of narrow, ivory-white petals, with white stamens surrounding a green stigma, visited by little, black pollen beetles.

M. × *loebneri* 'Leonard Messel' is a hybrid, with *M. stellata* as one of its parents, so the flowers are a similar shape, but it is a stronger grower, forming an upright, open tree. It has long, slender, pink buds opening narrow petals, white inside, but as they open flat to the sun the effect from a distance is tinted pink, since you can still see the backs of the petals.

Cornus mas, the Cornelian Cherry, is not frequently seen in gardens. A native of central and south-east Europe, it eventually forms a large shrub or small tree, up to 6m/20ft tall. Where there is room, as in a wood, its open framework of bare branches makes a delightful screen through which to view the distant scene. It provides such a spring-like atmosphere, so early in the year, as every curving branch and twig is wreathed with puffs of yellow, starry flowers. I confess I admire this cloud-like effect almost

Above: *Hamamelis mollis*, the Chinese Witch Hazel, opens scented tassels of narrow petals, rolled like wood shavings, early in January.

Right: *Cornus mas*, a native of Central Eastern Europe, follows in March, with clouds of tiny yellow flowers forming a screen of blossom among dark shadows.

more than that of *Hamamelis mollis*, which flowers earlier. It took several years before the three specimens of *Cornus mas* I had planted began to think of flowering. They grew healthily but there were no signs of flower buds. One we moved, and the shock caused the plant to smother itself with flower buds, its priority changed to seed production in case of sudden death. It did not die, but neither has any of the shrubs produced a crop of fruit. Careful searching revealed an isolated, small, plum-like fruit which dropped off while still green. Perhaps our sneaky spring frosts prevent pollination. The other bushes we dug round with a spade, about 60cm/2ft from the trunk, to check the growth and encourage the production of flower buds.

Cornus mas 'Variegata' is much slower-growing, doubtless because its very attractive foliage, variegated cream and green, means there is less chlorophyll to encourage strong growth. For the same reason, probably, it comes into flower sooner. Quite a young shrub will create a haze of yellow flowers in early spring, continuing to be a delicate feature for the rest of the summer. Mine has now made a small standard tree, about 2m/6½ft tall, attractive in mid-winter with tan-coloured, peeling bark. Six years ago I planted at the entrance to the Wood Garden a group of the striking form of our native Dogwood, *C. sanguinea* 'Midwinter Fire', which is readily available in garden centres. One alone makes a feature; where there is room, three make a spectacular display (see pages 180–1).

The red-rimmed, drooping bells of *Helleborus foetidus* contrast with the veined leaves of *Arum italicum* 'Marmoratum'. These two much-loved winter plants look handsome for months and last long into spring.

Ribes laurifolium, although not an outstanding shrub, has value in winter, both of foliage and flower, in a mixed shrub planting, perhaps against a north wall where its sprawling habit could look well swirling across a path, or against steps, softening the hard lines. In the Wood Garden it took several years to produce something worth writing about. It slowly formed a low, spreading bush consisting of several layers of branches clothed their entire length with evergreen leaves, with clusters of pale-green flowers that in shape are like those of the well-known flowering currant, conspicuous against the glossy, dark leaves. They repeat the colour of nearby *Helleborus foetidus* whose pale-green bells give that same quickening feeling of life beneath the surface in winter. But I have seen a much finer version of this ribes in the garden of my artist-friend John Morley, well known for his collection of snowdrops as well as other choice bulbs. John's plant came originally from the garden of Amy Doncaster and is not commercially cultivated (please do not kill my friendship with John by badgering him for it). His single specimen planted several years ago against a wall is still only knee high. It is a very fine form with much larger and more conspicuous drooping clusters of pale-green flowers on less densely leaved branches. John had another, which could be the same as mine, but looked better because it was growing through another bush

which helped support the lax branches. I write about other flowering currants when they scent the air in February (Chapter 2).

Viburnum farreri (syn. *V. fragrans*) had a struggle to get going, preferring a moister soil, but deep, sandy soils enable plants to plunge their roots into cooler depths, and now my viburnums are growing reasonably well. They produce stiffly upright, shaggy, chestnut-brown stems, which gradually branch outwards to present a free-flowering, bouquet-like effect, making room for more upright replacement branches from the base. I also have the hybrid, *V. × bodnantense* 'Dawn', with larger clusters of much deeper rose-pink buds and pale-pink flowers, equally sweet-scented, and *V. opulus* 'Fructu Luteo', the yellow-fruited Guelder Rose.

No garden is static – the picture changes with each season from day to day, even hour by hour. In the ten or so years since we started creating the Wood Garden, I have planted more trees and shrubs (listed on page 186), which I describe as I take you to the awakening garden and share its unfolding through the year.

With a graceful shape and variegated foliage, *Cornus mas* 'Variegata' creates a focal point in spring and throughout the summer, retaining bright colour as the tender greens of early summer deepen to a more uniform shade beneath the developing overhead canopy.

2 | Awakenings

T HIS BEAUTIFUL SUNDAY MORNING in early February is the moment I have been longing for – to walk to the Wood Garden to see the picture I have been imagining throughout the winter, of aconites, snowdrops and the little *Narcissus* 'Cedric Morris' disappearing into the distance between the lichen-green boles of oak trees.

I walk with my back to the sun, feeling its warmth, but it is too cold to linger in the Little Grassy Wood to observe the cyclamen's endless variation in leaf patterns. So far it has not been a bad winter (no winter at all, some of us say) – only a few flakes of snow, the occasional frosty morning, nothing long-lasting – therefore soil temperatures have never been very low. This means roots and bulbs carry on developing beneath the surface throughout the winter and the garden awakes several weeks earlier than it did in the years when frost penetrated a foot or more into the ground, when you could not put a fork into the rock-hard soil until the thaw came. It is several years since we had such conditions.

It is a thrill to see among the leaf litter yellow drifts of winter aconites (*Eranthis hyemalis*) mingling with opening bunches of snowdrops. Neither was

Left: A sight to chase away the winter blues: sheets of yellow aconites, *Eranthis hyemalis*, one of the first flowers to welcome another year in the garden.

here ten years ago. A debate goes on in my mind as to whether I prefer to keep them in separate groups. I love to see an uninterrupted flood of one or the other – but then I come across a patch where they are mixed and haven't the heart to separate them. Perhaps partially intermingling drifts is the thing to aim for, avoiding a polka-dot effect.

Winter aconites I associate with my childhood, vying with my brothers to see who would discover the first one as we peered through the railings of an old, neglected garden. Because the soil has never become really cold, I can already see thousands of seedlings scattered around the parent plants; just two tiny leaves emerging from each seed that fell last year. Among them are two-year seedlings with frilly ruffs, which will make sheets of yellow flowers next year. I am delighted to see them spilling into the pathway: my light sandy soil suits them, but not all soils, it seems, are favourable. I must watch this invasive habit as the lusty foliage, before it dies down, might smother something more delicate later on. Where space will not permit such colonization I plant *Adonis amurensis* 'Fukujukai', from Japan, which flowers a little later, with semi-double, golden, buttercup-like flowers.

The Wood Garden is waking up but an icy wind is stinging my hands and face. Bending to pick a posy of snowdrops for the house, I marvel at their perfect shapes, marble textures. Later I arrange them simply in a small, pewter jug with black-strap leaves of *Ophiopogon planiscapus* 'Nigrescens', pink-flushed catkins of *Salix × stipularis* and tiny, young leaves of *Arum italicum* 'Marmoratum' ('Pictum'). By evening the warmth of my workroom has lifted the snowdrops' outer petals and they glisten under the bright light. Outside I can see a huge, full moon slowly rising above the nursery wall. I put out the utility-room light, unlock the back door and step outside to watch the moon flooding my little backyard with cold light, picking out the rope-like pattern of the now leafless vine, *Vitis coignetiae*, trained across the wall.

THE FIRST DAFFODIL

There is usually some competition between us to see who will be the first to spot the opening buds of a special little daffodil growing in the garden. We call it *Narcissus* 'Cedric Morris'. Almost always we are able to pick a few buds that will open for Christmas day. It was brought home from Spain more than forty years ago by my great teacher and friend, Sir Cedric Morris. This is how it was discovered. A friend of Cedric's, Basil Leng, a renowned plantsman who lived and gardened in Provence, was driving along a coastal road in northern Spain. Stopping to make a picnic inevitably meant botanizing among the grassy, rock-strewn slopes, and there he came across a little, wild daffodil he

Here is *Narcissus* 'Cedric Morris', just losing the distinctive green shading which marks the back of the petals, showing the exquisitely twisted petals and frilly-edge trumpets that form thimble-sized flowers.

had never seen before. It appeared to be the only one of its kind in the vicinity, so he dug it up, and continued his journey to join Cedric in Portugal. (Cedric spent most winters painting around the Mediterranean, to escape cold East Anglia.) After some years Cedric had increased his stock of this daffodil enough to be able to give me a bulb, from which our present stock has been developed.

The bulb produces very narrow, green leaves, the flower stems short at first, but continuing to lengthen until by the end of February they are about 25cm/10in. The flower is in perfect scale, a truly miniature trumpet daffodil, not dwarfed, which to me implies deformed. The lemon-yellow, pointed petals twist slightly around the frilly-edged trumpet, while the base of the corolla is stained green. It has not set seed with us, but I have a friend in North Carolina, John Elsley, who tells me it seeds freely in his garden. Perhaps our late frosts damage the developing ovaries, or prevent pollination taking place. In very frosty weather the flowers lie flat on the soil, but rise again, seemingly unhurt, after they have thawed out.

The bulbs increase slowly but after several years the clumps can be divided. It is important to choose the right site for them. They thrive in average garden soil, and in grass, provided it is not too coarse. They appreciate a dressing of well-made compost. Most important of all, they need protection from the narcissus fly which, in May, lays its eggs at the base of the leaves where the emerging grub can burrow down into the bulbs, eating them away to a hollow shell. To avoid this disaster, never plant the bulbs in an exposed situation, but beneath the shade of trees or deciduous shrubs, or alongside herbaceous plants whose leaves will provide protection. I offer this advice from harsh experience. It took many years to build up sufficient stocks to be able to offer this narcissus for sale. No sooner had I put it into the catalogue than we found almost all our stock bed had been devastated by this wretched fly. I can still feel those empty husks of eaten-out bulbs. This taught me to put all species daffodils in semi-shaded situations.

Basil Leng kindly gave me permission to name his discovery after Cedric Morris, and many years later I had the pleasure of taking a potful of this special daffodil to Cedric on his ninetieth birthday – he had by then lost all his stock.

UPLIFTING SNOWDROPS

Right: Snowdrops and cyclamen gleam against brown leaf litter and the dark-hued leaf rosettes of ajuga. In February sunshine the large, cupped sepals of *Galanthus* 'S. Arnott' flare wide open to show the strong, green arch at the top of the inner petals.

Merely the thought of seeing the first snowdrop pulls me through the dark months of winter. When the flowers start to fade, we divide the large bundles of established bulbs, replanting them in little clumps of three or so, and immediately I look forward to their flowering next spring. Left alone, one clump stays much the same, and some, such as *Galanthus nivalis* 'Viridapicis' (easily recognized by its distinguishing mark – a dab of green, like nail varnish, elegantly tipping the outer segments), produce fewer flowers, even die out, if allowed to become overcrowded. Splitting the clumps encourages the formation of new, strong bulbs. By continuing this process you can have sheets of snowdrops in a comparatively short time. I like to spread the more vigorous types far away into the centres of large beds, beneath deciduous shrubs, where they show up from the pathways, rather than stringing them like necklaces round the path edges.

Few snowdrops, in my experience, self-seed, but I am told it is possible to encourage seed formation in some forms by hand pollination. I haven't tried! But snowdrops are so amenable – after division, they flower cheerfully the following spring as if they had never been disturbed in full leaf, whereas bulbs

Galanthus 'Wisley Magnet' draws attention by its large outer petals, 3.5cm/1⅜in long, which sway from the long, thread-like pedicels.

that have been lifted and dried may take two years to recover; some never do, but pine away.

Snowdrops occur in the wild throughout Europe, from Russia, through Turkey, Yugoslavia, Germany and far south in Spain and Greece. Our common snowdrop, *Galanthus nivalis*, is not native to Britain but has become naturalized, and includes doubles. Porcelain buds open pointed petals, poised above narrow, grey-green leaves, all in perfect proportion. We all know special wooded places, ignored for the rest of the year, to which we make a pilgrimage in January and February to see them by the thousands, or even millions, smothering an ivy-carpeted floor.

Over many years species have been collected and hybridized, so now not only are there some really fine selections, but we can also have snowdrops in flower over a long season, from October to the end of March. Readers not yet infected with snowdrop mania may be astonished (and disbelieving) to hear that recently I read in *The Times* of a new snowdrop being found at East Lambrook Manor in Somerset, home of that great plantswoman and engaging garden writer, the late Margery Fish, thus adding yet another named form to more than five hundred already recognized. 'What!' they will exclaim, 'There are two types of snowdrop, the single and the double. *Five hundred!* That's mad.' So thought I, until 28 January 1975 when I took my first exhibit of winter flowers and foliage to the Royal Horticultural Society Show at Westminster Hall in London. On a small table nearby were pots and pans of snowdrops, differing slightly, yes, but uninitiated as I was I could scarcely tell one from another, until a galanthophile appeared and started gently to tip them up and show me their distinguishing features. The differences are often small, yet enough to have created an addiction in many collectors, which must seem incomprehensible to those not infected. The latest monograph presents 'a new look at the histories of more than 450 cultivars'! David Ward, my Nursery Manager, and I have a very soft spot for snowdrops, but we need to be selective, to grow the ones which make good garden plants and are distinctive. As well as those I describe below, a few more which do well for us, available from specialist nurseries, are listed on pages 196 to 197.

The snowdrop season lasts for many months. With me it begins in October–November with *Galanthus reginae-olgae* subsp. *reginae-olgae*, which we used to call *G. corcyrensis*. This grows wild in Sicily and Greece, enabling it to flourish in a warm, well-drained site where many other snowdrops would fail. Next I am looking out for *G. elwesii* var. *monostictus* Hiemalis Group a week or two before Christmas ('hiemalis' means winter-flowering). The typical species, *G. elwesii*, does not appear until February when I look out for its bunched buds reminding me of penguin beaks pointed skywards as they huddle together against the icy blast. G. 'Atkinsii' opens in January, before *G. elwesii*, and flowers to the end of February. Large, pear-shaped buds open to lift horizontally, like little helicopters, long, narrow 'petals', twice as long as the inner segments. It increases quickly, making strong, free-flowering clumps. We were unable to find a recognized name for the snowdrop that appears last of all, creating a snowfall effect in March with big, bold clumps of well-formed flowers on 20cm/8in stems, producing two flowers to each bulb. We called it 'Finale' but recently the name of *G. plicatus* 'Washfield Warham' has been chosen by the authorities.

All snowdrops give something special when held intimately in the hand and it is always worthwhile to tip up any unfamiliar snowdrop, since the green markings vary. Many have the bold 'V' sign, like green lipstick, at the tip of each inner segment, but in some the green may extend to the base of the petals, like a stocking. *Galanthus nivalis* 'Blewbury Tart', for example, is quaint almost to the point of being grotesque, compared to the classic snowdrop. This double snowdrop splits open wide from the centre to show overlapping layers of green segments faintly rimmed with white. *In situ* this overall green colouring makes it almost invisible, but held in the hand, or shown in a small vase, its upturned face looks not unlike a green double primrose.

An exceptional single is 'Mrs Thompson'. A large and fascinating hybrid, she cannot make up her mind, sometimes producing two flowers on the same stem; more strangely still, she sometimes has five large outer segments protecting four inner segments, suspended delicately on extra-long pedicels so that they hover, when wide open, shivering in the slightest breeze.

Among the many doubles I have a soft spot for 'Lady Beatrix Stanley'. She flourishes beneath the Great Oak in the Long Shady Walk and has increased so well, and has such presence, that she can be seen from the house as a snow patch far away. She starts early but stays into March. Her long, narrow outer segments are lifted like a hen's wings to shelter the neat, tightly double, green-rimmed centre. 'Lady Elphinstone', found in Cheshire by Sir Graeme Elphinstone, is smaller (about 12.5cm/5in tall) and of a more delicate constitution. She will surprise you with many layers of creamy-yellow petticoats, with here and there a touch of orange. Every year I tip up some of the heads to make sure they have not reverted to green. Newly planted bulbs have alarmed us by doing just that, but left undisturbed they have increased and produce a good proportion of yellow centres. Soil conditions may affect their stability; we grow them in acid sand enriched with compost beneath the canopy of an ancient oak, together with cyclamen and *Erythronium dens-canis*.

Galanthus plicatus 'Washfield Warham' makes vigorous clumps of broad grey leaves, above which dangle quantities of large flowers.

Above: *Galanthus elwesii* 'Cedric's Prolific' is a robust grower which increases well.

Right: If I had to choose one double snowdrop I think it would be *Galanthus* 'Hippolyta' with beautifully formed rounded bells filled with green-edged petticoats – until I look at 'Desdemona' and 'Dionysus'. It would be as hard to choose between these for preference as it is to describe them adequately. I cannot have favourites!

We grow some of the double snowdrops raised by H. A. Greatorex of Norwich and named after Shakespearian characters. Such names seem appropriate, since they make me think of full-skirted gowns, underpinned with layers of petticoats. It has to be said that, at a glance, they appear very much alike, all with neatly arranged rows of inner segments, edged with broad, green 'V' markings, but the gardener recognizes their individual mannerisms as a mother knows her children. The first to open with us is G. 'Hippolyta'. Long outer segments are folded round a fat bud, opening to show tightly packed petticoats evenly edged with green. Sometimes more than one flower is produced from each pair of wide, grey-green leaves on 20cm/8in stems. G. 'Desdemona' quickly catches up, with flowers on taller stems, 30–35cm/12–14in, held well above large clumps of grey-green leaves. She holds her outer 'petals' wide open, even reflexing the tips to show off green-stained petticoats. Both these forms increase vigorously and flower abundantly.

Some snowdrops have remarkable foliage. Most have fairly narrow, grey-green leaves. A few have flat, shining, green leaves. G. *ikariae*, a native of the Aegean islands (also from Turkey and the Caucasus), has short, bright-green leaves which curl back abruptly as if to make way for rather chubby flowers with dark-green markings on the inner segments, almost covering them. To my delight this pretty snowdrop seeds itself around. G. 'Washfield Colesbourne' stands out above the crowd, both for foliage and flower. It has exceptionally broad, grey-green, ribbon-like leaves, above which stand tall stems (30–35cm/12–14in), on which long 'petals' are suspended from a conspicuous, dark-green ovary, with the inner segments entirely green, edged with white, the reverse of most forms. G. *elwesii* 'Three Leaves' draws attention as each bulb has three broad, bluish-grey leaves instead of the usual two. Rounded, chubby flowers have inner segments almost entirely green.

The naming of snowdrops can be confusing both to experts and amateurs. We have recently learnt that the snowdrop we have long called *Galanthus caucasicus* should now be called *G. elwesii* var. *monostictus* of which there are numerous variations. Our form, originally from Cedric Morris more than forty years ago, has large, concave petals, their outer tips washed faintly green, sheltering inner segments marked with a dark-green 'V'. John Morley considers it to be a distinct cultivar. For the purpose of this book I propose calling it *Galanthus elwesii* 'Cedric's Prolific'.

We have a special snowdrop of our own. It occurred here many years ago, a perfect, globular shape and scented, especially when brought into a warm room. It opens its first flower almost at ground level, not very impressive at first, but slowly the stems lengthen and the flower expands. A second flower

follows from the same bulb, prolonging the season well into March. We are surprised and pleased to find that this snowdrop seeds true. Several years ago we sent it to a panel of experts at the Royal Horticultural Society to determine if it was already known. No one could put a name to it. My good friend Graham Stuart Thomas suggested it be named after me, and so it has been recorded as *Galanthus plicatus* 'Beth Chatto'.

FEBRUARY SUNSHINE

Already February is flashing by too quickly! We are into double figures, and can have tea in the daylight. It has been cold with winds mainly from the north-west but we have had more than our usual share of sunshine for this time of year. Too often we are submerged for weeks in winter beneath sullen, grey skies. Like a dustbin lid it feels, pressing on my heart, but when the low sun beams through and touches every twig, raindrop, bird's wing and my writing table, my spirits fly up like a jack-in-the-box, and everyone on the nursery is smiling.

It is Saturday morning. The garden is empty of people. (We are not open to visitors on Saturdays until the beginning of March.) The wind has dropped, the sun is warm; there is a feeling that spring is around the corner. The Wood Garden is alive with birds vigorously claiming their territory. Noisy blackbirds scrape frantically in the leaf litter, in the distance a great tit monotonously rings his bell and a robin drops on to the path beside me, hoping I might have brought a fork to give him the chance of picking up a worm. Overhead blue sky and mountainous, white clouds can be seen through a tracery of bare twigs and branches. Dried heads of the lacecap *Hydrangea macrophylla* 'Mariesii Perfecta' (syn. *H. m.* 'Bluewave'), bleached to pale straw colour against a shadowy background, appear to float in empty space. They are as effective now when every shape and shade is valued, catching my eye from far away, as when in fresh flower.

I am sitting on a plank bench, close to a straight-stemmed oak; its lichen-green trunk is swathed in the russet stems and twigs of *Hydrangea anomala* subsp. *petiolaris* still holding on to some of its lacecap flower heads, now bleached paper-brown, contrasting with a dense shrub of Common Box (*Buxus sempervirens*) which makes such a comfortable-looking mass of lively green behind the bare tree trunk. Nearby *Daphne laureola*, our native Spurge Laurel, found on chalk and limestone, has made low, evergreen bushes, about 1m/40in tall. Their tip shoots are crowded with clusters of pale-green, tubular flowers tucked beneath the dark, shiny leaves. Glossy-black berries will appear later in the year.

Above: The papery seed heads of *Hydrangea macrophylla* 'Mariesii Perfecta' glimmer like pale ghosts of summer on dark winter days.

Right: *Hydrangea anomala* subsp. *petiolaris* took several years to put down a root system vigorous enough to encircle the bare trunk of an oak with brown flaking stems. I appreciate the climbing hydrangea in every season (illustrated on pages 4, 129 and 164).

THE WOODLAND FLOOR

Although many plants and bulbs still sleep beneath the leaf litter, the woodland floor has endless patterns to catch my eye, formed by the combination of deciduous and evergreen plants. Robust stands of *Arum italicum* 'Marmoratum', with lush-looking, marbled leaves, emerge though trapped oak leaves. *Fragaria chiloensis* 'Chaval', a kind of mat-forming wild strawberry, makes carpets of neat, evergreen leaves. The drifts of snowdrops and aconites are enhanced by plants which keep good leaves in winter. With or without flowers, this woven-tapestry effect is very satisfying. I love to see living plants stretching across the brown carpet of leaf litter. Epimediums, burnished bronze by cold, but still well preserved, curve away from the path's edge towards the centre of a large area where summer plants are resting, where the hybrid *Narcissus* 'February Gold' will dance soon in seemingly empty spaces. The small-leaved periwinkle, *Vinca minor* 'La Grave', contrasts with frosty carpets of lamiums, while a pretty cream-speckled ivy, *Hedera helix* 'Luzii', throws a pale carpet between deciduous shrubs or spreads across a pathway. Some ajugas turn beetroot-red in winter; so does *Tellima grandiflora* Rubra Group. This handsome plant makes spreading mounds of round, scalloped leaves, green above, purple beneath, changing to rich red-purples and bronze at the first touch of cold. Above large, round, burnished leaves stand the glistening-yellow, bowl-shaped flowers of *Ranunculus ficaria* subsp. *chrysocephalus* and, in patches of low sunlight, the dark-brown, polished leaves of *R. f.* 'Brazen Hussy', discovered in a wood by Christopher Lloyd, will soon set off shiny-yellow flowers, before retiring out of sight in early summer. (I describe other celandines on page 207.)

All of these plants make winter landscapes to set off early bulbs, but I need to see collapsed fronds of deciduous ferns removed since they may smother them. Also last year's epimedium foliage should be cut down at the beginning of February to avoid shearing off the delicate flower stems that emerge well in advance of the new leaves. If the old leaves are left, you will scarcely see the crowded flowering stems – once they have been removed, you could be astonished in March and April at the hazy effect made by the tiny, columbine-like flowers in myriad shades from pale yellow or white to rosy pink or pale purple. I describe many of these much valued foliage plants on page 194.

Feeling chilled by a white mist seeping between the tree trunks, as I leave the Wood Garden I make a detour to an adjoining strip of untouched woodland to pick young nettle-tops and then to my vegetable garden to dig six good leeks. With two potatoes I have the ingredients for my favourite nettle soup, a beautiful colour, good flavour and very comforting.

Of the many different epimediums, *Epimedium* × *perralchicum* 'Frohnleiten' is one of the best in poor conditions (dry shade) for producing handsome foliage all the year round, with sprays of bright yellow flowers in spring, if you have revealed them by removing the old leaves in February.

Ice-coated buds of *Ribes sanguineum* 'Albescens' will open undamaged bunches of pale pink flowers (illustrated on page 64). If picked a few weeks earlier and brought indoors, they open pure white.

EARLY SCENTS

For me the scent of flowering currant, *Ribes sanguineum* 'Albescens', is part of the awakening garden. I like to pick long, curving branches just as the flower buds begin to swell. I bruise the stem ends, put them into a large jug with a few pieces of *Euphorbia amygdaloides* var. *robbiae* and stand it on a low table by a glass door opening on to my outdoor sitting area. Within a few days tiny, fan-shaped, pleated leaves will be unfolding along the bare, polished, brown stems, followed by drooping tassels of white flowers. In the Wood Garden these flowers will open pink, but brought on indoors they slowly unfurl from pale green buds to white, making an unusual bouquet for St Valentine's Day. Each morning I go to look at them, to see that more flowers have opened, the clusters lengthening. Some people find the smell objectionable; I have to sniff hard to detect it once it has settled down in the house, but keen-nosed visitors say, 'Ugh! Cats!'

Despite rooty conditions beneath a Silver Birch, stands of *Fritillaria imperialis*, the Crown Imperial, find enough moisture and nourishment to make increasing clumps of flowering bulbs. Later, when the soil dries out, the bulbs become dormant. At the base of the birch *Fritillaria verticillata*, with pale-green bells, pencilled inside with brown veins, are just going over. Lush green leaves of *Colchicum* 'Rosy Dawn' mark where waves of pink goblets will flow through this area in September.

The strangely pungent smell of Crown Imperials, *Fritillaria imperialis*, we suddenly catch on the air even before the bulbs have begun to thrust their fat buds through the soil. Another early perfume is the sweet, spicy scent from the fat, sticky buds of the Balsam Poplar, *Populus balsamifera*, wafted on the air from far away.

More mysterious is the perfume from a group of small, insignificant shrubs which you may not have noticed as you walked past, so modest are they in appearance. Then, several yards away, downwind, you are suddenly stopped by a curiously sweet scent, half-spice, half-almond perhaps. Turning back, you will see only low, box-like shrubs marking the entrance to the Wood Garden. Actually I have planted two species of Christmas Box, one on either side of the path. The first, *Sarcococca hookeriana* var. *digyna*, has long, narrow, evergreen leaves with purple-stained, young stems, so I am presuming my plants are the cultivar 'Purple Stem'. The flowers are practically hidden, tucked into the axils of the leaves. They consist of tiny clusters of ivory-white stamens and stigmas emerging from rose-tinted tubes of minute petals, held in reddish-brown calyces. The visual effect of this without a magnifying glass is minimal, but the perfume carried on a cold air-stream is powerful. This shrub comes from Sichuan and Yunnan, grows to about 1m/40in tall, and slowly increases, forming thickets. The other sarcococca I grow is, I think, *S. confusa*, known only in cultivation. It is not so tall, about 75cm/30in, and has glossier, elliptical leaves with wavy edges. The white flowers, just tiny tassels, are tucked into every axil along the length of every twig, to be followed by shining, black berries, many of which remain until new flowers arrive to push them off the following winter. This shrub does not appear to sucker. I value the foliage of both these sarcococcas, as well as the perfume, in small winter vases.

Viburnum × *bodnantense* 'Dawn' produces pale-pink, sweetly scented flowers on bare wood throughout the winter. Hard frost damages some of them but many more are to come and it is at its best now, before the leaves break. David Ward and I had never seen a fully grown specimen of this viburnum. Imagine our astonishment, once again in John Morley's garden, on coming across what appeared from his entrance gate to be a precocious apple tree loaded with blossom, at least 6m/20ft tall, towering over cyclamen and snowdrops. It is both humbling and inspiring to see what life might have in store for us, if we can live long enough. Before Christmas we may occasionally see trusses of flower opening on *V. farreri* (syn. *V. fragrans*) but now, in the last week of February, clusters of pale, almost-white flowers appear to float on the air, opening from rosy buds, adding to the spring-like scene begun by *Cornus mas* nearby, while a warm, still day brings out a sweet perfume.

LENTEN ROSES

There is something heart-stopping about the earliest flowers, particularly the snowdrops and Lenten Roses (*Helleborus × hybridus*). At this bleak time of year they evoke strong emotion, often more intense for me than the 'gaudy flowers' of summer. Is it because they return unfailingly with the coming of the light, their delicate beauty concealing an unshakeable life force? Or just that there is comparatively little else at this time of year?

Hellebores make an entrance by the end of February, taking over from the fading drifts of snowdrops. Odd flowers can be found on precocious plants throughout winter, a few, especially creamy-white forms, appearing in autumn. After planting they take several years to build up a large plant capable of supporting many flower stems. One has to have patience; but on an old clump, more than ten years old, I have lost count of the number of flower stems. For my first show in the RHS Hall at Westminster (25 January 1975), I dug up one of these great plants and wrapped its huge rootball in hessian (burlap) to make a feature on my stand. I discovered, much later, that you cannot replant such an old boy successfully. It is much better to divide up the rootstock, retaining the outside pieces which will have plenty of young root, and throw away the woody centre. Each piece will establish without fail if divided in either spring or early autumn when new roots are being formed. Replanted in fresh soil, they will take several years to make mature plants.

A spotted Lenten Rose, *Helleborus × hybridus*, with white flowers heavily peppered with pink and distinctive white margins.

We have been planting good forms of *Helleborus × hybridus* in the Wood Garden for the past five or six years. I am not experienced in careful and observant breeding programmes, as is my good friend Elizabeth Strangman, whom I first met more than forty years ago in Cedric Morris's garden. I consider her to be unrivalled in her understanding and development of hellebores in recent years. Her meticulous nursery of many rare species plants has been much admired by serious gardeners who, with me, will wish her good health and happiness as she has now retired from the demands of nursery management.

For many years I have been selecting hellebores which I considered to be improvements on those I already had. By this largely hit-and-miss method, David Ward and I have built up a stock of mother-plants of distinctive shape, colour and vigour, which are included in our catalogue and some of which are listed on page 199. We have not named them, but identify them thus:

'Apple Blossom' is one of many pale pink selections of *Helleborus* × *hybridus*. From groups of seedlings, flowering in their third year, we select those we like best, but all are seductive with subdued shades and degrees of speckling.

primrose-yellow, sloe-purple, wine-red, speckled-white, apple-blossom and so on. These are propagated vegetatively to enable visitors to obtain exactly the same plants they may have seen in the garden. Unworthy plants – those with poor shape or weak colour – are scrapped, but on the whole what is a worthless hellebore? Such is their subtle charm, you might reach out eagerly for something we decide to dump!

The very dark, almost black-purples with a grey patina are highly sought after, and are indeed curiously magnetic when you stoop to tip up their faces and see the pale-cream stamens sheltering there, but like other dark flowers (I am thinking of some of the Mediterranean fritillaries) they are almost lost in the garden, fading into the dark tones of the soil. I have used Spring Snowflake, *Leucojum vernum* var. *vagneri*, to draw attention to one of our darkest selections, a sloe-black-purple, filled with cream stamens. We also plant them among pale ground cover, perhaps the silver-leaved *Lamium maculatum* 'White Nancy', or the yellow-leaved comfrey, *Symphytum* 'Goldsmith', which is now thrusting carpets of bright, new leaves through bare soil.

We sometimes hear visitors wishing the hellebores would not droop their

A pale green form of *Helleborus* × *hybridus* planted beneath catkin-like flowers of *Corylopsis glabrescens* var. *gotoana* and the warm tones of *Spiraea japonica* 'Goldflame' in the background.

heads; indeed some breeders are doing their best to develop upright forms, but I have never lost the thrill of tipping up these modest flower heads to marvel at the diversity of freckling and shading. Elizabeth Strangman has bred a beautiful strain with white, red-rimmed, cup-shaped flowers veined both on the back and the inside, where wine-coloured, capillary-like veins lead down into a ring of dark nectaries. Heavenly! Doubles are beginning to flow like a tide from several specialist nurseries, many I suspect originating from Elizabeth's work. We have not been immune, and have added some of her blood to our stock, but although I can admire the doubles, none has the heart-stopping perfection of single flowers.

As I look around the Wood Garden I see green selections of *H.* × *hybridus* making clumps, all attractive, in various shades of green. They probably have as parents two species, *H. viridis* subsp. *occidentalis* and *H. odorus*. I particularly admire *H. odorus* with large, apple-green, flat-faced flowers, while *H. viridis*, although smaller, has cup-shaped flowers lined with a faint bluish tinge. One of the earliest *H.* × *hybridus*, most welcome in mid-January, belongs to the Kochii Group. The plant we have selected produces quantities of short,

I have seen *Helleborus argutifolius* growing wild in openings in the Sweet Chestnut woods of Corsica. Its great heads of lime-green flowers illuminate the garden for months, from late winter until the seedpods are bursting in early summer.

branching stems carrying nodding buds which open small, shallow saucers of primrose-yellow. This possibly is a parent of some of the very fine, almost lemon-yellow forms now available.

Perhaps the most dramatic of all the hellebores is *H. × nigercors*. It is much admired for its large, open-faced flowers looking up to the sky. Having as parents *H. niger* and *H. argutifolius* (*corsicus*), it produces several stems like *H. argutifolius*, bearing multiple heads of green-shadowed, white flowers, the same shape as those of *H. niger*, the backs of the flowers tinged with bronze as they mature. Well-grown plants produce eight or ten stems, about 30cm/1ft tall, each carrying large trusses of flower, with new buds opening to carry the display over many weeks; still handsome well into spring. Unfortunately this cross is sterile. We propagate it by division, or the cross can be made again by hand pollination. *Helleborus argutifolius* flourishes almost anywhere in the garden, in both semi-shade or full sunlight, but in my experience does best in free-draining soil with additional compost. Each spring it produces many stiff stems, clothed in claw-shaped foliage of cool jade-green. The following winter these tend to fall out from the centre like the spokes of a wheel to make way for the next season's shoots. By January every stem carries a large cluster of jade-green, cup-shaped flowers forming an irregular garland around the imaginary rim of my wheel, remaining handsome well into May. The effect of tying up these wayward stems is, I think, disastrous. Just a little ingenuity is needed to place the plants to their advantage, perhaps on a bank where they can flop among ground-cover plants, and where their handsome foliage in summer will create a focal point above a medley of carpeters. Our old friend *Helleborus foetidus* still makes its mark in mid-March through to May, though by then it is forming seed pods.

All hellebores are liable to be attacked by a fungus disease, botrytis, which causes a kind of breakdown in the leaf surfaces, resulting in ugly, black blotches. We cut off the leaves of *H. × hybridus* before Christmas, even if they look healthy. They will have done their work of feeding the rootstock by then. Removing them will prevent infection attacking the flower stems and newly emerging leaves in spring.

A bowl of mixed hellebores selected from seedlings.

As I leave the wood with a bucket of hellebore flowers, I stop at the vegetable garden to gather salad. My late-winter salads are some of the most exciting of all the year. Although we are subject to very cold winds from across the sea, our light soil is an advantage, while shelter made from hoops covered with polythene is enough protection, especially in recent mild winters. A few degrees of frost under cover does less harm than alternate wetting and freezing.

Back in the kitchen, the hellebore flower heads are quickly arranged in a flat bowl, with a few marbled leaves of arum to set off their faces looking up at me like an end-of-term school photograph. The salad repeats exactly the rich colours of the hellebores. A narrow-leaved chicory, 'Rossa di Treviso', turns wondrous shades of ruby and plum, the innermost hearts pale-rose and tender. 'Pain de Sucre' (Sugar Loaf) makes large plants shaped like a fat cos lettuce, continuing to grow throughout winter to make tight hearts of folded leaves, reminding me, as I unwrap them, of permanently pleated fabric. These inner leaves are blanched to the colour of primroses, exactly the same shade as some of our hellebores, while the centre of each crumpled leaf is glistening ivory. Next in my salad bowl I put the deeply cut leaves of rocket, *Eruca vesicaria* subsp. *sativa*, and small, hot-tasting, teaspoon-sized leaves of Mega Cress (*Lepidum sativum*), both of which add vibrant green. What a luxury to brighten the dark evening with such colour, and to be able to grow such good things to eat! (*Not* the hellebores: they *are* harmful if eaten.)

3 | Spring Enchantment

I<small>T IS A CALM</small> M<small>ARCH EVENING</small>, the air full of bird song – blackbird, robin, chiffchaff and a green woodpecker yaffling in the distance. In the blink of an eye we have passed from winter gloom and cold to such a quantity of flowers. Amelanchiers and flowering currants form graceful fountains of delicate colour here and there among the largely leafless trees and shrubs, perfect in scale and tone, lifting the eye above early-flowering bulbs. Young forget-me-nots (*Myosotis sylvatica*), seeded in places along the path edges and beneath deciduous shrubs, often where I would not think of planting them, make waves of green that will turn sky-blue in April and May. Most of the snowdrops are over, but the late form, *Galanthus plicatus* 'Washfield Warham' (which we originally called 'Finale'), is at its best, a really good garden plant, making vigorous clumps of broad, grey leaves above which dangle quantities of large flowers.

Young stems and unfolding, crumpled leaves of peonies are bursting through the soil. I enjoy every stage of their development, especially the Caucasian beauty, *Paeonia mlokosewitschii*, familiarly known as Molly the Witch. Its pinkish-bronze stems and emerging leaves are in rich contrast to the pool

Left: The Caucasian wild peony, *Paeonia mlokosewitschii*, is a joy to watch every day through all its stages of development, from the moment the pinkish-bronze stems burst through the soil until the mature, grey-green foliage sets off the beauty of round flower buds that unfurl pale-yellow, silk-textured petals (illustrated on pages 80 and 109).

Above: This pulmonaria was found as a seedling in the garden by my nursery manager who cherished it and found that the variegation remained stable, so we have named it after him *Pulmonaria rubra* 'David Ward'.

Right: A glimpse of the Little Grassy Wood in April, with forms of the wild Wood Anemone, *A. nemorosa*, creating pools of pale blue and white, studded with cream and white narcissi, including *Narcissus* 'Jenny' and *N.* 'Thalia'. Seedlings of *Fritillaria meleagris* are beginning to form little colonies.

of deep, pure blue formed by *Scilla siberica* seeded freely among the peony clumps. Nearby a dark-plum-purple form of *Helleborus* × *hybridus* adds yet another exotic tone to this picture.

Soon waves and ripples of yellow daffodils will flow between the tree trunks, lighting up the wood floor. Emerging with them is *Milium effusum* 'Aureum', Bowles' Golden Grass, whose delicate foliage is almost the same colour and, from a distance, looks like patches of sunlight between the leafless trees. It has spread by seedlings, easily identified and removed if you have too many, but as the cover plants develop you need to watch to make sure there will still be enough spaces for such welcome seedlings to find a home.

The pulmonarias (lungworts), among the first plants to open an eye, regardless of weather, are slowly unrolling funnel-shaped flowers from dense terminal clusters of buds. Those of *Pulmonaria officinalis*, the old garden species commonly called Soldiers and Sailors, fade from pink to light lilac-blue, but varying clones and interbred seedlings make for considerable variation in foliage, and flower colour ranges from pure white and pale blue to gentian blue and deepest pink. At this time of year the leaves are small, all along the flowering stems, and are best cut down as the flowers fade to make way for the basal rosettes of leaves which continue to grow and form a feature throughout the summer. The foliage is generally dark-green, bristly and variously spotted in shades of lighter green or pale grey, sometimes totally silvered. *P. rubra* 'David Ward', for example, forms huge, flower-like rosettes of long, pale-green leaves with wide, white margins; its coral red flowers appear from March to April. (I describe some other good pulmonarias on pages 206-7). All prefer leaf-mould soil in full or part-shade among shrubs, at the front of the border or on a grassy bank. In dry conditions they are prone to attack by mildew, which disfigures the handsome basal foliage that can provide such a valuable feature later in the year. Work is being done in the USA to produce mildew-resistant forms.

A MEDIEVAL TAPESTRY

In early March, after a few days of mild temperatures (10–15C/50–59°F), the floor of the Little Grassy Wood suddenly looks like a medieval tapestry. Every day in March and into April I come to see it and share the gasps of pleasure I hear as visitors turn a corner and find this feast laid out before them. With the sun behind me slowly dropping along the west boundary of the neighbouring farm, I sit on my little fishing stool to enjoy this multi-coloured carpet, knowing how fleeting some of the flowers will be. I can hear a bumblebee and see a lone honeybee foraging half-heartedly among the erythroniums.

The small *Narcissus minor* naturalizes well in grass, as does the Dog's Tooth Violet, *Erythronium dens-canis.* Both can be lifted before the leaves have disappeared to make swirling patches of colour elsewhere.

Each spring I search expectantly in the short turf, hoping to see more and more Snake's Head Fritillary, *Fritillaria meleagris,* to marvel at the flowers' strange shapes and colours: square-shouldered, drooping bells, matt-purple, chequered in pale and dark maroon, with occasional pink or white forms faintly checked with green. This fritillary is a native of Britain and most of Europe; remnants spared from agriculture can be found wild in low-lying, damp meadows. It is easily grown, in sun or part shade, provided the soil never becomes parched. Ours are beginning to form colonies of seedlings now that we have learnt how to deal with an over-blown population of pheasants. Handsome as these birds are, they are a disaster among choice bulbs, digging them up with their strong spurs, or nipping off the flower heads, preventing any setting of seed. The seedlings, promise of flowers for next year, are easily distinguished from grass. They have narrow, grass-like leaves, but are grey-green, while those sending up a stiff flower stem hold their leaves horizontally, presenting maximum surface to the light.

The daffodils, anemones and primroses will carry on for several weeks yet, but the unexpected haze of cyclamen-pink Dog's Tooth Violets (*Erythronium dens-canis*) is ephemeral. A week ago it was hard to find the pointed tips pushing through the short turf. Now fist-sized clumps are spreading wide, smooth, oval, matt leaves, marbled chocolate and jade-green, while just above them flutter small, pinkish-mauve, lily-shaped flowers, their pointed petals reflexed like those of cyclamen to show navy-blue stamens thrusting forward. Already some of these delicate flowers are browning at the tip, possibly caught by an early-morning frost, and perhaps next weekend they will be shrivelled, but the attractive leaves will play a part for some while yet. Even when the flowers have gone, the clusters of marbled leaves, still beautifully marked, are worth stopping to admire. I can't say I have ever seen seedlings, but after flowering we lift and divide established bundles of corms to spread them further afield and lay down a sprinkling of colour elsewhere. The corms resemble a dog's canine tooth, being much the same shape, smooth, polished and white. Now, after several years of spreading them around, we see them creating a delicate wash of pink between dwarf narcissus (*Narcissus pseudonarcissus* subsp. *pseudonarcissus*), primroses and our native wood anemone, *Anemone nemorosa*.

Scilla bithynica is making ever-widening pools of blue, composed of loose heads of small, starry flowers from pale to deep blue, on 15cm/6in stems above narrow leaves. It is seeding well, even among the coarser grasses in my grass-floored wood, and I feel it is safer to use this charming little bluebell than our native *Hyacinthoides non-scripta*, which seeds rampantly and whose lush foliage smothers out plants intended to provide interest later in the season.

Sitting in the Little Grassy Wood in early April, glad of the sun on my back to counter the chill wind, I look across to pools of blue scattered throughout the grass floor made by two types of wood anemone. From a distance it is not easy to distinguish one from the other, but if you walk towards them, facing the sun, you will see the backs of their petals, a cold greyish-white in the case of *A. n.* 'Robinsoniana', while the backs of *A. n.* 'Allenii' have a purplish stain that gives a deeper, warmer shade of lavender-blue as the petals open wide to the sun. Both make a breathtaking sight whether carpeting short grass or growing in open borders in the Long Shady Walk where they are planted beneath deciduous shrubs, covering the naked soil which later will be hidden beneath great leaves of hosta. By the time the grass grows tall or the hostas fill the same space, the anemones will have nourished their bundles of brown, twig-like rhizomes, extended their colonies and disappeared.

I am pleased to see a free-flowering, single, white, bronze-backed form of

Anemone nemorosa 'Robinsoniana' has pale silvery backs to its light blue flowers, while *A. apennina* has darker blue flowers with narrower petals. Primroses and cowslips seed around them.

Primroses (*Primula vulgaris*) with *Anemone apennina*.

Anemone nemorosa marking the path edge in the Little Grassy Wood. It is competing well with the short grass, overwhelming it at this stage with bronze-tinted, finely cut leaves. There are several named cultivars of our wild white Wood Anemone. The largest we grow, *A. n.* 'Lady Doneraile', flutters pure-white flowers, 5cm/2in across, on dark-stained stems above cushions of dissected leaves, echoing the white drifts of *Narcissus* 'Thalia'. *A. n.* 'Vestal' is a double white, each flower having an outer circle of large sepals surrounding a centre of overlapping white petals, looking like tiny Victorian posies standing above carpets of finely cut leaves. *A. n.* 'Virescens' slowly spreads clumps of divided leaves entirely covered with curiously attractive green flowers. Instead of the normal white flower, each consists of overlapping layers of modified calyces, all finely divided. Intriguing to look down on, it is irresistible to a flower arranger. Later the 'flowers' will be flecked with white.

Successfully competing with the grass, colonizing by means of creeping rhizomes, are two yellow-flowered anemones. *Anemone ranunculoides* 'Pleniflora' has small, bright-yellow, semi-double flowers while from thin, horizontal rootstocks *A. × lipsiensis* bears pale, sulphur-yellow flowers of good size, held above finely cut, bronzed leaves.

Anemone apennina takes over as *A. nemorosa* is fading, thrusting its mounds of neatly cut leaves above the rapidly growing spring grass, each daisy-like flower made up of many narrow, rich-blue petals revealing cream stamens around a green ovary. *A. blanda* is similar, and obtainable in white, blue and pink, all easy and a delight for weeks in semi-shade or open situations.

For gardeners who dare not let vigorous colonizers, however attractive, through the gate, there are two more anemones I love and can safely recommend. The first, similar to *A. nemorosa*, is *A. trifolia*; aptly named, it makes neat cushions of pointed leaves held in threes, buried in April beneath flat, white flowers whose purity is emphasized with white stamens. The other runs and seeds acceptably in open spaces in the Wood Garden, where it forms drifts of white flowers. Its delicate, pointed, white petals turn into bundles of cream, fluffy seed heads. It is the Snowdrop Anemone, *A. sylvestris*.

ACCIDENTAL EFFECTS

Towards the end of March, as the early yellow daffodils, including the little *Narcissus minor*, are fading, sprinklings of primroses take their place. Is any flower lovelier or more appealing, especially in a natural setting? It has taken several years for the primroses I introduced to make themselves at home in the Little Grassy Wood. Now I am delighted to see babies scattered around them, even establishing in the hard-trodden grass path which meanders through this flowering carpet of shade-tolerant plants. You need to look closely at your primroses to check you have a mixture of pin- and thrum-eyed plants. Pin-eyed flowers show a tiny, dot-sized pistil; thrum-eyed show slightly recessed clusters of anthers. Presumably they cross-pollinate, since I notice that where either grows in isolation there are no seedlings. I am always glad to see the things I have planted doing well, but it pleases me more to see self-sown seedlings appearing among them, especially here, where young primrose plants are flowering for the first time, competing with the grassy turf.

Because the Wood Garden slopes slightly from north to south, seedlings of plants such as primroses, cowslips, violas and aquilegias are washed along the pathways, germinating in little trails, or as isolated specimens. It is interesting to see varied hybrids arising from self-made crosses among primroses and cowslips. One of the best, appearing this year, must have *Primula* 'Guinevere' as one of its parents. Although the flowers nestle low-down among bronze-tinted leaves, pretending to be pink primroses, it is actually a polyanthus: that is, it carries several flowers on each stem. The stems and calyces are stained purple and the lilac-pink flowers have large, yellow eyes. A few yards away on the path edge stands a new addition to the Wood Garden, a robust clump of green leaves, carrying forty purple-stained stems, 25–38cm/10–15in tall, with multiple heads of creamy-yellow flowers. Across the path another sibling has made an even larger plant, with heads of clear-yellow primrose flowers, pin-eyed, whereas the first is thrum-eyed. We must watch out for seedlings.

Looking like a specially fine form of the Sweet Violet, *Viola odorata*, is *V. septentrionalis* which comes from moist pine woods in north-east America. It claims its space in my Wood Garden by forming dense masses of fat, creeping rhizomes, which suddenly erupt in spring with china-white, chubby flowers, followed by carpets of large, round leaves. Scattered around, even in the path, are welcome seedlings. As children we looked on shady banks and in hedge bottoms for our native *V. odorata*, so I thought the Wood Garden would be an ideal home, but to my astonishment plants here produce quantities of fine foliage but few flowers, whereas scattered about the garden in open situations they produce sheets of flower, hiding the leaves.

Accidentals often create a natural effect, better than some calculated plan, but too many plants left to their own devices can sometimes result in chaos and confusion. This problem puts the responsibility of decision making on both the gardeners (the carers) and the creator of the garden, especially when the garden has, like mine, grown too big for me to hold all the reins in my own hands.

Top: *Primula vulgaris* subsp. *sibthorpii* with *Chrysosplenium davidianum* which, at first glance, looks as if it is a bright carpet of tiny euphorbias.

Above: *Anemone nemorosa* 'Vestal'.

Top: *Corylopsis glabrescens* var. *gotoana* dangles fat, catkin-like clusters of tiny yellow flowers above green hellebores.

Above: *Corylopsis sinensis* var. *calvescens* f. *veitchiana* has looser clusters of tiny, cowslip-like flowers that create a haze of creamy-yellow.

FLOWERING SHRUBS

More delicate shades of yellow than some of the strident forms of *Forsythia* are to be found in the genus *Corylopsis*, related to the Chinese Witch Hazel (*Hamamelidaceae*). Corylopsis grow wild in scrub and forest edges on the mountains of Japan. The first to flower in my garden is *C. sinensis* var. *calvescens* f. *veitchiana*, which has slowly made a wide-spreading bush about 2.4m/8ft tall and across. From a distance it is a haze of pale creamy-yellow, made by a mass of twisting, twiggy branches, densely hung with catkin-like clusters of greenish-yellow flowers – tiny, bell-shapes strung on thin threads, pushing out dot-sized, brown anthers. *C. glabrescens* var. *gotoana* flowers a little later with primrose-yellow tassels of cowslip-like flowers, about 5cm/2in long, strung from leafless branches. It makes a delicate feature standing above cream hellebores. Colonies of *Narcissus minor* thread their way among the brown carpet of dry oak leaves whose warm colour is repeated more intensely in the unfolding amber leaves of *Spiraea japonica* 'Goldflame'. I love this little shrub, especially at this time of year, so effective as a single plant, or in small groups that, like newly lit lamps, invite us into the still chilly Wood Garden. As the days grow longer and the light stronger, these 'lamps' go out when the leaves mature to form a neutral green background for something else.

Another shrub which links *Corylopsis glabrescens* var. *gotoana* and the small spiraeas is the well-known *Amelanchier lamarckii*, which is especially attractive early in spring, and again in autumn when its leaves turn to vivid shades of cherry and peach. It prefers damp acid woods or scrub on sandy soil, but I am pleased to find that given time to put down roots, and helped with a mulch of leaf mould or compost, it is coping well enough in my dry corner of Essex. Eventually it will make a large deciduous shrub or tree, up to 10m/33ft tall (unlikely with me), but it can be controlled by pruning where there is shortage of space. My bushes are about five years old, with good extension growth gracefully arching to form overall roughly pyramidal shapes. Short lateral branches carry drooping clusters of flower buds, and tiny, silky, emerging leaves, all softly tinted pinkish-brown. Although I will enjoy the effect in a few days' time of myriad cherry-like, white flowers warmed by young, bronze-tinted foliage, I admire now its delicate shades on fine structure.

I am not comfortable with camellias, especially doubles, and have yet to find one that looks right in my garden, apart from *Camellia* × *williamsii* 'J. C. Williams' with flowers like a large, single, pink rose, but it is planted on the sunny, west wall of my house, so does not belong in this book. In a north-facing border, shielded from early-morning sunshine, I planted *C.* × *w.*

'Donation' with inexperienced enthusiasm. Today it is about 5.5m/18ft high and 3.5m/11ft wide, laden with semi-double, rich-pink flowers, making an amazing display of exotic blooms which many visitors enjoy and giving me the luxury of cutting long branches to make simple but sumptuous arrangements for the house. However, I have to admit it is overpowering in my garden setting. Since it is backed by well-shaped conifers, I am thinking I might reduce it in size, to be in scale with its surroundings. I think double camellias are more suited to fine architectural settings, such as paved courtyards surrounded by mellow brick walls, or planted in containers, either in a conservatory or outside, which can be moved under cover when frost is forecast.

Much more to my taste than camellias in the Wood Garden are the flowering currants, natives of north California and British Columbia, where they grow in openings in thuja and pine forests. I have already mentioned *Ribes laurifolium* as a shrub for the understorey in the Wood Garden. After a mild winter the pale-pink *R. sanguineum* 'Albescens' is at its best, every branch

Above: *Spiraea japonica* 'Goldflame' unfolds new leaves in shades of amber and caramel. A light prune in March, removing any twigs which have reverted to green, encourages better foliage.

Left: *Amelanchier lamarckii* makes a large, graceful shrub, with beautiful spring foliage and cherry-like blossom (see page 80). In autumn its leaves turn to vivid shades of cherry and peach (illustrated on page 165).

Above: The Flowering Currant can be found in shades of pink, from very pale, as *Ribes sanguineum* 'Albescens' shown here, to deep loganberry pink.

Below: We watch the new scarlet shoots of *Pieris japonica* 'Tilford' almost daily in case it should be damaged by overnight frost in April.

hung with trusses of flowers opening shell-pink, with deeper-pink buds waiting to open. This is the currant I pick in early February, in tight bud, to watch it open pure-white, pendulous flowers in the warmth of the house. The white-flowered currant, *R. s.* 'White Icicle', creates a most graceful focal point above daffodils. It is truly white, with not a hint of pink in its dense bundles of little flowers suspended along every arching bough, and tiny pleated, fan-shaped leaves setting off the pearly whiteness. The newly emerging trusses of flowers on *R. s.* 'Brocklebankii' are raspberry-pink, fading to a lighter shade, a stunning combination with the yellow leaves which will stand out all summer against a dark background, needing enough light to retain that pale colour, but not direct sunlight to cause scorching. Some people dislike pink and yellow together. Personally I like mixing reds, pinks and yellows, but much depends on the intensity of colour and size of flower. With small flowers one can often get away very agreeably with savage stabs of colour.

Other yellow leaves for contrast are provided by several different types of bramble. *Rubus idaeus* is the wild raspberry, familiar in mountain woods in Britain and throughout Europe. The yellow-leaved cultivar, *R. i.* 'Aureus', grows no more than 30cm/1ft tall, dwarfed presumably by lack of chlorophyll. I love it for its bright colour in spring and early summer, when it seeps like shafts of sunlight through more mundane ground cover. I value it too for the shape and size of the leaves, which appeal to the flower arranger. But I have to admit it is not for small, restricted areas (unless you can contain it), since it spreads enthusiastically by underground shoots. *R. cockburnianus* 'Goldenvale', with bright lemon-yellow leaves which turn pale green in shade, is a delight in the right place (perhaps in a large container, if you haven't yards of empty space).

Among the most desirable yet tantalizing of spring-flowering shrubs are species and cultivars of *Pieris* whose natural homes are in Japan and south-west China. They need conditions similar to those required by rhododendrons: that is, acid soil and damp conditions – in both air and soil – plus protection from spring frost. Obviously I should not think of growing them, but like many gardeners I am tempted to break my own rules (Nature's rules really). Dry summers and spring frosts are my problem. The first I adjust with plenty of mulch and occasional watering. The second I can do little about except hope that developing overhead canopies and surrounding shrubs provide protection from all but severely low temperatures. In the eight years or so since I planted *Pieris japonica* 'Tilford', my shrub has grown to about 2m/6ft 6½in tall and 1m/40in across. Its new growth has been frozen more years than not, but it stoically starts again, slowly increasing in height and girth

until now it forms a remarkable feature, dangling large clusters of lily-of-the-valley-like waxen bells above groups of greenish-white hellebores growing around it. (This is a *Helleborus* × *hybridus*, selected by Eric Smith, one of the best of plantsmen, who did much to raise interest in the genus. I particularly like this hellebore for its pointed, curving petals, looking free and graceful fluttering above the brown leaf litter.) The shoots of the pieris are small still, a heavenly shade of coral, becoming enamelled scarlet as they develop, before softening to pink through cream to yellowish-green and finally turning dark evergreen. With the temperature dropping fast, and the radio forecasting wintry conditions, I shall be coming every day to admire this vulnerable beauty, hoping it may be spared a cruel frost.

I also have *Pieris japonica* 'Rosea'. So far it has grown slowly, making a smaller shrub, with clusters of pink flowers which appear brownish-pink as I look down on them because they have reddish-brown-tinted petioles, but when I tip them up and look underneath, each tiny pitcher is white, fluted with rose-pink, and scented, I think, but the air is too cold to tell.

On the first evening of changing clocks to summertime, I walked back to

The white-flowered currant, *Ribes sanguineum* 'White Icicle', forms a graceful fountain of pure-white flowers among the largely leafless trees and shrubs, lifting the eye above early flowering bulbs such as *Narcissus* 'February Gold'.

Large, heart-shaped leaves of *Trachystemon orientalis* make bold contrast among small-leafed ground-cover plants, like periwinkle (*Vinca*) and tiarella, as well as carpeting large, inaccessible areas between shrubs.

the welcoming warmth of the house, put fresh logs on the wood-burning stove and listened to the companionable sound of crackling wood. Now I could smell the strangely-sweet, spicy scent of pieris, both pink and white, hanging in clusters from a pale-blue vase like a swarm of bees. Later I tried to wipe off the spots of 'water' shining on my writing pad, but they remained – I tasted sweet nectar, fallen like dew.

ROBUST GROUND COVERERS

I have learnt to value invasive plants in my Wood Garden which might well be considered thugs in a restricted setting. Since I began with no stoloniferous grasses or deep-rooted weeds such as docks and dandelions, I have aimed to keep it that way by using plants I value for their appearance, which protect the soil surface from the effects of the weather – be it sun, rain or wind – and keep many square yards entirely weed-free, allowing precious time and effort to be spent where it is needed. All of these labour-savers could be easily dislodged if (or when) I decide to use their site for something else.

Invaluable to me, but possibly the most gross, is *Trachystemon orientalis*, found wild in woodland in Turkey and eastern Europe. Forming dense colonies of large, heart-shaped, pointed leaves, rough in texture, heavily veined, it covers large areas of poor soil, disappearing into the distance beneath rooty shrubs and shady canopies of oak trees where no unfortunate gardener should be asked to go on hands and knees. Attractively pale-green in spring, the foliage will darken later. Well before the leaves emerge, it produces pink stems of curious, dart-like flowers that, like those of *Symphytum* to which they are related, begin as clusters of tightly rolled buds. By March the leaves are already pushing aside the early flowers, which have dropped their curled-back, blue and white petals to leave needle-like, mauve pistils protruding all over the plants, making a fuzzy effect while there are many more hairy buds waiting to open. As I write, a large, fat bumblebee with golden waistband and bottom is buzzing noisily among the flowers, enjoying a late supper.

Vinca minor 'La Grave', which for years was called *V. m.* 'Bowles' Blue', makes a dense, evergreen carpet between shrubs, awash with deep-blue, dark-eyed flowers. By the end of March fresh-green, leafy, trailing stems are coming through so fast they begin to overwhelm the tide of blue, punctuated here and there with fat clumps of the luscious-looking leaves of colchicums. I welcome the appearance of these squeaky-fresh leaves in early spring, long before other bold, contrasting leaves have begun to think of making an appearance, and already I look forward to warm days in September when I catch my breath at the sight of rosy-mauve goblets opening their hearts to the sun. Yet I know that by the end of May or early June the dying of their leaves will be an eyesore to more tidy-minded gardeners. My answer is to look the other way! There is always something else to draw your attention, while bulb foliage must be allowed to die peacefully.

Just now, on the opposite side of the path, clumps of grey-green leaves of a snowdrop make attractive contrast growing through a purple-flowered periwinkle, *Vinca minor* 'Atropurpurea', together with the dark-purple-leaved violet, *Viola riviniana* Purpurea Group. It contributes interesting dark shadows to this group. Spreading from beneath the winter-flowering *Sarcococca hookeriana* var. *digyna* are trails of the white-flowered periwinkle, *Vinca minor* f. *alba*, interspersed with clumps of *Narcissus* 'Jenny'. We trim the vincas in late summer, removing enough foliage to give a better view of the flowers before new growth overwhelms them in late spring.

Sweet Woodruff (*Galium odoratum*), one of the prettiest of the ground-covering plants, makes pale-green carpets of tiny, narrow, pointed leaves, arranged in whorls along short stems, about 12cm/5in tall, carrying open heads of white, starry flowers in early summer. It colonizes any piece of bare, shady soil with wiry, underground rhizomes, so must be watched where space is limited, or where it might overrun fragile neighbours. Taller plants grow easily through it, including hellebores, *Thalictrum aquilegiifolium*, colchicums and, of course, shrubs.

A small, robust vertical I value in shade or part shade is *Reineckea carnea*, related to Lily-of-the-Valley, but rather shy-flowering. It has short sprays of starry pink flowers in early summer, easily missed but a pleasant surprise when you find them. Its value for me is the year-round contrast it makes with its upstanding colonies of fresh-green leaves.

In the Little Grassy Wood *Euphorbia amygdaloides* var. *robbiae* (Mrs Robb's Bonnet) is at its best edging a mixed planting of shrubs, which form a background to the west-facing side. This euphorbia grows wild in the woods of north Turkey and, so the story goes, was named after a Mrs Robb who smuggled the plant home to England in her hatbox. We are indebted to her awareness of the value of this plant, for its handsome rosettes of dark, evergreen leaves and loose heads of yellowy-green flowers, which have typical saucer-like bracts surrounding minute, starry flowers in the centre. The spring-like colour and graceful habit of the flower head make this my favourite euphorbia to use in spring vases, adding cream or white daffodils (*Narcissus* 'Jenny' or *N.* 'Thalia') with a few twigs of some shrub with leaf-buds just opening, and, inevitably, to balance, two or three leaves of *Arum italicum* 'Marmoratum' ('Pictum'). However, I have to admit this euphorbia is invasive.

In the Little Grassy Wood *Euphorbia amygdaloides* var. *robbiae* provides armfuls of luminous yellow-green to put with bunches of spring flowers. It smothers rough grass with its rosettes of evergreen leaves and needs to be restricted from overrunning its neighbours.

Its wandering roots supporting evergreen leaves make it invaluable ground cover in dry shade, even in dry, rooty soil, which is where mine thread their way around the skirts of shrubs beneath the summer shade of oaks. I need to keep an eye on it and remove invasive pieces before they intrude too far into the grassy floor. Despite that one drawback, I would not be without this euphorbia. Early in the morning, or, as now, on a still, cold evening after a shower, it radiates light, back-lit by the sinking sun, its hundreds of flowering stems the same lovely yellowy-green shade we love to see in other members of this family, many of which prefer sunnier situations.

I enjoy the sight of *Allium ursinum* (Ramsons) on the wilder boundary of the Wood Garden, among bluebells and pink campions, and the taste in a salad (taking care to chew parsley afterwards). This wild garlic is found in Britain and throughout Europe in damp woods and meadows. The leaves could be mistaken for those of Lily-of-the-Valley (also found wild in woods) until you crush them and smell the strong garlic odour. The bulbs produce sheets of white blossom formed by round heads, the size of a golf ball, composed of radiating, starry, white flowers, equally odoriferous. It is said to have remarkable medicinal powers.

GRACEFUL NARCISSUS

Narcissus 'Cedric Morris' looks amazingly good still in early March, having been in flower for more than eight weeks. Much depends on both the soil and air temperature for a sight of the next yellow daffodils. *N.* 'February Gold' rarely opens much before the beginning of March in our part of England. After a comparatively mild winter it does not stir itself any earlier. It is always a thrill to see the first buds open. A glimpse of yellow with plenty of unopened buds to come is perhaps the most heart-stirring moment, the sign that winter is truly behind us.

On the whole I prefer species daffodils in a woodland setting, since most increase well and create a natural effect. But some hybrids retain the grace of their parents and are so attractive I could not be without them. *Narcissus* 'February Gold' is a hybrid between *N. cyclamineus* and *N. pseudonarcissus*. It is taller than either, retaining the swept-back petals of *N. cyclamineus*. The Lent Lily, *N. pseudonarcissus*, a native of English damp meadows and found in woods, meadows and hillsides throughout western Europe, varies in shape and shades of yellow. The form we grow, *N. pseudonarcissus* subsp. *pseudonarcissus*, has pale-cream, slightly twisted petals surrounding a lemon-yellow trumpet. I am pleased to see seedlings appearing among the bulbs I originally planted. They will probably flower next year.

Narcissus cyclamineus catches everyone's eye despite being tiny (15–20cm/6–8in tall). It prefers damp, peaty soil – the best you are likely to see are at Wisley, the RHS garden in Surrey, where a low-lying meadow is full of them, like buttercups. They remind me of miniature Christmas crackers poised on short stems. Each flower has a narrow, frilly-edged trumpet while the pointed petals flare behind, imitating the shape of the trumpet, all in the same tone of clear yellow. Although my bulbs have survived many years beneath an ancient oak, they have not increased, as they would have done in more favourable conditions. We hope to remedy that by finding a damper spot for them.

A seldom-seen daffodil which opens at the end of February is *Narcissus pallidiflorus*, given to me more than forty years ago by Cedric Morris. It is easily recognized by its slender, cream buds pointing defiantly skywards, gradually lowering as they unfurl pale-primrose-coloured flowers on 15–20cm/6–8in stems. Another small, much-loved daffodil I had from the Cedric Morris garden is *N. minor*. Low, swirling clumps of grey-green leaves are packed with perfect, little light-yellow trumpet flowers on 15cm/6in stems. They increase most satisfactorily and look enchanting planted in drifts.

Narcissus 'Tête-à-tête' is aptly named. Like Siamese twins, two dainty flowers are held back to back atop each stem. Deservedly popular, it is another *N. cyclamineus* cross, having light-yellow, recurved petals behind neatly frilled, deep-yellow trumpets. It is very tolerant of conditions, whether open borders or shade. It thrives in the carpet of blue periwinkle (*Vinca minor* 'La Grave') edging some of my Wood Garden paths.

At the end of March 2000 I was thrilled to count about a hundred flowers on slowly increasing clumps of *Narcissus* 'Eystettensis' (Queen Anne's Double Daffodil). Although she is a double, I cannot help admiring her, primarily for her colour, slightly deeper yellow than primroses nearby, with layers of chiffon-textured petals of different lengths lying flat on each of the six outer 'petals', each section pinned neatly together at the centre. They stand on stems 20–25cm/8–10in tall. *N.* 'Rip van Winkle' is another small double of a deeper yellow, not so neatly layered, but with narrow and slightly twisted petals, not at all coarse, worth looking at closely. The old cottage-double daffodil of my childhood I grow out of a sense of nostalgia, but still think it is coarse and messy. Hybrid daffodils are legion. We have but a few. Among those showing *N. cyclamineus* as one of its parents is a late-flowering form with both corolla and trumpet the same light, clear yellow, the flared-back 'petals' revealing a long, narrow trumpet. We have been told it is called *N.* 'Englander'.

Although I have a preference for species plants, I like to use some cultivars

This picture illustrates the value of combining various shapes to form a satisfying whole. The eye travels upwards from the ground-covering, white-flowered *Pachyphragma macrophyllum*, through the golden *Philadelphus coronarius* 'Aureus', just breaking bud, to the dark conifer in the distance. In the foreground lush leaves of a colchicum are growing through a small, speckle-leaved ivy, *Hedera helix* 'Luzii', edging the narrow, crushed-bark-covered path, which runs diagonally across the view.

Overleaf: Self-sown plants of Bowles' Golden Grass, *Milium effusum* 'Aureum', introduce patches of sunlight beneath leafless trees and shrubs, their colour repeated in *Narcissus × odorus* 'Double Campernelle'. The flowering stems of pulmonarias will be followed by impressive clumps of new basal foliage.

Leucojum aestivum 'Gravetye Giant' is a selected form of the Summer Snowflake, a native of Europe and South West Asia, found in woods and swampy places. In most soils, except the very dry, it makes hearty clumps of leaves topped with bell-like, white flowers. It is most effective planted in drifts among crimson dogwood stems but solitary groups make bold yet graceful features which are a pleasure to meet anywhere in the garden.

where they seem appropriate, but care needs to be taken when mixing the two, else one will appear weedy, the other coarse. There is nothing coarse about the impressive *Narcissus* 'Beersheba'. It creates a bold effect seen at a distance among leaf-losing shrubs, since it does not require your close attention. It increases well, producing impressive flowers whose long, creamy-yellow trumpets gradually fade to white, matching the broad petals.

Waves of cream and white daffodils take the place of yellow forms, their colours intensifying the effect of the white-flowered wood anemones, which have spread themselves like sheets laid out to dry. The narrow, yellow trumpets of *Narcissus* 'Jenny' are fading now to the same ivory shades as her swept-back petals, while *N.* 'Thalia' is just opening and will look good for some weeks to come. On modestly bent necks, she carries two flowers to a stem; the dainty, pointed petals and short, frilled trumpets are the same shade, glistening white. 'Thalia' and creamy-white *N.* 'Tresamble' enhance the bouquets of shining, white flowers on *Exochorda* × *macrantha* 'The Bride'.

Flowering at the same time, in April and into May, well-established clumps of *Leucojum aestivum* 'Gravetye Giant', the Summer Snowflake, are eye-catching in full flower. This bulb has surprised me by making huge clumps in the Little Grassy Wood, since it also thrives elsewhere in my garden on heavy soil near water. It looks good between bushes of red-stemmed dogwood (*Cornus stolonifera*), flowering before too much foliage obscures the flowers.

THE LONG SHADY WALK

At one end of the Long Shady Walk, where I planted my first collection of shade-loving plants, there is an area screened by a big weeping willow, *Salix alba* 'Tristis'. In early April masses of slender, tumbling branches threaded with small, yellow-green leaves and minute catkins create a see-through curtain. The willow, partnered by an ancient oak on the opposite side of the grass walk, keeps the sun off a mixed planting of shrubs which separates the main garden from the nursery stock beds lying beyond. In early spring this is an enchanted spot, dependent almost entirely on shapes and shades of green.

The focal point is a beautiful small tree, *Cornus controversa* 'Variegata', now about 4.5m/15ft tall, forming a pagoda-like shape with horizontal branches held in distinct layers. The young leaves, delicately variegated with wide, white margins, are well displayed along the branches, while clusters of cream flower buds stand upright above them. The spare, elegant shape, accentuated by the pale foliage outlined against a dark yew, creates for me a living sculpture, which no statue could replace. Nearby *Weigela* 'Looymansii Aurea' opens coral-edged leaves, which slowly mature to lemon-yellow. Small, evergreen

shrubs of our native *Daphne laureola* have been eye-catching for weeks with terminal shoots carrying clusters of small, green, tubular flowers, but these are now forming bunches of pea-sized fruits which will finally turn shining black.

While admiring these congenial companions I was stopped in my tracks by a froth of white flowers flowing between and beneath them. *Pachyphragma macrophyllum* is a joy, planted to follow fading snowdrops, with a thousand and one heads of cress-like flowers flooding the area with patches of white, like snowfall. I welcome the spread of this plant in rooty, shady places, gradually concealing the leafy clumps of snowdrops which will fade away unseen until next year. As the 'snow patches' of pachyphragma 'melt' away, overlapping, large, round leaves replace them for the rest of the year with weed-proof ground cover. Several robust clumps of a deep-gentian-blue pulmonaria make good accents in this pale colour scheme.

At the back of this group *Staphylea × elgans* has formed an erect, open, tree-like shrub clothed in handsome leaves, mostly divided into three leaflets. In April from the axils of the leaves appear long racemes of wax-textured flowers, ivory-white at first, flushing faintly pink as they fade. As the

As snowdrops steal away, snowy patches of *Pachyphragma macrophyllum* take their place, followed by carpets of round, green leaves backed with purple which provide good ground cover beneath trees. The early-flowering *Spiraea thunbergii* echoes the pachyphragma with its sprays of little white flowers.

Staphylea × elegans makes a tall, upright shrub bearing white, wax-like flowers held in clusters; these elongate over several weeks, thus showing off the individual flowers more distinctly.

internodes lengthen they make me think of long, elegant earrings, remaining good for several weeks, still handsome and commented on in mid-May.

It is mid-April, cool and sunny, with enough moisture beneath the trees to sustain good foliage and choice woodland flowers. A skein of colours, mostly blues among cream and yellow, is woven throughout this border against a backcloth of emerging foliage. *Brunnera macrophylla* teases you into thinking it is a forget-me-not, since its long sprays of blue flowers are very similar, but the foliage is quite different. Each large, heart-shaped leaf provides important contrast of form among small-leaved creepers, like Sweet Woodruff and Golden Creeping Jenny (*Lysimachia nummularia* 'Aurea'). Of the variegated brunneras I like best *Brunnera macrophylla* 'Hadspen Cream'; light-green leaves are irregularly bordered with primrose, which dissolves partially into the centre. Whether planted singly or as a group, this plant makes a gentle accent later in the year among many shades of green when flowers in shade are few. *B. m.* 'Dawson's White' has more striking green-and-white variegation, but needs careful placing, protected from sun scorch or wind damage, which turns the white parts brown. An enthusiastic plantsman, Dr Tony Rogerson, gave me the plant we call *B. m.* 'Langtrees', named after his garden in Devon. Its large, rough-textured, dark-green leaves are bordered with a pattern of silvery-grey spots, as if a paintbrush dipped in aluminium had been used. Long sprays of forget-me-not-like flowers hover over them for weeks in spring.

Along the path edge low washes of blue are made with *Omphalodes cappadocica*. This choice plant from the Republic of Georgia and north-east Turkey forms clumps of oval, green leaves, above which float sprays of intense gentian-blue flowers, larger than forget-me-nots, reminiscent of blue speedwell. *O. c.* 'Cherry Ingram' is an extra fine selection, the flowers larger than the type. In *O. c.* 'Starry Eyes' pale-lilac petals have a star of dark-blue bars pinned to the centre of each flower, very eye-catching if you can grow it well, but in my experience it is not such a reliable grower. My conditions might be too dry. Omphalodes needs leafy, retentive soil, in part shade. Being evergreen, it also needs some shelter as it can be damaged by hard frost. In the

Wood Garden I planted the European *O. verna* (hardy to −15C/5°F) since I know it to be more invasive. Its spreading carpets of pointed, heart-shaped leaves make good ground cover for bulbs to grow through. In spring it is sprinkled with small, forget-me-not-like flowers in both blue and white.

On the east-facing bank where we replaced the ditch with a drainage pipe and plenty of compost, *Omphalodes cappadocica* runs up the slope between rusty trusses of tightly curled fern fronds. *Ajuga reptans* 'Catlin's Giant' makes dark shadows around the pools of blue. Nearby groups of our best selections of *Helleborus × hybridus* are heavy with fat seed pods which must be removed quickly before they have the chance to fall and produce a rash of seedlings, making unnecessary weeding of plants in the wrong place.

APRIL HIGHLIGHTS

The weather in April can be fickle – blue skies one minute and the next the light turns menacingly yellow, the sun almost doused by black thunderclouds. The garden changes by the minute, by the hour, according to the light, driven on by the urgency of spring. To miss even a day is a loss, so much will have advanced in twenty-four hours. In 2000, winter arrived the day after we changed the clocks to summertime, bringing ten days of sleet, rain and bitterly cold wind out of the north-east. Miraculously the pieris was undamaged, in spite of some overnight frost. One night the sky was starlit when I went to bed, but I was relieved when I woke to find the garden shrouded in heavy mist rather than white with frost.

Despite grousing about the weather when it is cold and miserably wet, I do enjoy the drama of April skies. One evening I was walking through the nursery, among the tidy array of potted plants, where the sky above is vast and uninterrupted. The sun was struggling to escape between dark banks of cloud driving in from the west. Ahead of me the sky was still blue, a landscape of huge, cottonwool clouds, top-lit with flecks of sunlight, while the foreground was interspersed with low, ash-grey 'barges' sailing in menacing fashion towards the Wood Garden, where I was heading. I had hoped to stand and take in the view beyond the nursery, a stage-like backdrop of mixed deciduous and evergreen trees and shrubs leading to the Wood Garden. Over the past thirty years or so, where once was bare land (after the removal of brambles), the open, empty sky has been 'painted' with a backcloth of contrasting shapes and shades. Silver Birch, various wild crab apples, chosen for their wealth of spring blossom and autumn fruit, contrast with the dark shapes of conifers and deciduous trees to make an interesting screen all the year round. I stood waiting for that magical moment when the reluctant rays of sun bring the scene to life, illuminating the diaphanous veils of colour as tiny leaves unfold – pinkish-bronze of poplar, euphorbia-yellow of emerging oak, pea-green ribbons of weeping willow, all pulled together into a meaningful design with dark accents of shapely evergreens. I knew that in a week this picture would be gone. My reverie was interrupted. The temperature dropped dramatically; from behind me, icy rain swept across the nursery and I ran for shelter.

Now I am passing a tall Silver Birch I planted perhaps twenty years ago. Its white bole and branches soaring into a blue sky are leafless still, but laced with fringes of curly, yellow catkins. A climbing rose, *Rosa* 'Hidcote Gold', is now halfway up the trunk, while last summer's extension growth cascades over the poor sandy soil beneath, transformed now with a shawl of blue periwinkle (*Vinca minor* 'La Grave') curving across the path. The clumps of colchicum leaves seem especially lush this year. Individual bulbs have increased to form large clumps, punctuating the blue carpets of periwinkle, pulmonarias and *Omphalodes verna*. I am lucky to have the space to plant bold groups of individual species which in turn help us by maintaining a regular carpet of foliage in various shades, textures and forms.

Any out-of-the-way piece of shaded soil which can be left bare to allow *Claytonia sibirica*, which formerly we called *Montia*, to seed will become an area you will seek every spring. This charming little woodlander is an annual I have seen in flower, frothing like the wave's edge, beneath the dark shade of a pine forest, where little else can grow and where there is no competition for the seedlings. Each plant forms a loose rosette of narrow, slightly succulent leaves, from which rise airy sprays of pink or white flowers, about 20cm/8in tall. Closely related is *C. perfoliata*, known as Winter Purslane or Miner's Lettuce since its clusters of bright-green, fleshy leaves can be used in salad, but fond as I am of gathering wild plants for salads or flavouring, this is one we wage war against on the nursery stock beds where it can become a pest.

There are numerous cardamines that are not difficult to grow in light shade. Cardamine, correctly pronounced *kär-dam'i-né*, is the collective name for lady's smock, or cuckoo flower as we called it as children when damp meadows alongside the river were full of them, together with buttercups and Wood Avens (*Geum rivale*), and tiny golden frogs, small as moths, jumped ahead of us in the long wet grass. These scenes have mostly gone since the meadows were drained during the war years to grow more food.

Cardamine quinquefolia spreads quite quickly with underground shoots, very useful where there is room. When established it forms attractive mounds of overlapping, pointed, finger-like leaves, welcome early in the year when much of the ground is bare, and topped with trusses of bright-mauvish-pink

Cardamine quinquefolia grows wild in damp shady places in the Caucasus. It spreads by means of underground shoots, but is well worth the space since it flowers very early.

flowers which show up well from a distance. *C. pentaphylla* is more widely known, another delight in early spring, adding a warm colour to the cool clumps of snowdrops. Its finely cut leaves, purple-tinted at first, unroll together with clusters of flower buds which open nodding lilac flowers, larger than those of *C. quinquefolia*, the petals flaring open to reveal paler tones within. *C. kitaibelii* has chalk-white flowers above low mounds of light-green, palmate leaves. *C. bulbifera* produces colonies of slender stems, 25–38cm/10–15in tall, lightly dressed in narrow leaves, topped with spires of pretty lilac-coloured, cruciform flowers. It is native to Britain, growing in damp patches in oak woods. It can become a menace in the wrong place, since it spreads by underground roots and by little brown bulbils held in the leaf axils, but it is a delight to come across in a low-lying part of the Wood Garden where it can proliferate among primroses, followed by coarse plants such as the Giant Hogweed, *Heracleum mantegazzianum*, and the American Poke Weed, *Phytolacca americana*.

Fragile-looking plants sometimes surprise me by turning up year after year with little or no help from me. I am thinking of various forms of corydalis, some of which I first saw in Cedric Morris's garden more than forty years ago. Both he and the plants he gave me have passed on, but every spring new generations turn up regularly to take me back to Benton End, which exists only in the memory of those who visited and loved it – maybe that is another precious thing about gardening. We all pass on, our gardens change, many disintegrate and disappear. That is not important. What matters is the continuing cycle of sharing and learning about plants, and perhaps a little bit of us remains with our plants. I still feel very much the spirit of Cedric as his plants return here year after year, knowing they are thriving and giving pleasure in many other gardens. They are not Cedric Morris plants, Gertrude Jekyll plants, Beth Chatto plants or anyone else's, but are universal. However, when I first read a book by Gertrude Jekyll, I felt so strongly her presence through the way she expressed her love for plants that I almost said aloud, 'Don't worry, we still feel as you did, we still tend your plants.'

Corydalis solida, despite its name, seems an ephemeral plant to provoke such ponderous thoughts. The epithet, *solida*, refers to the tubers which make me think of small new potatoes, except that they are yellow and easy to find when digging around. Early in spring, before the wood anemones appear, I am looking out for this plant's pretty, distinctive foliage: mounds of finely cut, blue-grey leaves of just the right tone to set off heads of long-spurred flowers, deep lilac in colour, with tiny, gaping, white mouths. On the floor of the Little Grassy Wood, this corydalis increases slowly by seed as well as by making more

Corydalis ochroleuca, the white relative of the well-known Yellow Fumitory, seeds into dry, shady crevices, old walls or stony soil.

Top: The flowers of *Corydalis cava albiflora* stand well above a nest of light-green, finely cut leaves.

Above: *Corydalis cheilanthifolia*, despite its fragile appearance, maintains its role in shady places by means of self-sown seedlings with finely cut, fern-like leaves that look very appropriate in a woodland setting.

tubers underground. These spread more readily elsewhere in the garden where there is less root competition.

The tubers of *Corydalis cava* are identified by being rather hollow on the upper surface. The flowers are more conspicuous than those of *C. solida*, standing well above a nest of light-green, finely cut leaves. The short, leafless stems, about 15–20cm/6–8in tall, are topped with a flight of long-spurred, lipped flowers, the spurs a rich dark pink, with paler, frilly lips opening to reveal a white throat. *C. c. albiflora* is a little taller, 20–30cm/8–12in, its spires of creamy-white flowers so delicate they are almost transparent. Although fragile-looking, these plants have endured here for forty years, finding niches by seeding among other plants, completing their lifecycle before being overwhelmed by vigorous neighbours. While writing these notes I picked flowers of *C. cava* and noticed for the first time how sweetly scented they are, a spicy perfume reminding me of the buds of the Balsam Poplar (*Populus balsamifera*). Now I shall always look to bring a few stems into the house to have that unexpected pleasure.

The flowers of *Corydalis malkensis* are a little larger but similar to those of *C. cava*, short-spurred, creamy-white, hovering on 15cm/6in stems, just above finely cut, green leaves, creating a pretty, tumbled effect. This plant is new to me and, now that I have learnt to smell its fresh, primrose-like scent, I have planted it on a raised bed against the east-facing wall of the greenhouse. It seeds readily, but needs to be preserved from invaders. A cool pocket in a rock garden would suit it well. *C. cheilanthifolia* produces 20cm/8in spires of canary-yellow flowers, conspicuous above attractive, fern-like foliage whose green tones are sometimes touched with bronze. It has no scent that I can detect, but makes good contrast among the grey leaves of snowdrops and emerging leaves of trilliums. I am so glad this corydalis preserves itself by seeding around (it does not make tubers). Carpets of plants like tellima and cranesbill would prove too much for tiny emerging seedlings, but where there is still a bit of open space they make the most of it.

As long as we are spared severe late frost, *Dicentra spectabilis* makes luscious plants with many glossy, hollow stems bowed with horizontal fringes of deep-rose, heart-shaped flowers. It is known variously as Bleeding Heart or Lady in the Bath: if you turn a flower upside down and pull aside the two halves of the 'heart', you will expose a tiny, white figure with head and drooping shoulders – fun for children of all ages! It still amazes me to see dicentras doing well in my Wood Garden, since fifty years ago when I coveted them in West Country gardens there was no way I could keep them in the dry, chalky boulder-clay of my first married home, 11km/7 miles from here. The white

D. s. 'Alba' is not quite so robust, but is cool perfection, dripping with pure-white lockets strung along green stems, among pea-green leaves, and heart-stopping as it emerges from a carpet of Sweet Woodruff, keeping company with one of the bluest of hostas, young and immaculate now, covered with a waxy, blue bloom, and with partially unfurled ferns. We have recently acquired *Dicentra spectabilis* 'Gold Heart' with leaves of a rich, ochre-yellow. It will provide good foliage contrast if it retains this colour. I'm not certain of this combination with raspberry-red lockets, but my eye is taken by a solitary yellow-leaved seedling, so apparently it comes true from seed.

I make the most of fragile-looking dicentras, aware that a sudden overnight frost may leave them lying blackened and broken on the ground. I think much depends on how long the early-morning frost lasts, as well as on planting to avoid direct sunlight. After frost, innocently the sun rises on a scene of destruction, warming the chilled air. I clear away the damage and carry the remains to the compost heap, sad to see such beauty cut off in its prime. Some weeks later I am astonished, and grateful, to see new – if fewer – flower shoots emerging as the underground rootstocks make every effort to reproduce themselves.

The lovely *Dicentra spectabilis* 'Alba', with pale green leaves and stems, flowers for weeks in late spring and early summer.

AMERICAN WOODLANDERS

April is the month for erythroniums and trilliums, with dangling tassels of uvularia joining the scene towards the end of the month. All February and March I look forward to these North American woodland plants, and the possibility of a warm day to linger among them, but here in my Essex garden I still associate them with chilled hands and a wind-proof coat. Just as well, because apart from the European Dog's Tooth Violet (*Erythronium dens-canis*) most of them come from the western states of North America where they grow in mountain woods and on meadow slopes, plentifully supplied with moisture in spring, even if they may be dried out later. Erythroniums need

adequate moisture and feed to make large, smooth corms, much the same size and shape as my thumb. When they are established it is very satisfying to dig out a handful of fat, pointed corms where once there was one. In North America they have descriptive common names, such as Avalanche Lily, Lamb's Tongue, Adder's Tongue and Glacier Lily. These indicate the habitat – high up on glacier-capped mountains, emerging as the snow melts on the lower slopes – or refer to the handsome leaves, usually two to each bulb, long, tongue-shaped, often strikingly mottled with brown. Most generally grown in gardens are selected forms or hybrids between native species.

Erythronium californicum 'White Beauty' is the shortest, standing about 25cm/10in tall. It clumps up quite quickly, producing quantities of soft-cream, lily-like flowers, which open to the sun, sweeping pointed petals backwards to display rust-coloured markings that form a jagged ring at the base, exposing downswept pistils and stamens. The leaves are faintly mottled. *E.* 'Sundisc' is taller, up to 45cm/18in, flaunting several clear-yellow flowers quivering on bare brown stems held well above lush-looking, tongue-shaped leaves, variously marbled in shades of brown. Tip them up to see the reddish-brown disc surrounding the stamens and ovary. The well-known *E.* 'Pagoda' is similar but slighter, the flowers a paler yellow without the red disc and with attractive green backs to the petals. These two hybrids have *E. tuolumnense* as one of their parents. It carries several smallish, deep-yellow flowers above pale-green leaves, and has given its height to the hybrids, but tends to be shy-flowering in cultivation.

Erythronium revolutum has become naturalized in moist, woodland conditions in Britain, including in two famous Surrey gardens, the Savill Garden in Windsor Great Park, and the Royal Horticultural Society Garden at Wisley. In damp, peaty soil, without too much competition from bulky plants, the lilac-pink flowers freely set seed. It delights me as much to find colonies of seedlings around my parent plants as it does to see the flowers. They just need to be left undisturbed – no hoeing – but with a mulch of leaf mould or crushed bark to mark them. Seedlings vary in tone: opening cream, they blush to shades of pink as they mature. Some selections are deep rose pink from bud.

Trilliums (Trinity Flower or Wood Lily), many from North America, like the same cool conditions as erythroniums, in rich, leaf-mould soil that does not dry out, especially in early summer. Patience is needed to establish handsome clumps, which are slowly formed by underground rhizomes. As the name implies, they are distinguished by the division of three – three leaves at the top of a bare stem, above which are three calyces and three petals. There

Top: *Erythronium* 'Sundisc', with handsome mottled leaves and clear-yellow flowers on brown stems.

Above: *Erythronium revolutum* reflexes lilac-pink petals to show its cream heart.

Left: *Amelanchier lamarckii* lifts the eye above a patchwork quilt of trilliums, erythroniums, hellebores and *Paeonia mlokosewitschii* coming into bud.

are several species and selections available. With perseverance, not to say obstinacy, we have spent many years establishing improved microclimates in the garden and now are managing to grow some of these woodland treasures tolerably well, although I know they would establish more quickly in a damper climate. The best-known Wood Lily is *Trillium grandiflorum*. Wild in woods in eastern and central North America, usually on limestone, it makes a dome-shaped plant of veined and shining leaves which set off pure-white, open-funnel-shaped flowers. Pale pink *T. g.* 'Roseum' is a treasure, with foliage also warmly tinted. *T. g.* 'Flore Pleno' is breathtaking in April, with perfectly formed, double, white flowers, as lovely as little camellias. I confess these are still growing in the shelter of our shady Maternity House, a long, Netlon-covered tunnel where choice shade plants are propagated and nursed in raised beds until stocks have increased. We thought the site we had chosen for this tunnel, on low-lying land, was ideal, and so it proved to be during many typical dry summers, with only 25cm/10in average rainfall in winter and the same in summer, but the considerably wetter winter months of the past two or three years have caused the water table to rise too high and rot stock plants of trillium. Fortunately David had young replacements in the pipeline, but it was a hard lesson to suddenly find, in spring, almost empty beds that previously had been crowded with mature plants. As with many plants which need moisture in the growing season, it is vital to ensure they are not waterlogged when dormant.

Right: The flowers of *Trillium chloropetalum* vary in shades of wine, from light to dark, while the leaves too show greater or lesser degrees of marbling.

I have been looking in my plant 'bible', *Perennial Garden Plants* by Graham Stuart Thomas, for confirmation of the name of another trillium we grow. It is *Trillium chloropetalum* from the western United States, which grown from seed is very variable. We pick out the most distinctive and find we have a choice between good flowers and plain leaves or indifferent flowers above dramatic, strongly marbled leaves. Now I am looking down on a clump growing along the Long Shady Walk, planted about three years ago. There are five stems 25cm/10in tall. On the top of each are presented horizontally three large, heart-shaped leaves, up to 30cm/1ft across, mottled grey and green, pinned in the centre with upright, tulip-shaped flowers of a fine wine colour, light and dark as sunlight passes through them. They emerge from a froth of forget-me-nots hiding now the fading leaves of snowdrops. In *Bulbs* by Martyn Rix and Roger Phillips there is a splendid picture of a very similar trillium labelled *T. sessile*. However, that is the name I prefer to use for my very best form, and quoted by Graham as being a very similar species, but from the eastern states of America. I obtained this plant more than forty years ago from Messrs Hillier. On very short stems (15cm/6in) the emerging leaves are held

close to the dark soil, exquisitely marbled in shades of jade on a chocolate background, bearing dark-plum-coloured, upstanding flowers. The white selection of *T. chloropetalum* I originally grew from seed and it was worth waiting eight years for the first flower. Three broad, wavy-edged leaves, plain green but interestingly veined, form a handsome 'collar' to set off creamy-white flowers, wine-stained at the base, with fine veins bleeding upwards into the petals. It pleases me now to see seedlings – small, three-leaved versions of the parent plant – growing nearby.

A trillium I still long to grow well is *T. rivale*. Few gardeners could resist reaching for their wallet on seeing a panful of pale, pink-washed flowers held above small, pointed, green leaves, all no more than a few centimetres/inches high. Imagine how we felt, Christopher Lloyd and I, several years ago when we were in Australia, visiting a garden near Melbourne, and came across wide patches of this gem growing as freely as aubrieta might in England. But I should remind myself that the garden sloped down to a wooded valley filled with tree ferns and wonderful mosses, where we slithered and slipped on sodden paths. In the wild this plant grows in California and Oregon, in rocky places by streams or in the shade of pine forests, plentifully watered from the Pacific. There must be favourable situations on this side of the Atlantic, in the West Country or Wales; Scotland might be too cold. So far we have been fairly successful here in the Shade Tunnel where this plant has made a sizeable patch by means of underground rhizomes. It also does well in pans, plunged in a shady frame, but my aim, as a gardener, is to see most of my plants fending for themselves outdoors.

On another occasion, I was in California where I spent a magical weekend canoeing on the black, shallow water of a virgin forest of Swamp Cypress (*Taxodium distichum*). I also attended a meeting where I was shown lists ordering many thousands of trilliums, which were to be collected from the mountain woods of California, to supply the hunger of gardeners throughout the temperate world. This shocked me, as does the wholesale digging of bulbs from the wild, till I stopped to consider that mountainous regions can sustain only a very poor living for the local people. Why not gather a harvest supplied by nature? All this was more than ten years ago. Today there is a greater awareness of the need to conserve and preserve whole ecological associations, for the benefit of all life – insects, animals and plants. To this end there have been established some schemes (there need to be more) to train local people to collect seed, propagate and produce plants where conditions are ideal, to supply the gardening trade. Trilliums germinate easily from seed, but take several years to make flowering-sized plants. They are worth the wait. No

Trillium rivale from damp, shady places in Oregon and California is a very dwarf member of the genus; its flowers, standing 15cm/6in tall and 4cm/1½in across, are palest shell-pink. It is seen here with the curious, double-green form of Wood Anemone, *A. nemorosa* 'Virescens'.

television programme can convey the thrill of seeing that first bloom, an emotion similar to your child's first day at school, both events being the culmination of care and attention for at least four or five years.

Uvularias, although related to the robust Solomon's Seal, are smaller woodland plants. They are easily grown in well-drained, humus-rich soil, but benefit, I think, by careful placing, perhaps in a cool pocket in the rock garden, or on a shaded raised bed where you can look closely into their delicate features. Bellwort, *Uvularia grandiflora*, is found wild in woodlands of the eastern United States and eastern Canada. In spring narrow, pointed leaves unroll along olive-green, arching stems. Between them, at the upper end, hang tassel-shaped flowers composed of slightly twisted, sharply pointed, yellow petals, delicately transparent. The lovely *U. g.* var. *pallida* has paler, almost creamy-yellow flowers whose pointed tips flare wider than the type. *U. perfoliata* is similar to *U. grandiflora*, but not quite so robust. The flowers are pale lemon-yellow, and appear about a fortnight later. All the uvularias make slowly increasing clumps of closely packed stems.

4 | Early-Summer Profusion

BENEATH THE CANOPY OF NEWLY FLEDGED oak leaves, still bright yellowish-green, the whole wood floor is heaving with life in every shape and form. For flower and foliage I think the Wood Garden is at its best, the most varied, at this time of year. Evening light is low, subdued. Mornings are magical, totally still, every leaf still wet with dew, the fast-developing canopy overhead shielding everything from the glare of the sun. Tiny insects hover motionless or sway from side to side as if listening to the constant concert of bird song, dominated by a thrush atop the tallest tree, practising over and over again new trills. Now and then there comes a duet as another thrush far away offers a theme, which the first one takes up and embellishes with variations.

On the first still, balmy evening in May 2001, after an exceptionally wet winter, I struggle to find words to describe the sudden transformation from spring to summer. A cold, sodden April did nothing to encourage dallying among longed-for spring flowers, but now a warm air stream from the south-west has suddenly enveloped us. Everywhere gardens and countryside are exploding with new life, sparkling-fresh and abundant. During the past seven

Left: *Enkianthus campanulatus* from Japan is an ericaceous plant, so needs a lime-free soil which does not easily dry out. It forms an upright shrub with horizontal branches hung with pretty, bell-like flowers, while above them appear the new season's leaves that turn to shades of red and amber in the autumn (illustrated on page 164).

Tiarella cordifolia spreads welcome carpets of pale-green, heart-shaped leaves, easily dislodged if they stray too far, half hidden in spring and early summer beneath spires of creamy-white flowers.

months, since November, we have had 68cm/27in of rain. (I make no apology for repeating that our normal yearly average is 51cm/20½in!) Some plants will have benefited greatly, with moisture reaching deep into congested bundles of roots where light rain seldom penetrates. But there are areas of waterlogged soil where rainwater spills in from the surrounding farm, which may result in casualties. Here we plan to lay more pipes to improve the drainage.

The scene changes from day to day, even hour by hour. My two *Enkianthus campanulatus* have made very attractive shapes, their branches held in tabular fashion, in spaced layers, and the undersides of every branch and twig is fringed with clusters of small, bell-shaped flowers, creamy-green with pale-coral tips. The overall effect of this shrub is modest, probably passed by if mistakenly planted with flamboyant azaleas, but on this May evening it takes my breath away caught in low sunlight and underplanted with *Vancouveria chrysantha*, whose shield-shaped leaves on wiry stems are also coral-tinted. Being ericaceous, *Enkianthus* needs a lime-free soil, which luckily I have, but with low rainfall in most years I have had to find a deep pocket of humus-rich soil where there is less risk of it drying out.

Just now curving edges of the bare, trodden pathways are softened with carpets of the American Foam Flower, *Tiarella cordifolia*. A few pieces planted two or three years ago have spread most satisfyingly. Similar in habit, but smaller in scale, is *Mitella caulescens*, from conifer woods in British Columbia and one of the daintiest trailing plants. It runs like *Tiarella cordifolia* but has much smaller, heart-shaped, lobed leaves. In May short stems carry inconspicuous flowers creating a low haze of pale green. It thrives in cool leaf mould, in part shade. Forget-me-nots and the lovely blue *Omphalodes cappadocica* carry the eye into the distance with intermittent washes of blue, where earlier trilliums called out for attention. Leafy symphytums float drifts of pink, white and blue flowers in the shade cast by shrubs, and ferns are beginning to unroll their crosier-like, furry stems, compelling me to stop and stare.

The warm, humid air carries a sweet, citrus-like scent reminding me of the days when I staged my Chelsea exhibits. It is borne by a North American woodland plant, *Smilacina racemosa*, that makes slowly increasing colonies of leafy stems, reminiscent of Solomon's Seal (*Polygonatum × hybridum*) to which it is related, but from which it differs dramatically in having tapering heads of massed, fluffy, cream flowers. Nearby, making bold ground cover, is a cultivar of Lily-of-the-Valley (*Convallaria majalis* 'Hardwick Hall'), with a similar perfume, its bold leaves rimmed with yellow-green. We also have a colony of the handsomely striped *C. m.* 'Albostriata', which appears to retain most of its variegation, but is not totally reliable.

Smilacina racemosa, the sweet-scented relative of Solomon's Seal, makes slowly increasing colonies of leafy stems, with unfolding fern fronds tucked among them.

I turn round on my stool to face another colonizing plant, *Dicentra* 'Bacchanal'. One small piece, rescued from elsewhere in the garden where it had become almost buried beneath shrubs, has now spread about 3m/10ft along the path edge, shaded by a hazel bush that we have kept young by selective pruning each winter for pea sticks. The dicentra dangles dark, wine-red lockets above soft sheaves of pale-green, finely cut leaves, while arching stems of Solomon's Seal above carry neat rows of little cream bells edged with green. Sitting on a stool gives me a new perspective. Standing up I can see only part of the cool, wax-like flowers suspended over neighbouring plants, including one of the improved heuchera introductions, *Heuchera* 'Chocolate Ruffles', whose superb foliage, bronzed at this stage, with many tones of tan over dark shadowed green on the surface, rich-wine-red on the back, harmonizes with the dicentra flowers nudging up to it. What a combination! And if that were not enough, a huge clump of *Arum italicum* 'Marmoratum' with still perfect foliage has put itself into the picture. Shall I let it stay? Altogether these plants make a perfect combination at this moment, but the arum needs to be controlled: it loves my warm, light soil and too many will obscure or smother lesser beings before I have noticed the intrusion.

I have just pulled three handsome seedlings of a pink-flowered balsam, *Impatiens (Balsaminaceae)*, out of this group, since if left there to flower and seed they will obliterate it. Their hollow, leafy stems stand more than 1.5m/5ft tall, bearing sweet-scented flowers, shaped like Roman helmets, that

Doronicum pardalianches, the Great Leopard's Bane, spreads drifts of lemon-yellow daisy flowers until you feel obliged to say enough is enough.

eventually catapult black, round seeds far and wide. They must be relegated further back, against a boundary of bamboos, cotoneasters and birch trees.

The biennial honesty, *Lunaria annua*, including the variegated form (see page 94), pops up around the perimeters of the garden where its rash of seedlings can do little harm. More restrained and desirable, I think, is the perennial *L. rediviva* with loose heads of scented, pale-lilac, stock-like flowers held above layered skirts of oval, pointed leaves. One specimen plant, 75cm/30in tall, creates a good effect among blue aquilegias and will produce interesting, elliptical, papery seed heads, pale and effective in autumn.

Flowering at the same time is the Great Leopard's Bane, *Doronicum pardalianches*. Although its tuberous roots are invasive, I admire this plant's ability to thrive in thin woodland, even in grass. The effect of a glade of yellow daisies on tall, branching stems is a delight where they fill the space taken earlier by snowdrops and daffodils.

Where there is sufficient moisture, *Polemonium caeruleum*, found wild throughout the northern hemisphere and long cultivated in gardens as Jacob's Ladder, will thrive in full sun, but makes an attractive, small vertical in part shade above low-growing cover plants. It forms a tidy base of narrow leaflets arranged in pairs on long stems (representing 'ladders'), above which stand branching stems, 60cm/2ft tall, carrying a profusion of blue, open-bell-shaped flowers centred with orange stamens. *P.* 'Lambrook Mauve', originally from the garden of Margery Fish, carries heads of the prettiest, silky, lilac-mauve flowers, which are perfect among flowering ajugas, aquilegias and Bowles' Golden Grass (*Milium effusum*). *P. carneum*, from woods in the coastal ranges of north California and Oregon, is a delight to find on a cool border edge, where it makes a mass of tumbled stems smothered with loose heads of shell-pink saucers, opening from cream buds, fading to soft mauve.

QUAINT AQUILEGIAS

Aquilegias, fascinating in their diversity of colour and form, create valuable verticals above carpeting plants. *Aquilegia vulgaris* var. *flore-pleno* 'Adelaide Addison' has old-fashioned, Granny's Bonnet-type flowers. Behind its sheltering outer 'petals', or bracts, peep through the short, curled spurs of the inner modified petals, which resemble little, blue trumpets with flaring, white lips. Of none of this are you aware as you pass by their prim blue-and-white heads. Only if you stop and tip one up will you discover this curious adaptation that has evolved to seduce some foraging insect which will ensure good pollination. According to Graham Stuart Thomas, 'Aquilegia and Columbine refer to the shape of the flowers, the petals being like the extended wings of an eagle or dove below the spurs of the flowers, which resemble neck and head.' I must go and look at some of the aquilegias in the garden, to see if I recognize the bird-like shape!

What is remarkable is that this complicated-looking flower belongs to the buttercup family, *Ranunculaceae*, as do delphiniums, which may surprise you too, but if you take a delphinium flower and gently push your finger into the centre to push back the 'hood' you will find that the small sepals and petals which form the hooded shape will press open to represent a typical six-petalled buttercup flower. In the rare double form, *Delphinium* 'Alice Artindale', each flower consists of many layers of unmodified petals, perfectly shaped, to make little blue rosettes, tightly attached to long, slender branches.

Aquilegia vulgaris var. *stellata* 'Nora Barlow' has nodding heads consisting of layers of narrow, modified petals and sepals that are a combination of raspberry-pink and cream with green tips. From Mrs Rita Douglas of County Armagh I was sent seed of an aquilegia so dark purple it is almost black, most exciting now as its slender, branching stems stand up to 1m/40in tall, a little colony of them self-sown. Their dark flower heads repeat the colour of *Geranium phaeum* 'Samobor' which also acts as a good background for *Dicentra spectabilis*, just going past its best. This selected form of the Mourning Widow geranium has handsome, lobed leaves, the centre and margins of which are light green, each strongly marked with a wide, chocolate-coloured band.

This unusual aquilegia with dark, blackish-purple flowers was sent to me from Northern Ireland. Unfortunately I have no name for it.

THE LITTLE GRASSY WOOD

After weeks of cold and wet weather, we suddenly have a mini-heatwave! Outside in the open it is already hot early in the morning. Inside the Little Grassy Wood it is cool, shower-fresh. Droplets of dew sparkle like diamonds – minute flashes of green, blue and red – among the rapidly growing blades of grass that are smothering the last carpets of blue anemones. It is good to see the primroses pushing aside the grass with healthy, vigorous-looking clumps of leaves. They will be establishing sturdy crowns and root systems before they are finally overcome and disappear until next winter. We can be thankful for a cool, wet April for lush growth all round, and in the case of the primrose family, all variants of *Primula vulgaris*, for the absence of the red spider mite which sometimes debilitates our plants, especially in warm, dry spells. This tiny creature, almost invisible to the naked eye, breeds on the back of the leaves, quickly establishing colonies of sap-sucking young. You notice the effect when the rich-green leaves turn yellow and spotty.

Replacing blue anemones are drifts of bluebells, our native species *Hyacinthoides non-scripta*, and the Spanish *H. hispanica*, in shades of blue, pink and white. The latter differs from the former in holding erect spires of more open flowers above broader leaves. The two species will interbreed. Elsewhere, on the edge of the Wood Garden, I have only the native bluebell, where it will not be diluted. Above the bluebells rise stately camassias. In the wild these bulbous plants grow in damp meadows, from British Colombia to central California. They do not thrive in dry, hungry soil. Ecologically they do not belong beneath English oaks, but they are growing well, groups of them scattered here and there in sunny openings, the tall spires of blue, starry flowers creating welcome vertical shapes above the rapidly rising tide of grass. *Camassia leichtlinii* subsp. *suksdorfii* Caerulea Group is the ungainly title for an especially good form I brought home as seed from Oregon where it grows wild on waste land. It carries spires of dark-violet-blue, star-shaped flowers on the upper two-thirds of stout, bare stems. Long, lax leaves are lost among the grasses. Also standing 60-90cm/2-3ft tall is the cream-flowered typical subspecies, *C. l.* subsp. *leichtlinii*, not yet opened. Primly upright stems carry spires of tightly folded buds, caught now in low shafts of evening sunlight. They make intriguing verticals long before their star-shaped flowers have opened.

Among the rapidly rising grasses, vetches and clovers I see one of my most disliked weeds, relentless Sticky Willy, or Cleavers (*Galium aparine*), its long, trailing stems adorned with whorls of little leaves. Both square-cut stems and leaves are covered in minute hooks which catch in your skin or anything else, enabling the plant to lift up tiny, white flowers which quickly become round seed cases, also coated in hooks – a clever way of transferring its seed to the coats of passing animals. Already where I sit at the main path edge I see far too many young plants of this weed where a few days ago there were none. Very soon I hope my gardening girls will walk through this area to pull all they can see before the seeds have formed. Some years ago I was in Ireland with Christopher Lloyd, heading for the Burren, when we were shocked to see Sticky Willy smothering roadside hedges like curtains spread out to dry.

Another much prettier but equally dangerous weed in the wrong place has already been greatly reduced. It is *Anthriscus sylvestris*, the early kind of Cow Parsley; we call it Queen Anne's Lace but that is the common name my American friends use for wild carrot. Along the lanes now, leading to the village where I do my weekly shopping, it is a picture, with banks and green swards frothing with this graceful, delicate umbellifer, its creamy-white heads merging with hawthorn, which is heavy with clusters of flowers, rich as clotted cream. We still have a few flowering plants, previously missed, but they will be

removed before they set seed, otherwise they would take over the entire area.

Other very lovely umbellifers we have allowed in and I describe them on pages 134-6, but here I must include an attractive introduction that also needs controlling, both in the Little Grassy Wood and the Wood Garden. The biennial *Smyrnium perfoliatum* (Perfoliate Alexanders) has looked handsome for some weeks now, fooling visitors into thinking it is a euphorbia, since both leaves and flowers are a symphony of those same yellowy tones. But look at the flower heads and you will see it is an umbellifer (*Apiaceae*). Each side stem branches at the top where plenty of light above the surging grasses turns the

In the background is *Smyrnium perfoliatum* pretending to be a euphorbia, but if you look carefully you will see it is an umbellifer. Seeded among it are the purplish-pink and white forms of honesty (*Lunaria annua*), while in the foreground are a thousand spires of *Tellima grandiflora*.

topmost leaves an electrifying shade of yellow, to match the lacy heads of tiny flowers. Combined with bluebells, both our native and the Spanish Bluebell, they make a lively colour harmony.

As the days lengthen the Little Grassy Wood becomes a waving mass of feathery flower heads with fading Martagon Lilies in shades of purple and white standing above them. We wait for later blooms, of white lilies (*Lilium speciosum* var. *album*) and the orange-and-brown speckled turkscap flowers of *L. hansonii*, to finish their display before cropping the grasses with a strimmer at the end of June.

BENEATH ANCIENT OAKS

On 16 April 2001 I noted yet another frustrating day for gardeners, photographers and writers – as well as visitors. The Atlantic air-stream had been piling up successive thunderstorms, interspersed with brief but exquisite periods of sunlight. It is no wonder ancient peoples worshipped the sun, and still, in our various ways, do we. After the exceptionally wet winter and spring, with almost three times our average rainfall, new growth on everything had attained an almost overwhelming luxuriance. But now, in mid-May, I stand in wonder beneath the ancient oaks in the Long Shady Walk, watching alternate patterns of sunshine and shade as sunbeams escaping the flying clouds are filtered into this winding glade. I marvel at how the plants have developed in recent years to fill their space, forming complicated tapestries on the ground or sky-reaching shapes above my head. All around me are tiny, unfolding leaves, so tender that the light passes through them to reveal endless delicate shades of green. It is breathtaking, the more so since this moment is fleeting: it will not come exactly the same again. From hour to hour the light changes, from day to day the soft tones of green darken as the leaves gradually mature. Strong contrast to indeterminate green shapes is made as moving shafts of evening sun pick out the corrugated trunks of ancient oak, surging hostas and pyramidal, dark-toned hollies. There are no harsh elements, no straight lines, just gentle curves, which are repeated in the undulating effect of height and hollows formed by the shapes of trees, shrubs and plants beneath them, leaving spaces for us to catch glimpses of the view beyond, and for the birds to fly through.

Beneath the Great Oak, cyclamen and snowdrop leaves are fading now, pushed aside by colonies of the little, purple-leaved, unscented violet, *Viola riviniana* Purpurea Group. Seeded among them are bright-yellow patches of *Tanacetum parthenium* 'Aureum' (syn. *Chrysanthemum parthenium* 'Aureum'). The pink-flowered Honesty, *Lunaria annua* 'Variegata' (syn. *L. biennis*

'Variegata'), with strongly variegated leaves, makes a gaudy splash of colour and the dozens of seedlings dotted around make me think of day-old chicks darting around their mother. In the distance a more tranquil effect is achieved with thick colonies of the green-leaved, white-flowered honesty (*L. a.* var. *albiflora*) growing beneath a white-stemmed birch. *Melica uniflora* f. *albida*, one of the prettiest woodland grasses, makes clumps of soft-green leaves above which float pale, glistening flower heads like sprays of tiny rice grains, the effect as soft as fur against other smooth leaves.

On either side of the winding path there are patterns made with contrasting leaf shapes and textures, including the parasol-shaped foliage of hardy geraniums and the handsome purple-leaved *Ajuga reptans* 'Catlin's Giant', flowering now with 20cm/8in spires of close-set, dark-blue flowers, the colour intensified by purple-brown calyces. After flowering, new rosettes of glossy leaves, twice as large as those of other ajugas, will assume the same dark hue. A drift of paler blue is formed by the forget-me-not flowers of *Brunnera macrophylla*. Sprays of tiny blue flowers float above heart-shaped, matt-green leaves. *Saxifraga* × *geum* selections are easy and most satisfying plants, quickly establishing weed-free carpets of close-packed, evergreen rosettes, studded now like a pincushion with thin, red stalks opening airy sprays of tiny, pink stars with dark pin-eyes. Alongside a path's edge are the shining, green, arrow-shaped leaves of *Arisarum proboscideum*, the Mouse-tail Arum. Now, in May, if you look closely, you will see the long, curling 'tails' emerging – whip-like tips of small, brown arum flowers looking like the round backsides of mice which have dived headfirst inside to hide!

Making bold contrast with the small-leaved carpeting plants are the large, fresh, finger-shaped leaves of *Helleborus* × *hybridus*, pushing aside now their ripening seed heads, which still remain attractive in subdued shades of cream, green and faded purple. As a background to this group is the yellow-leaved *Weigela* 'Looymansii Aurea' with Golden Hop, *Humulus lupulus* 'Aureus', carrying the bright colour up into a dark-leaved holly.

A white *Clematis montana*, formerly called *C. spooneri*, now *C. montana* var. *sericea*, has taken its time to scramble up the gnarled trunk of one of the ancient oaks. There is too little light for it to produce many flowers on its way up the trunk, but where it has reached some of the lower branches they are wreathed in clusters of white flowers. As it ascends the tree by means of its long, vigorous shoots, more and more trailers will hang from the branches, carrying flowers at every joint. I had it so twenty years ago, when we could walk through a shower of flowers just above our heads, but the prolonged droughts of the mid-1990s killed it.

Melica uniflora f. *albida,* with shimmering sprays of pale green buds, makes unusual contrast with *Geranium phaeum.*

Overleaf: The golden leaves of *Philadelphus coronarius* 'Aureus' imitate sunlight in shadowy places beneath the fast developing leaf canopy. Arching stems of Solomon's Seal and fronds of *Matteuccia struthiopteris*, caught in alternate light and shade, lift the eye above the woodland floor. *Tellima grandiflora* forms tidy clumps among the swathes of forget-me-nots, lamium, *Dicentra* 'Langtrees' and *Ajuga reptans* 'Catlin's Giant' that fringe the path.

Handsome flower clusters of *Dipelta floribunda* in May will be followed by conspicuous bundles of pale-copper-coloured seed cases in late summer.

Exochorda × *macrantha* 'The Bride' makes an open bush of lax, arching branches densely set with little strings, 7–10cm/3–4in long, of round white buds opening rose-shaped, snowy-white blossoms, each the size of a buttercup with conspicuous, green eyes. In the Wood Garden my shrub has spread to 3m/10ft and I'm not sure what to do with it. Somewhere in the past I feel certain I have seen it thrusting through something firmer. Christopher Lloyd's plant I have known for the past twenty years, in the open, never higher than eye level on the side of a path, vigorously pruned directly after flowering, firmly kept in its appointed place. It certainly works with such a lax-growing shrub, but I still hanker for showers of white 'buttercups' above my head. In the Long Shady Walk I have the less often seen *E.* × *m*. 'The Pearl', which does not draw attention to itself so dramatically as 'The Bride'. It makes a firmly upright bush with sprays of round, pearl-like buds opening pure-white flowers among small, grey-green leaves but, in my garden, not as abundant. I find we need to reduce its height every few years to keep the flowers where we can easily see them, rather than thrashing up into the branches of the Indian Horse-chestnut, *Aesculus indica*. Incidentally, this horsechestnut is one of the most beautiful sights in spring when the sticky buds open young leaves shaded pinkish-brown and tan. The spikes of flower which follow are pink-flushed too.

Dipelta floribunda, from central and western China, has flourished on the opposite side of the path in the Long Shady Walk, where there is enough light overhead to encourage the production of flower clusters reminiscent of weigela, to which it is related. My shrub has formed six trunks, carrying arching branches sparsely clothed in narrow, pointed leaves and bearing now, in mid-May, clusters of tubular flowers with pink-washed backs opening white-frilled orange throats. By late summer these will have become conspicuous bundles of pale-copper, papery seed cases. It makes a great shrub, the lower half leafless, showing bark peeling off in long strips. If that worries you, plant in front of it, as I have, the yellow-leaved mock orange, *Philadelphus coronarius* 'Aureus', and be delighted with the handsome clusters of flower which emerge above its leggy companion. Our philadelphus had become too tall, the flowers almost out of sight, so we cut it to a framework about shoulder height. It has taken two years to refurbish itself, but is flowering now as never before. More correctly (when pruning is not left until you are aware of a problem), it is best to thin out old stems immediately after flowering.

LEAFY CARPETS

While you might mistake *Vancouveria chrysantha* and *V. hexandra* for epimediums, their differences make each worthy of a place in the shade. Although related to epimediums (which are almost all Asian), they are not so amazingly tough in dry shade, seeming to need kinder, damper conditions. They hail from Oregon and California, where they form low patches of evergreen leaves on wild, rocky hillsides or in pinewoods by means of their wandering underground rhizomes. Having found a cooler, damper spot for them, I am delighted in early summer to come across sprays of tiny white flowers standing well above the foliage of *V. hexandra*, while *V. chrysantha* has little yellow flowers floating on hair-thin stems above pale green leaves stained and edged rusty-red. The leaf shape differs too from that of epimediums, being shield-shaped and slightly lobed.

The USA is also the home of our garden phlox, which include the well-known cultivated Border Phlox, *Phlox paniculata*, that provide rich colour and heavy perfume in open, sunny borders. For partial shade there are species which form creeping mats and cushions and look comfortable with other American introductions, such as heucheras and tiarellas. *P. stolonifera* forms mats of fresh green leaves on creeping stems which root as they go, making good ground cover. Loose heads of flowers on stems 15–20cm/6–8in tall are held well above the leaves in May. *P. s.* 'Ariane' has heads of snow-white, yellow-eyed flowers, while those of *P. s.* 'Blue Ridge' are lilac-blue with a pin-eye of orange stamens. Another delight for cool soil and part shade in early summer is *P. divaricata* 'Blue Dreams'. Delicate, branching stems, about 30cm/1ft tall, carry deep-blue, narrow buds opening soft-blue petals. When suited this phlox increases by means of rooting stems, as well as setting seed. I welcome the colonizing habit of *P. pilosa*, which tolerates somewhat drier conditions. Slender flowering stems appear from underground shoots, carrying loose, pyramidal heads of soft mauve-pink, sweetly scented, making a low haze of flowers for weeks in mid-summer. The season is prolonged by new flowers appearing on a succession of side shoots.

Hard-wearing symphytums, members of the borage family, which we value primarily for their ability to spare weeding in spaces between shrubs in the Wood Garden, are now doing their bit, making drifts of pink, white or blue flowers. Leafy carpets of *Symphytum* 'Hidcote Blue' are almost obscured by branching stems carrying nodding heads of flower. The tiny, coral buds are held in tightly rolled clusters, as many as thirty to each head, opening narrow, tubular flowers, blue at the base, white at the tip. *S.* 'Hidcote Pink' differs in having scarcely a tinge of blue, so appearing as a drift of pink and white, imitating fallen apple blossom. While I value the slowly invasive habit of these plants in rough or awkward places, elsewhere they need watching, and ripping out – for example where they have crept down the north-facing clay bank at the end of the Long Shady Walk and threaten to overwhelm toad lilies (*Tricyrtis*) and other pleasures to come.

In contrast to the lower-growing symphytums, *S. asperum* makes a stately, eye-catching plant from a deep rootstock. Tall, self-supporting, leafy stems are topped with branching heads carrying typical crosiers of garnet-red buds, unfolding intense gentian-blue flowers: really impressive. *S. caucasicum* is similar but a softer, paler blue, a delight in rough places where its underground invading rhizomes will not be regretted. These two come from north-east Turkey and the Caucasus. *S. orientale*, a native of Russia and the Caucasus, has attractive, pure-white flowers early in May, tolerating dry shade. For the edge of woodland or shady paths, *S. tuberosum*, a native from Scotland and throughout Europe and east to Russia, makes low, creeping patches of matt-green leaves just now topped with cowslip-like clusters of pale-yellow flowers.

Tellimas and tiarellas might be dismissed as 'weedy' in the wrong setting, in the open among too many cultivars, but they add immeasurably to a fairyland effect in woodland – or in any cool, shady place. *Tellima grandiflora* forms tidy clumps of round, scalloped leaves and produces sheaves of slender stems up to 1m/40in tall, threaded with tiny, green bells with turned-back, whiskery edges, creating a filmy screen of green, insignificant as one stem but

Just opening its first flowers from tightly rolled bundles of buds is *Symphytum* 'Hidcote Pink'.

enchanting *en masse*. There are various sorts. *T. g.* 'Purpurteppich' has leaves which become veined and stained with maroon in summer, while *T. g.* Rubra Group is valuable for winter effect when its leaves change to rich red-purple and bronze. Finally we have one whose pale-green bells fill the air with a delicious scent, when the temperature is right. It is called *T. g.* Odorata Group. This plant was given to me by a kind stranger who came to my Chelsea stand, to tell me she had a form which smelled of *Dianthus*: would I like a piece? It duly arrived and has surprised and confused both visitors and staff who look around in vain for old-fashioned pinks in a woodland setting.

Tiarella cordifolia, spreads low trailing stems of small, hairy, green leaves, still with some short spires of starry, white flowers, which make an attractive setting for hostas and tall *Dicentra spectabilis*. This tiarella associates well with the ground-hugging evergreen *Asarum europaeum*, a native of European woodlands (not British) that I value as much as small-leaved ivies for ground cover in dry shade. It spreads slowly, so is useful where ivy could be too invasive. This wild ginger has round, green leaves, satin-finished, faintly veined, that curve round at the point where they rejoin each short stem leaving a tiny, round, dark hole down which all the veins disappear. In spring snowdrops dangle chilly bells above it, and in autumn and winter its rich-green leaves remain eye-catching.

Recently we have found new introductions of tiarella that are clump-forming. They include *T.* 'Ninja' which has bronze-tinted leaves with deep-cut edges, producing throughout summer spires of pink buds, opening to fluffy, white flowers. *T.* 'Tiger Stripe' has light-green, palmate leaves variously blotched along the veins as if with a sponge dipped in brown paint, fading with age to warm, rosy shades in winter.

Tiarella cordifolia, flowering still, spreads a carpet at my feet as I sit on this rough-cut plank bench, made from wood we cut down when starting the Wood Garden.

I must watch patches of colchicum leaves surging from great bundles of bulbs underground, benefiting obviously from the wetting they have rarely experienced here before, to the extent that their lush foliage is smothering pulmonarias and cranesbills which were originally planted to give their large, goblet-shaped flowers protection from mud splashes in autumn. As soon as the leaves begin to turn yellow we must dig up the bulbs and find a place where they can do no harm – an open situation in mown grass would be ideal. (Where can I find a meadow for a barrowload of colchicum bulbs?)

ELEGANT FERNS

Throughout the Long Shady Walk and the Wood Garden ferns are unrolling their tightly curled fiddle-necks. No other plant, apart from the trees themselves, evokes such a feeling of cool, tranquil woodland. Whether they are in shade or sunlight, there is something mysterious in the fur-backed thrusting stems and the fragility of pale, curled fronds.

These ancient plants, which evolved millions of years ago long before flowering plants appeared, range in size throughout the world from huge trees to slimy films covering tree trunks. Aeons ago they formed part of the coal measures, their frond patterns preserved in compressed layers of shining, black coal. Today they still occur in a vast range of size and shapes, in climates wet and warm enough to support them. Dry and windy Essex is not renowned for its ferns, either in the wild or in gardens. I always associated them with visits to the West Country or wet Wales, where horizontal branches are festooned with moss and the long, narrow leaves of the Common Polypody, *Polypodium vulgare*. However, this colonizing fern will make do with drier conditions. In the garden I value *P. interjectum* 'Cornubiense', a variant from Cornwall, with beautifully divided fronds creating a lacy effect that lasts throughout winter. Just now it is still dreaming. Last year's overwintered foliage, looking rusty and tired, should be removed while there is no sign of emerging buds, but come they will, in their own good time, to freshen the garden in August with beautiful, spring-green fronds.

Until years passed and I had created more kindly microclimates in my developing garden, this fern and the long-suffering Male Fern, *Dryopteris filix-mas*, were the only ferns I could consider. The ubiquitous Male Fern will survive and thrive in the driest and draughtiest of borders, even thrust into a hedge bottom, but if it is given slightly kinder conditions its effect compares well with the most choice of ferns, as it makes elegant sheaves of divided fronds, 90–120cm/3–4ft tall, remaining evergreen in sheltered situations. It has several choice relatives. The Golden Scale Male Fern, *D. affinis (D. pseudomas)*, is one of the most handsome of all hardy ferns. I stand looking at it as it emerges from a dim hollow between the forked roots of an ancient oak, at that perfect moment when each half-grown stem is backed with soft, rust-coloured scales set on either side with tiny green leaflets (or pinnae) still closed tight, like a baby's fists. The fiddle-neck tips remind me of a snail shell, or those paper whistles we had as children at fairs and blew into to make them unroll. I am sure if I could stand still long enough I would see these fronds move. Next morning, when I visited groups of the same fern in the Wood Garden, I found they had unrolled to the tips overnight.

The Golden Scale Male Fern, *Dryopteris affinis (D. pseudomas)*, is just beginning to unroll its fiddle necks enclosed in soft, rust-coloured scales.

I feel fortunate now to have a few more of the handsome varieties I used to covet in West Country gardens. I have been thrilled in recent years to find I can grow *Dryopteris erythrosora*, of the same genus, but originating in the Far East, from China and Japan. At the foot of east- and north-facing walls, together with clematis and hostas, also beneath a weeping willow among blue-grey and yellow-leaved forms of Dutchman's Breeches (*Dicentra spectabilis*), this fern attracts attention all the year round. New fronds are a warm reddish-brown, with flushes of colour retained as they expand. Small and delicate as those of a maidenhair fern at first, the fronds gradually open and toughen to become broad and glossy-green, some 45cm/18in tall and 25cm/10in across. Mature fronds carry rows of tiny, red spore capsules on their underside. To

The unrolling fronds – both stems and pinnae – of *Dryopteris erythrosora* are flushed red, becoming pale green suffused with red as they spread and develop. New fronds are produced throughout summer, so the fern retains a lively appearance well into autumn.

my surprise and pleasure new bronzy-red fronds continue to emerge until autumn as the mature ones lean aside to make room for them. Grandest of all is *D. wallichiana*, found in much of Asia and South America, and one of the last ferns to wake up. In its resting state, the tightly rolled buds are densely covered with soft, dark-brown scales, making them look like a cluster of furry creatures, huddled together for protection. As they slowly unfurl, tall, green stems clothed in almost black, scaly hairs are in marked contrast to the pale, golden-green tone of the opening fronds. Unlike the fiddle-neck tips of some ferns, the tips of this look like nothing so much as rolled-up hairy caterpillars. When well suited, in cool damp shade, in acid or neutral soil, the fronds can grow 1.2–1.5m/4–5ft tall.

Ferns are so captivating that they need a book to themselves. There are still more I would like to share, and, as yet, am not bored to write about, but if they are not for you, skip the next page or two and join me further along, among the flowery woodland plants.

The genus *Polystichum* provides yet more easily grown ferns, in cool, leafy soil, either acid or alkaline. *P. setiferum* is a native of Britain and Europe, found in deciduous woodland, often on limy soil. *P. s.* Plumosum Group has finely divided, lace-like fronds. In its winter resting state, after the old fronds are cut down in February, there is left a kind of rusty-brown nest made of old remains. The dormant buds lie huddled together in this 'nest', slowly unfolding broad, much-divided fronds attached to a stem densely backed with shining, copper scales. I picked a frond and ran my finger along, from base to tip. It felt sleek and soft as a cat's back. At this early stage this group of coppery-toned plants forms a contrast among the low carpet of Japanese anemone leaves and tall stands of *Thalictrum aquilegiifolium*, while near the path edge *Epimedium × versicolor* 'Sulphureum' echoes the copper tones with mounds of overlapping, heart-shaped leaves with reddish-brown marbling.

During the past exceptionally wet winter we moved (or thought we had) a colony of the Ostrich Plume Fern, *Matteuccia struthiopteris* (found in damp places all around the northern hemisphere), from a position where the sun's rays in high summer fell through a gap in the overhead canopy, causing the fronds to burn. Surveying the site now, I find many 'shuttlecocks' still standing, too advanced to move, but their turn will come, since this fern is invasive, extending by long, underground shoots. We moved most of it to the lowest part of the Wood Garden where we have left a broad strip some 12.9m/14yd wide to allow predominantly natives, like snowdrops and aconites, bluebells, pink campions, Lily-of-the-Valley and primroses, to colonize. Here was a wild place to plant a drift of matteuccia where heavy winter rain brings down rich

Right: Partially expanded fronds of *Dryopteris affinis* rise above the finely-cut, blue-grey leaves of *Dicentra formosa*, which is sometimes called Dutchman's Breeches on account of the baggy shape of the little pink flowers, held in pairs.

Spread like a lace shawl beneath the bold, leathery leaf rosettes of *Euphorbia amagdyloides* var. *robbiae*, topped with typical spurge flowers, are delicate-looking fronds of the hardy Maidenhair Fern, *Adiantum venustum*, bronze-tinted when young. Tucked between the two is *Arum italicum* 'Marmoratum', doubtless from seed dropped by a passing bird.

silt. Unlike any other fern we grow, it makes a basal stem or trunk from which ascend elegant fronds forming perfect shuttlecock shapes. Caught in alternate light and shade, they lift my eye above the wood floor and into the distance between the tree trunks. Swathes of forget-me-nots, washed down as seed from upper levels, fringe the path edge, making a paler, sharper blue than the haze of bluebells beyond.

As I was writing this, suddenly my trance was shattered by a family with small children who found the narrow, winding paths irresistible for a game of hide and seek, their shrill calls clashing with the unfazed birds still in concert overhead. When father joined in the chase I crept away, praying no damage would be done and knowing they soon would tire, preferring a promised trip to the coast 20km/12 miles away. In the cool of early morning another family, grandma, parents and two tots walked by me. Father asked the tiny girl if she knew the name of the plants they were passing. 'Ferns,' she replied. Impressed, I picked some of the furry fronds for her to touch. She thanked me and put them into her brother's pram. I felt indebted to this family sharing my little bit of heaven. (It is churlish of me to resent the occasional youngsters who let off steam, tearing round the garden as if it were a public park. The grassed area of the car park is not nearly such fun.)

Adiantum venustum closely resembles the maidenhair fern of greenhouses, which also did well in some of the unheated farmhouses I used to stay in (quite happily I hasten to say) when I was on the road giving talks or demonstrations of flower-arranging in the past. It has taken years to colonize the base of a shaded sandy bank, together with violets, Golden Creeping Jenny, the double, white wood anemone, and self-sown *Lathyrus vernus* f. *roseus*, a bushy, little plant covered in spring with tiny, rose-pink pea flowers above neat, divided leaves. Left to look after itself, this fern has made a wide-spreading colony of lace-like, overlapping fronds, pale bronze as they emerge, acid green when mature, and finally rusty brown as they remain throughout winter.

After seeing *Adiantum pedatum* flourishing in damp woodland in Connecticut, I planted it on a raised bed on the north side of a greenhouse where it is flourishing as it never did in less favourable parts of the garden. It has made dense clumps of shining, black stems, each supporting a hand-like structure of fronds. Beside it flourishes another treasure for a cool, damp situation, *Athyrium niponicum* var. *pictum*, the Japanese Painted Fern. This exquisite fern holds its leaves almost horizontally, the better to show off its unusual colouring. Each frond composed of tiny pinnae (leaflets) is so pale it appears to be silvery grey, flushed with maroon on either side of the central vein, which is pinkish brown.

Other much-loved ferns, such as polystichums, the Lady Fern and irresistible forms of Hart's Tongue Fern, are described on pages 212-13.

PROUD ASTRANTIAS

Just now I am enjoying a group of white-flowered *Astrantia major* subsp. *involucrata* standing proud in an open space where sunlight enters through a gap in the overhead canopy. There are slight variations of flower size and shape between individual plants, so we must have planted seedlings to make the group. One is especially remarkable, reminding me of a photograph I admired years ago in one of Margery Fish's books. She called her plant *A. m.* subsp. *involucrata* 'Shaggy'. Mine stands over 90cm/3ft tall with upstanding, branching stems carrying curious, green-and-white flowers. The centre of each is filled with a quivering umbel of minute, pale-green, fertile flowers

Astrantia major alba, with upturned heads, each made of many narrow segments filled with quivering creamy centres, grows through a little 'meadow' of *Melica uniflora* f. *albida*, one of the prettiest woodland grasses.

which quickly develop into flat seed cases held on short, slender threads. It helps to visualize them if you know the plant is now classified as an *Apiaceae*, with *Chaerophyllum*, *Smyrnium* and the frothy annual *Ammi majus*. That is not all. Surrounding this centrepiece are long, pointed, twisted bracts, white with sharp, green tips, producing overall the effect of a daisy-shaped flower, the largest of them 9cm/3½in across. Caught in part shadow, swaying in a slight breeze, they are quietly mesmerising.

Astrantia major 'Claret', one of several selected wine-coloured masterworts.

None of the other plants in this group has such long or shaggy 'petals', but all are equally attractive, faintly flushed with pink. Being smaller, and perhaps having neater, more regular bracts, they are good for dried-flower pictures, since the centres, made of green seed cases on pink stalks, press neatly flat rather than becoming a squashy muddle as most daisy shapes do.

The flowers have gone now from the yellow-leaved *Dicentra spectablis*, but its foliage makes a focal point among dark-green hellebores, ferns and upturned seed heads of *Erythronium* 'Pagoda'. Elsewhere, nearer the path edge, is the smaller *Astrantia major* 'Rubra', standing 45–60cm/18–24in tall, whose ray-like 'petals' are soft purplish-red, much the same colour as we see in some plum-coloured *Helleborus* × *hybridus*. There are several named variants of this colour form available now, including *Astrantia major* 'Claret' and *A. m.* 'Ruby Wedding'. I have walked with Piet Oudolf, a Dutch nurseryman and garden designer of repute, through rows and rows of flowering astrantias, grown from seed, all looking very similar, but noticing here and there something a little lighter, or darker, or larger. As with hellebores, although I am fascinated by the dark cultivars, I think the lighter colours make more garden-worthy plants since they show up better against the dark soil or from a distance.

FLEETING PEONIES

Unlike the heavy double cultivars, single peonies are ephemeral creatures, dropping all too soon if caught in strong sunlight. But in cool places, between shrubs or beneath light overhead shade, they look their fragile best, and last longer. From the moment they burst through the soil in March and April I enjoy every stage of their development, especially the Caucasian beauty, *Paeonia mlokosewitschii*, or the more pronounceable Molly the Witch. Now her mature, grey-green foliage sets off the beauty of cool, lemon-yellow flowers filled with gold stamens. Another unusual peony was originally given to me as *P. emodi* by my good friend Cedric Morris, but we have since learnt that this plant is *P.* 'Late Windflower', a cross between *P. emodi* and *P. veitchii*, made in 1939 by Dr A. P. Saunders of New York. Finely cut foliage, bronze-

tinted when young, sets off branching stems of white, sweetly scented, single blooms, exquisite backed by ferns and surrounded by a blue wash of forget-me-nots. The true *P. emodi*, introduced from north west India in 1862, I obtained from Elizabeth Strangman. It differs in having slightly smaller flowers, without the bronze tint to the foliage. The other parent, *P. veitchii* from China, comes readily from seed, producing several flowers per stem that vary in size and shades of pink, from deep magenta to the delicate tones of wild rose. It is not difficult to select and keep the best large-flowered forms to enhance a cool, semi-shady situation.

Another peony, *P.* 'Avant Garde', given to me many years ago by Eric Smith, late of *The Plantsmen*, and raised by him, also has petals the colour of the wild rose, flushed at the edges, paling towards the centre where fringes of pale-orange stamens spring from a base stained ruby-red, looking like an eye surrounded by long eyelashes.

All peonies take time, as do hellebores, to settle down and make a stout rootstock, so that each succeeding year we may hope to count more numbers of flowering stems. Not all soils or aspects please them. I think both do best

Paeonia mlokosewitschii thrives in well-drained, humus-rich soil, in sun or part shade, but the fleeting lemon-yellow flowers last longer in shade. In autumn, fat seedpods split open to reveal blue-black, pearl-like seeds, set against a crimson 'silk' lining.

Overleaf: *Paeonia* 'Late Windflower' hovers above *Dicentra formosa*, flowering at the same time as *Smilacina racemosa* and self-sown aquilegias (not seen in the photograph). The Welsh Poppy, *Meconopsis cambrica*, has just found a toehold and will add to the scene if it can find space and enough light to form a little colony.

and look well in partial shade. Certainly the single peonies last longer in a cool situation, in soil well-enriched with plenty of organic matter. From then on it is a matter of patience.

Last year on the anniversary of Andrew's birthday (he would have been ninety-two years old on 18 May 2001), I went early into the garden to pick yellow peonies in memory of him. Nearby was growing *Smyrnium perfoliatum* whose airy sprays of flowers and new foliage repeat, in slightly deeper tones, those of the peony. I added a few dark peony leaves and I dropped this hand-held bouquet into a tall jug placed on a low table against a glass door. The peonies opened spun-silk petals, translucent against the light, each scented flower 15cm/6in across. Two friends arrived for lunch on this special day. Despite being perceptive gardeners, for a moment they thought the flowers were made of silk, exclaiming with delight when closer observation showed them to be alive. This arrangement lasted five days. Admittedly the weather was cool, cool enough for me to light the wood-burning stove for my friends. For the first time since Andrew's seventieth birthday we had lunch indoors instead of beneath the magnolia tree (*Magnolia × soulangeana* 'Alba') where previously our family had gathered to celebrate.

FLOWERING SHRUBS

After an exceptional 75mm/3in of rain over the Bank Holiday weekend, combined with wind and hail, I find the Wood Garden suddenly looking dishevelled. The paths are littered with twigs and young oak leaves wrenched off by wind-driven hailstones, while some shallow-rooted plants, like foxgloves and fluffy-headed thalictrums, lie broken in open spaces where sudden gusts lashed them. On a day too cold and wet to make notes outside I picked a basketful of dripping branches to take indoors and write about in comfort! But it is such unusual weather for May, almost June. To complain seems sinful when normally we would be praying for rain. Instead I am concerned by the abundance of lush growth everywhere, very aware of this rapidly changing canvas, thinking about what can take over and what must be restrained or removed.

Rubus 'Benenden' (*R. tridel*) from a distance looks like a huge rose bush up to 3m/10ft tall and wide, as its bronze-tinted, arching canes are bowed to the ground, carrying large white flowers (up to 7cm/3in across), along the entire length. There are no thorns to savage you, but soft, bright-green, lobed leaves show off the purity of the flowers. This ornamental bramble was raised by Captain Collingwood Ingram, whose garden I visited with Cedric Morris long ago. He was known as 'Cherry' Ingram because he introduced many

Japanese flowering cherries, among them *Prunus* 'Taihaku', the Great White Cherry. Years ago I remember Captain Ingram telling the story of finding it in a remote monastery garden and how he risked life and limb to get the first cutting back to England. Recently I have been told that he found it in a Sussex garden in 1923! Apparently, the full story can be found in his book, *Ornamental Cherries*.

The unusual *Weigela middendorffiana* (1.5m/5ft), a seldom-seen native of north China and Japan, is not nearly so showy as the well-known pink-flowering weigelas, but always attracts curious glances. It does best in part shade where it can obtain some protection from early frost, since it tends to start early into growth. It makes a sturdy framework supporting arched branches, the better to display matt-green leaves above which stand clusters

Weigela middendorffiana, with clusters of pale-yellow, chubby flowers flaunting deep-orange throats, usually attracts the eye of a keen plantsperson.

of pale-yellow, chubby flowers flaunting deep-orange throats. In retentive soil this is a modest shrub compared with, for example, a bright yellow azalea, but is cool and graceful above unfolding ferns and a scattering of lemon-yellow Welsh Poppies (*Meconopsis cambrica*).

We grow a compact weigela, *Weigela* 'Florida Variegata', less often seen than the type. Its narrow leaves appear more brightly variegated and it is less vigorous (1.2m/4ft tall and wide). The leaves look as if someone had painted them individually, the centres in shades of light and deeper green, the edges irregularly bordered with creamy-white. Despite an obvious shortage of chlorophyll, this little shrub is bowed down with clusters of flower all along the arching stems. Wine-coloured buds open pale-pink, trumpet-shaped flowers, making a most attractive combination of colour and form. I have already mentioned *W.* 'Looymansii Aurea', with large, lemon-yellow leaves, which retains its even colour to provide contrast long after the flowers have gone. Cherry-red buds opening pale-pink flowers are well displayed against the pale foliage which will scorch in strong sunlight. I used to grow *W. florida* 'Foliis Purpureis', slow-growing and compact (1.5m/5ft), its chocolate-stained leaves making a good background for pale purplish-pink flowers, but through carelessness, have lost it. However, it needs an open situation to colour well so does not really belong here.

One of the most handsome forms of weigela, *W.* 'Gustave Malet', is loaded in June with rose-pink blossoms.

A pink-flowered hybrid weigela, given to me with no name but which could be *Weigela* 'Gustave Malet', has made big (1.2 x 1.8m/ 4 x 6ft) ebullient shrubs, loaded in June with bunches of large flowers opening soft rose-pink blossoms from cherry-red buds. It is strange how much we can miss in the garden, often rushing past in a hurry to do or see something else. Sitting in the warmth of the house (since it is wet and cold outside), I can hold a branch in my hand and observe the subtleties of colour, tone and texture for the first time. Everything about this shrub is matt, from the rich-green, oval leaves to the almost crêpe-like texture of the petals, which develop paler shades of pink as the flowers mature. *W.* 'Mont Blanc' (1.2 x 1.8m/4ft x 6ft) is another fine, very free-flowering hybrid, opening large

The hairy calyces of *Kolkwitzia amabilis* continue to make a fuzzy feature after the flowers have fallen and the seedpods are developing. Also called the Beauty Bush, and well named since it forms a large, graceful shrub, in summer its arching branches are festooned with shell-pink blooms. *K. a.* 'Pink Cloud' has deeper pink flowers.

clusters of scented, creamy-white flowers from green-tinted buds. One petal within is washed with yellow, like spilt pollen, possibly to tempt insects inside to brush against the protruding white anthers and stigma.

Kolkwitzia amabilis, the Beauty Bush, could be mistaken for a fluffy weigela, both being members of the family *Caprifoliaceae*, which includes honeysuckle, all having flowers of a similar construction. It was introduced from north China by Ernest Wilson, to whom we are indebted for the introduction of many garden-worthy shrubs. We grow the cultivar *K. a.* 'Pink Cloud', a seedling raised at Wisley, which eventually makes a large bush (2.5 x 2.5m/ 8 x 8ft) consisting of overlapping layers of branches. The young wood and new foliage are attractively stained red. The previous year's wood carries clusters of rose-pink buds opening light-pink, bell-shaped flowers with flaring petals, their throats invitingly peppered with yellow. The calyces and flower stalks (pedicels) are conspicuously coated in silvery hairs, giving a faint fuzzy effect overall. I like to come across it in an open space in the Wood Garden where its graceful habit and delicate colouring look appropriate.

Diervilla × *splendens* is a modest shrub in comparison with the larger and more showy weigelas, but I value it for its foliage rather than for the small, honeysuckle-like yellow flowers which appear in mid-summer and again in autumn on new shoots. You may, like me, have wondered what the difference was between diervilla and weigela. (Do you still say 'weigelia'?) If I had been

Although not in the first flight of ornamental shrubs, I value *Diervilla* × *splendens* for its foliage in spring and again in autumn. Its drawback is its suckering habit, but if controlled and the old wood is pruned out in winter, the spring flush of reddish-bronze leaves is quite dramatic. A quieter display comes in autumn with a fresh burst of new tips setting off a late crop of small yellow flowers.

more observant, I would have noticed that whereas in weigela the flowers are borne on shoots from the previous year's growth, in diervilla the flowers are produced on the current season's growth. It makes a slowly suckering clump – needs the spade round it from time to time to keep it in its place, and pruning in late winter to cut out old wood and promote plenty of fresh spring growth clothed in pretty, pointed, bronze leaves which slowly fade to yellowy-green.

Stephanandra incisa 'Crispa' comes from Japan and is related to spiraeas. Its small, maple-shaped leaves have prettily cut edges, while coral-tinted, new shoots carry sprays of tiny, cream flowers in early summer. It is reputed to have good autumn colour, but mine has not been remarkable. (Perhaps I should try it elsewhere.) In winter it forms a ground-hugging hummock of pale, tangled branches, a pleasing contrast to winter carpeting plants when it is sunlit or gilded with hoar-frost. I used to have *S. tanakae*, which makes a larger shrub, most graceful with arching branches, deeply veined leaves, and larger, cream flowers. I must try it again. Both need thinning to encourage new growth since it is their habit and attractive foliage which make them garden-worthy.

MAINTAINING BALANCE

It is necessary to observe closely the changing conditions in early summer when all about the garden, whether in sun or shade, new growth is extending, especially after an unusually wet spring. We need to make sure there will be enough space, light and air for some of the herbaceous plants which will continue to provide interest later in the season. I am often reminded of David Ward's comment as we stood two years ago in the Gravel Garden where plants form undulating hills and hollows, spaces for the birds and butterflies to flit through, with elegant verticals rising among them, all creating a permanent picture, or landscape. While we were enjoying the effect together, David, father of four children, put my thoughts into words when he said that this, our baby of ten years, was rapidly becoming a rebellious teenager. So it is with the Wood Garden of a similar age. You can no longer see through the empty aisles of my church and I feel enclosed in a green world from floor to sky. Trees and shrubs which seemed to sit still, suddenly astonish me by their bulk and height and I feel concern for what needs to be done to contain and direct so much bursting vitality. In natural woodland, not controlled by man, it takes several generations for the dominant trees to overtop and smother out the understorey. Sometimes, where there is enough space and light, a close pair of trunks will together make a handsome canopy, like Siamese twins, each forming half of the umbrella-like head.

Shrubs that bear flowers on the previous year's growth and have finished flowering (such as the weigelas and deutzias) need pruning by cutting out all the branches which have flowered to encourage the production of new branches to flower the following year. Evergreens should be cut back now while I can see the congestion or where they are smothering herbaceous plants. We may even have to remove some.

By taking out a surplus oak in the Wood Garden, we exposed a good form of *Clematis montana* struggling to climb another oak with three trunks and plenty of lateral branches higher up. I am delighted to see the clematis growing strongly, with plenty of deep rose-pink flowers, 7cm/3in across. Since it has three trunks I thought this tree could support an autumn-flowering climber, so we planted nearby, in a good, deep hole, *Pileostegia viburnoides*, a member of the hydrangea family but without the conspicuous bracts. Once established its stems cling firmly to their support (elsewhere we have it covering a north-facing wall) and climb quickly, furnished with long, pointed, evergreen leaves, bronze-tinted when young. The flowers are most welcome later in the year, very like elderflowers: wide, flat heads composed of tiny cream flowers.

We had rain almost every day from October 2000 to April 2001 and had to abandon our plan to cut back some of the evergreens that form a windbreak along the Long Shady Walk. Observing how much these background shrubs were encroaching over the plants they were meant to protect, we took the risk of damaging some of the plants on the ground (rather than waiting till the following autumn), and during May 2001 reduced the height and spread of some of the laurels (*Prunus laurocerasus*) which were flowering overhead. Although we were obliged to cut hard back, we were careful to ensure that enough remained to maintain a background screen, while in future we aim to prune more regularly to maintain the right proportions between the shrubs and the herbaceous plants and bulbs in the foreground.

Also in the Long Shady Walk a *Pieris formosa* var. *forrestii*, planted some thirty years ago, is vast now, about 4m/13ft tall and the same across. When undamaged by late frost it is a wonderful sight as each terminal cluster of new leaves resembles small poinsettias, enamelled in shades of cherry-red and fading as they mature to creamy tones before finally turning green. Heavy clusters of small, ivory, bell-shaped flowers of waxy texture weigh down the branches. Flowering above it stands *Liriodendron tulipifera*, the Tulip Tree, planted at the same time and now 12m/40ft tall. Both these handsome features merit a park-like setting, but while valuing the noble aspect they give to the garden, we also need to maintain a balance between all plant forms, for both aesthetic and cultural reasons. The pieris can be reduced without loss of presence, which will relieve its herbaceous neighbours in danger of being smothered out, and removal of low branches on the Tulip Tree will let in more light while still retaining a good framework of branches high in the sky, valued in winter as much as in summer.

Left: The self-clinging climber *Pileostegia viburnoides*, with long, pointed evergreen leaves, grows well on north walls, over tree stumps, or anything you wish to hide. Its branches of frothy cream flowers are a bonus later in the summer.

Above: I think this is *Pieris formosa* var. *forrestii*, which we planted in moist, silty soil more than thirty years ago. It has made a vast shrub and is a wondrous sight when every new leaf is enamelled cherry-red.

After tea, sitting on my stool without raincoat, wellies or umbrella, suddenly I become aware of a deathly stillness, until a robin's shrill song split the silence, followed by the first spattering of rain. Strange, coppery light squeezing between rafts of cloud casts a faint glow into the shadows, picking out still-fresh shades of green, the pale blue of forget-me-nots and the lemon globes of *Paeonia mlokosewitschii*, until the moment when the ink from my pen is washed down the page. Ugh! I take shelter beneath a laurel, but it is too much. Rain soaks my shirt. As I run for home the smell of new growth – wet leaves, wet flowers, warm, wet earth – envelops me: Nature's aromatherapy, there for everyone who is privileged to grow a garden.

5 | High-Summer Tapestries

A S SUMMER PROGRESSES AND THE OVERHEAD canopy casts increasing shade, light-green or variegated leaves become more important than flowers on the woodland floor. Much as I value spring and early summer flowers, it is foliage that keeps my canvas fresh and varied throughout summer and into autumn. For much of the year, grasses, grass-like plants and ferns contribute to the interplay of shapes and textures, but now they become key players. I am heartened when visitors say they like the Wood Garden in high summer. After the continual excitement of spring-time and early summer, I wonder if they might think it dull; but there is charm, I think, in the peace and simplicity of cool greens, both overhead and carpeting the floor, and I enjoy sitting beneath the trees, absorbing the sights, smells and sounds without distraction. A willow warbler repeats endlessly its falling scale, answered faintly, by its mate, perhaps, or a rival. If I sit long enough I sometimes see a tree creeper – a glimpse only – like a little mouse scampering up a tree before it vanishes round the far side of the trunk.

Much-needed verticals, lifting the spirits and leading the eye into the distance, include drifts of white foxgloves, fluffy-headed thalictrums and various

Left: *Gillenia trifoliata*, with clouds of pointed, white petals captured on wire-thin stalks, creates a delicate screen through which to view more robust plants.

Thalictrum aquilegiifolium makes interesting verticals, the slender stems rising above surrounding greenery and flaunting clusters of fluffy flowers, reminiscent of candyfloss.

lilies that contribute now and into autumn. Arching above ground-hugging plants are various types of Solomon's Seal, *Polygonatum × hybridum*, including *P. odoratum* 'Silver Wings'. *P. falcatum* 'Variegatum' has slim, white edgings outlining every rounded leaf, reminiscent of old-fashioned, gold-rimmed spectacles (in fashion again now: nothing is new!). In a shaded corner among the filigree foliage of *Actaea spicata*, the stems and partially unfurled leaves of *Polygonatum × hybridum* 'Betberg' are stained in shades of brown, with clusters of tiny, cream flower buds dangling from the leaf axils. Earlier, in May, sharp-eyed visitors spotted the milk-chocolate-brown shoots of this special Solomon's seal pushing through the leaf-mould soil. It was given to me by Isbert Preussler, who was trained originally by the famous German plantsman Karl Foerster, and later was chief propagator and hybridizer for Countess von Stein Zeppelin at her nursery in the Black Forest. Herr Preussler found this handsome and unusual plant on his beloved mountain, after which he named it.

One of the loveliest feature plants is *Aruncus dioicus*, Goat's Beard. It grows in mountain woods around the northern hemisphere. It is superb in foliage and flower from the moment its elegant sprays of pale-green, fern-like leaves emerge in spring. I like it best just as the flowers are opening. Long, tapering spires of tiny, green buds become cream seed pearls, finally bursting into a plume of frothy blossom towards the end of June.

Gillenia trifoliata looks entirely appropriate in semi-shade, a delight to come across as you turn a corner and find it unexpectedly, although it will do well in almost any soil and position provided it is not scorched. An American native, introduced to Britain in the early eighteenth century, its dark-tinted, branching stems (1.2m/4ft tall) are scarcely visible. They carry neat, pointed leaves, supporting airy sprays of white, starry flowers that appear to float around the plant like a cluster of moths.

Nearby stand the narrow spires of *Digitalis lutea* whose colour is repeated in *Hypericum* × *inodorum* 'Ysella'. I first saw this small, yellow foxglove growing wild along the edges of woodland in the Swiss Alps. The individual flowers are small, much smaller and narrower than those of our native Common Foxglove, *Digitalis purpurea*, and close-set to form narrow spires, 75–90cm/ 2½–3ft tall. At seeding time they will colonize any available empty space, providing delicate-looking verticals above the leaves of hellebores, violas and Sweet Woodruff.

GROUND-COVER CARPETS

A group of plants I rely on, whether in flower or not, is the hardy cranesbills. They seem to flourish in almost any situation, apart from the hottest and driest. Even in considerable shade between shrubs they provide attractive ground cover, while in half-shade, and where there is sufficient light, they seem to be in flower most of the summer months and well into autumn.

The vigorous *Geranium phaeum* 'Samobor' (see page 91) is one of the first to flower. *G. nodosum* is not spectacular but is very obliging, thriving anywhere, even in dark shade. Throughout summer and into autumn it produces small, light-purple flowers whose pale centres are enlivened with crimson veins and pale-blue stamens, appearing to float on wire-thin, dark stems above smooth, maple-shaped leaves. *G.* × *oxonianum* 'Claridge Druce' is extremely vigorous and will colonize wide areas where space permits. I allow mine to clothe open, bare spaces in the Wood Garden while I am waiting to decide on new plant introductions. It is a relief to pass by totally weed-free areas covered with low mounds of dark-green, divided leaves crowded with pink flowers, the colour deepened by a network of hair-fine, magenta veins. In June this geranium makes a sea of upturned, pink faces mingling with the snowy clusters of *Rosa* 'Bobbie James' which hang down to ground level from the tall ash tree. Near my front door, in a north-west-facing border, a sweep of intense colour sprawls across the gravel path throughout July and August. Almost everywhere I have planted it, this geranium gives a sprinkling of jewel-like colour into autumn.

Overleaf: *Heuchera* 'Ruffles' and a low-growing type of Solomon's Seal, *Polygonatum odoratum* 'Silver Wings', make a pleasing combination, together with white Martagon Lilies, against a background of ferns.

Behind the plank bench is a massed planting of *Geranium* × *oxonianum* 'Claridge Druce', while at the base of the tree *Geranium* × *cantabrigiense* 'Cambridge' sprawls into the pathway.

Geranium × *cantabrigiense* 'Cambridge' makes another low carpet of small, pale-green, parasol-shaped leaves which contrast with the darker, willow-shaped leaves of *Buglossoides purpurocaerulea*. As the blue of the buglossoides begins to fade, the bright rose-pink geranium flowers take over. Throughout the summer the flowers come and go, rising and falling in seesaw fashion, but the leaves remain, creating patterns of light and dark shades of green.

Among the many hardy geraniums I grow, perhaps the one I value most is *Geranium macrorrhizum*. It is one of the very best ground-covering plants, thriving in sun or shade. It spreads by means of rooting stems, creating dense carpets of scallop-edged leaves, strongly aromatic, especially when you crush them a little when working around them. By autumn many of the felty leaves turn to shades of red and yellow, the rest remaining green throughout winter. There is variation in flower colour. I particularly like *G. m.* 'Album'. It has pale-shell-pink flowers which contrast well with deep-coral-coloured calyces and long, protruding stamens and pistil. Another lovely form is *G. m.* 'Ingwersen's Variety', with soft-lilac-pink flowers. If cut back after the first flush of flowering, they quickly regrow, creating cool-green carpets around the skirts of shrubs, such as the deutzias and flowering currants, and give a second display of flower.

Buglossoides purpurocaerulea (which formerly we called *Lithospermum*) spreads to make a dark-green, irregular border in place of the blue wash of forget-me-nots that blurs the edges of the winding pathways. When they fade to mildewed grey, the forget-me-nots need to be removed once enough seed has dropped for another year. *Buglossoides* has small, bristly, evergreen leaves on lax stems carrying clusters of small, deep-gentian-blue flowers. It has a different habit from *Lithodora diffusa* 'Heavenly Blue', which makes a low, ground-hugging carpet smothered in early summer with larger, wonderfully blue flowers, but it needs moist, acid sand in sun, whereas the *Buglossoides* will tolerate either limestone or dry, sandy soils, and its open habit leaves spaces for other plants and bulbs to grow through.

Teucrium scorodonia 'Crispum Marginatum', an attractive variant of Wood Sage that was found in the wild by Eric Smith, makes pretty, pale-green leaf rosettes, each leaf heavily frilled at the edges, a paler green than the rest of the mossy-textured leaf. Spikes of tiny cream-lipped flowers are attractive in midsummer. This teucrium is surprisingly drought-tolerant in shady places. Sweet Woodruff (*Galium odoratum*) continues to form ground-covering mounds by the edge of a path or below leggy shrubs. The filigree effect of its narrow leaves, joined to make seven-pointed stars threaded to form necklaces on lax stems, is offset by swathes of *Pachyphragma macrophyllum* whose large, round leaves run back into the shade of oaks.

It sounds dangerous to recommend of all things the pestilential weed Ground Elder, but the variegated *Aegopodium podagraria* 'Variegatum', with handsome cream-and-green leaves and lacy heads of tiny, cream flowers, will transform the poorest piece of soil where little else does well. I first fell in love with it seeing it planted in a narrow strip at the foot of a north-facing wall where it was neatly controlled by mowing up to the border edge. It does spread, I admit, left to itself, but is not uncontrollable.

We are slowly introducing some of the strangely seductive arisaemas, relatives of the arum, mainly distinguished by having divided foliage. They need well-fed, retentive soil in part shade, where they will intrigue the curious gardener. Although not at all flamboyant, they are fascinating both in foliage and flower. The first I came to know was *Arisaema triphyllum* (Jack-in-the-Pulpit) from moist woodlands in the eastern United States. Its narrow, arum-like flowers, about 15cm/10in tall, are basically green outside and variously striped inside in shades of purplish brown and palest green. Intensifying the

The narrow, pointed leaflets of *Arisaema ciliatum* form an umbrella shape which shelters the hooded, green and brown-striped arum-like flower, with a tip extending into an extraordinarily long, thin, brown tail.

Right: Plants doing well in the north-facing border at the base of a clay bank include this handsome pair: *Heuchera micrantha* var. *diversifolia* 'Palace Purple', which continues to produce fresh foliage after the veil of flowers has faded, with *Persicaria virginiana* Variegata Group providing cool contrast. This same combination is seen in context earlier in the year in the photograph on page 12.

Far right: Patience rewarded! After more than ten years, several smooth trunks of oak trees are girdled with blossom in June, provided by *Hydrangea anomala* subsp. *petiolaris.*

colour is the dark spadix protected beneath the overhanging spathe-tip (the 'pulpit'!). *A. candidissimum* needs careful marking, since it can always frighten you into thinking you have lost it, so late does it appear. Not until June will you see first bare, pink stems emerging to open narrow, white spathes, lined inside with pink-and-white candy stripes. Neatly wrapped round the base of each stem is a single leaf which unfolds three large lobes, resembling a great cloverleaf. A mound of these can be as striking as the beautiful flowers, lasting in good shape until autumn when they turn the colour of chamois leather. Quite unnerving to meet, almost at eye-level (about 75–90cm/30–36in), on a mid-summer evening is *A. tortuosum*. From a large, underground tuber there emerges a thick, purple-stained stem. Halfway up, two pedate leaves appear, while above them is poised a snake-like, hooded head – a narrow, pale-green spathe – and from beneath the curved lid flickers the long, thin, brown proboscis of the spadix.

Heuchera villosa 'Royal Red' makes warm contrast among many shades of green. Like a bolder, richer form of *H. micrantha* var. *diversifolia* 'Palace Purple', its large, vine-shaped leaves display several shades of dark and lighter tan, satin-finished on top, shining maroon on the reverse, all making a dark and glowing base for a forest of bronze flower stems whose top half carries whorls of tiny, pale-pink flowers, with mist-like effect. In recent years many variations of coloured-leaf heucheras have been introduced from the USA. As with hostas and other plants which have become fashionable, the choice can be bewildering. Two we have let in are *H.* 'Chocolate Ruffles' and *H.* 'Persian Carpet'. The latter has smooth, flat leaves to show off a sumptuous marbled effect; intricate veining over a dark-purple background slowly fades to silvery pewter, with plum-purple reverse. Superb, yes, but I have a soft spot for *H.* 'Ruffles', now making robust clumps of fresh-green, ruffle-edged leaves, above which stand tall, slender stems holding tiers of palest-green 'bobbles' – bead-like buds thrusting out minute stamens and stigmas – and creating an airy, natural effect along the path edge.

PILLARS OF BLOSSOM

Throughout the month of June, as the overhead canopy gradually blocks out the light and flowers on the floor disappear, climbers scrambling up tree trunks provide colourful focal points. Several specimens of the climbing hydrangea, *Hydrangea anomala* subsp. *petiolaris*, have now, after ten years, encircled the tall, straight trunks of supportive oaks, carrying large, flat heads of lace-like flowers 4.5–6m/15–20ft high into the branches. There were several exasperating years before they decided to make a move, but with solicitous watering and

Right: *Rosa* 'Paul's Himalayan Musk' Rambler is a tremendous grower, capable of reaching the tops of trees, from where it hangs thin, trailing stems festooned with semi-double, shell-pink flowers, sweetly scented.

Far right: Equally vigorous, *Rosa* 'Bobbie James' has long, fresh green, glossy leaves and large clusters of creamy-white flowers, gloriously fragrant.

mulching they finally established good root systems and now grow vigorously without further attention.

Climbing roses carry the eye into the heads of oak, ash and Silver Birch. They too have taken ten years, some of them reaching the topmost branches of their support. We use ex-army telephone wire covered with a cotton coating to lead climbers into trees, rather than plastering the trunks with wire-netting, as one sometimes sees. In too much shade roses do not flower well, needing space for light and air to surround them, so I must place them carefully, on an open-sided boundary of the Wood Garden, for example, or be prepared to thin more trees.

Needing the tallest, strongest tree is a 'Kiftsgate' rose, selected from *R. filipes*, native of western China. It is extremely vigorous, thrusting up strong shoots as tall as 6m/20ft in one season as it scrambles for the upper branches of the tree where it will dangle long, trailing stems festooned with airy bouquets, each often containing more than a hundred small, cup-shaped, creamy-white flowers, filled with orange stamens, borne on thread-like stalks – hence the name *filipes*, which is the direct Latin translation.

Another vigorous rose doing well as it romps towards the top of a tall ash tree, standing in an exposed position on the edge of a path, is *Rosa* 'Bobbie James'. It appeared by chance in the Sunningdale Nurseries in 1960 and was named by Graham Stuart Thomas (the renowned expert and conserver of old roses) after the Hon. Robert James in honour of his contribution to gardening, especially in the preservation of old roses. 'Bobbie James' is a wonderful sight when draped to ground level with large clusters of creamy-white flowers, larger than those of 'Kiftsgate', and slightly double, having an extra row or two of petals. On a warm June evening the sweet, fresh fragrance drifts for yards along the winding pathways.

On a solitary oak in full sun, opposite my kitchen window and far from the Wood Garden, I planted the equally vigorous rose, 'Paul's Himalayan Musk' Rambler. For some twenty years it has been a delight, from the moment the first dainty leaves appear and the first buds show colour until the towering cascade of blossom hides almost every leaf with sprays of shell-pink flowers – small rosettes, opening from deeper-pink buds, scenting the air long before the source is discovered. I wondered how long its support would last and decided it needed drastic pruning, even if it meant far fewer flowers in the coming year. We hired a hoist, a cage supported on a moveable arm, which reaches high into the tops of trees. Gerard, trained in the use of tree surgery equipment, cut away the huge beehive of tangled wood, leaving the main rope-like stems attached to the trunk and truncated branches of the oak. He warned me the tree might not last more than five more years, having been suffocated by the rose. I have taken that chance, hoping to see again this magnificent 'wedding bouquet' in June glory, but relieved also to see that a new view into the distance will be opened up when we are obliged to remove the rose and its worn-out support. Meanwhile, we have established another 'Paul's Himalayan Musk' on an oak at the edge of the Wood Garden.

Roses, especially the old shrub roses, remind me of Lady's Mantle, since they flower at the same time and go so well together. I surprise myself by finding I have not as yet planted *Alchemilla mollis* in the Wood Garden! There is still time, since it will grow in shade or sun, but

prefers some cool, of soil or aspect, such as a north-facing border where its froth of tiny, yellowy-green flowers are not scorched. Its smaller relatives are valued where space is limited. All come from European mountain meadows.

It was inevitable I would plant various forms of honeysuckles in the Wood Garden to clothe bare, pole-like trunks of younger trees, since our native *Lonicera periclymenum* was already there, scrambling over anything it could find to reach the light. Most of this we have removed, but I planted *L. p.* 'Graham Thomas', an extra-fine form found by Graham in a Warwickshire copse. Now, after ten years, its clusters of cream flowers, turning yellow as they age, are so abundant that they form a pillar of blossom, from top to bottom of a tall tree, filling the air with heavy scent on still, warm evenings when they are visited by moths. Another selection, *L. p.* 'Serotina', known as the Late Dutch Honeysuckle, is distinguished by its purple, twining stems clothed in dark blue-green leaves almost obliterated with clusters of garnet-red buds which open cream flowers, lovely to pick and put into a bowl of old roses, like *Rosa gallica* and *R.* 'Charles de Mills'. Valerie Finnis gave me this especially handsome plant. But while appreciating a somewhat cool situation these honeysuckles do not perform well in too much shade or too dry soil when they become disfigured with mildew.

On a shady north wall I have planted *Lonicera similis* var. *delavayi*. This evergreen climber is closely related to the better-known but less elegant *L. japonica*. Its young, bronze-tinted stems are clothed in long, pointed leaves, with clusters of creamy-white, scented flowers in the axils of every pair. Once a rope-like framework is established, creating an open pattern against the wall, it needs regular pruning to prevent it becoming a shapeless bundle.

I am fond of several honeysuckles which are not scented. (It is curious how some people switch off when you mention this fact, but they could be missing both choice and unusual climbers.) I grow *Lonicera flava*, from the south-eastern United States, on a shaded, east-facing wall where it gives two displays. In early summer the upper part of every stem carries a green cup formed by two leaves joined together, filled with a close bunch of orange-yellow flowers. By late summer there is an unexpected treat when you look up to see that these have become shining, red berries sitting in shallow saucers, as if held out for your inspection. So far I have not succeeded with one of the loveliest honeysuckles, *L.* × *tellmanniana*. The Wood Garden has proved too dry and shady for it and I am woefully short of walls. It needs a cool, humus-rich soil, sunlight, but not sun-scorch. When well suited it is a glorious sight, with extra-large flowers, deep yellow flushed with orange – it matters not that they are scentless: they are so handsome.

Left: Lonicera periclymenum 'Graham Thomas' flaunts its beauty against a blue sky. After several years this plant has made a vast, bushy shape against the trunk of an oak. It needs to be reduced by severe pruning of the old wood to encourage new growth from the base.

HANDSOME COW PARSLEYS

While we have learnt from experience to severely restrict, if not totally obliterate, the May-flowering Queen Anne's Lace, *Anthriscus sylvestris* (see page 14), which, unless you have ample space in a semi-wild area, is better left by the roadside, I do grow the irresistible *A. s.* 'Ravenswing' in a narrow, north-facing border where we can easily keep an eye on the seed. The dark-brownish-purple leaves, attractive in themselves, make ideal contrast for the lacy heads of white flowers which continue in succession for several weeks. (Grown in isolation, the seed produces a fair proportion true to type.) Regal lilies flower above it and slender, white tapers of *Actaea simplex* var. *simplex* Atropurpurea Group (formerly *Cimicifuga*) follow, repeating the same dark foliage in late summer.

Fortunately, as well as *Smyrnium perfoliatum* (see page 93), there are some desirable, less invasive umbellifers with finely cut, fern-like foliage which add grace and charm to cool shady areas. Astrantias, which I have described on page 107 (classified like smyrniums as *Apiaceae*), are probably the best-known.

Sweet Cicely (*Myrrhis odorata*) is a more substantial plant than Queen Anne's Lace, easily distinguished from other umbellifers by the occasional white splash on its soft, feathery leaves, looking (to my mind) as if a bird flying overhead had relieved itself, as can happen. But no, this is not contamination. Indeed, the leaves are sweet to taste, with a flavour of aniseed. Try adding them to salads or a bowl of hot plums or rhubarb. Heads of white flowers, held above leafy mounds on branching stems up to 1.2m/4ft tall, develop into large, crunchy seeds, edible and tasty when green. Eat them before they trouble you by seeding in the wrong place – but seedlings are easily recognized and as easily removed. Since it is a native, I let mine colonize among the wild bluebells and pink campions.

An unlikely looking umbellifer is *Cryptotaenia japonica* f. *atropurpurea*. Its rat-tail-shaped spires of tiny, purple flowers are insignificant, but I grow it for the handsome effect, even in deep shade, of trifoliate, astrantia-like leaves, purple as the leaves of beetroot. It seeds around in any vacant soil where a little colony can look attractive marching between low ground cover.

Seldom seen in gardens is another uncharacteristic umbellifer with the awkward name *Pleurospermum brunonis*, but it draws attention to itself on my north-facing clay bank at one end of the Long Shady Walk with a froth of chalk-white flowers above finely cut, green leaves, standing 60–75cm/2–2½ft tall.

Our native sanicle, *Sanicula europaea*, can be found flowering from May to August in deciduous woodland throughout Britain, and is common in beech woods in the south of England. It has shiny, dark-green, lobed leaves, with

Right: A delightful partnership in a narrow border at the base of a north-facing wall – *Anthriscus sylvestris* 'Ravenswing' contrasting with the fresh young fronds of *Dryopteris erythrosora*. Where one umbellifer with dark-brownish-purple leaves was planted, seedlings true to form have germinated around it.

Cenolophium denudatum is a handsome perennial umbellifer from Russia and north Asia. In an open situation, in retentive soil, it makes a strong, upstanding plant, with branching stems carrying lace-like, flat heads of little white flowers over a long period in mid-summer.

white or pale pink flowers held in very small, compact umbels on stems about 60cm/2ft tall. It will tolerate deep shade and quite dry conditions. In the Middle Ages it was used as a medicinal herb, from which its name is derived (*sano* means 'I heal' or 'I cure'.)

A very handsome, perennial umbellifer is *Cenolophium denudatum*. It is said to grow in any well-drained sunny border. That may well be so, but it delights me in not-too-shady places in the Wood Garden. Early in the year it forms an interesting mound of dark-green, fern-like leaves before making, in mid-summer, many branched stems topped with wide, flat heads tightly packed with green buds which slowly open tiny, white flowers. Caught by wind, they tend to flop among their neighbours – in my case *Skimmia japonica* 'Rubella' is conveniently near to help prop them up as they right themselves. It also looks good among astrantias.

Chaerophyllum hirsutum 'Roseum', the Pink Hairy Chervil, is the prettiest thing in early summer. It flowers from May onwards, growing to about 60–75cm/2–2½ ft. Over a base of feathery, apple-scented leaves stand branching stems holding a haze of tiny, lilac-mauve flowers. It prefers damp meadows or light woodland, so a dampish spot in sun or a cool, shady corner in the garden suits it well.

DRAMATIC FOLIAGE

Since we are making a wood garden as opposed to developing natural woodland, we need to pay attention to shapes and forms, and to use some plants which in themselves create a strong feature on which to focus. These pull the scene together, and rest the eye and mind, amid the formless confusion of small-leaved carpeting plants and twiggy bundles as deciduous shrubs start to lose their leaves. A statue or a fine urn can do this; in our case, we have a few simple benches strategically placed. But I like best to use plants as architectural features. After a long and complicated sentence it is a relief to come to a full stop. So it is in the garden. Plants with bold, simple shapes act as full stops at the end of statements made with a profusion of plants.

In summer, top of the list could be hostas. No other plant has the same impact. A well-established clump with many overlapping layers of large, simple leaves is for me what a fine boulder might be in gardens where such things can be found naturally but which would look totally out of place here in flat farmland. Unacceptable too in my Wood Garden would be some of the strongly variegated forms of hosta – there are associations for them elsewhere in the garden. Just now a blue hosta – it could be *Hosta* 'Blue Danube' or *H.* 'Halcyon' (both Tardiana Group) – makes a bold 'full stop' above the new growth of *Teucrium scorodonia* 'Crispum Marginatum' running around it. For spring and early summer I have included some of the gently variegated sorts, such as the lovely *Hosta fortunei* var. *albopicta*, whose leaves are marbled in shades of primrose, olive and pale green, turning totally green by mid-summer. Hostas that remain good-looking well into late summer and early autumn include *H. sieboldiana* whose crisp, robust leaves of a marvellous bluish-grey make a feature impossible to pass by. The variety *H. s.* var. *elegans* has superb leaves even more deeply veined and 'quilted', so the colour appears a deeper shade of blue-grey. Two plain-green-leaved hostas, tough-textured, which look suitably simple are *H. ventricosa* with broadly oval leaves, deeply veined, and *H. lancifolia* with layers of shining, dark-green leaves, narrow and pointed. Both make good impact plants on the curve of a path and both are handsome in flower. With a wealth of new introductions to choose from, these two old-fashioned species may seem unadventurous but they fulfil my needs in their situation.

We are often asked how we keep our hostas relatively free of slug damage. We try to avoid unfriendly chemicals as much as possible but I admit to using slug-bait occasionally: only a little is needed, tucked under the leaves. After that I think the mulch of pulverized bark helps, as do the many birds which live in the garden.

Hosta fortunei var. *aureomarginata* has found its way into the Long Shady Walk, where it looks well despite being variegated! Too many variegated or yellow-leaved plants massed together can look uncomfortably busy, but used sparingly among suitable companions they are invaluable. Here *Geranium macrorrhizum* 'Album' has crept around the hosta.

In the Long Shady Walk, where the crushed-bark-covered path turns left alongside the north-facing clay bank, is the shining evergreen *Magnolia grandiflora* (on the far left of the photograph) with the yellow-leaved *Weigela* 'Looymansii Aurea' for contrast. Dominating the scene is the tall columnar mass of *Persicaria polymorpha*, a perennial plant composed of strong stems crowned in mid-summer with widely branched heads of creamy-white flowers. Balancing the effect, planted on the clay bank, is *Acer negundo* 'Variegatum'.

Just one large plant of *Persicaria virginiana* Variegata Group will lift a quiet scene. Its oval leaves, softly marbled in shades of cream and green, are as good as a flowering plant among resting companions such as hardy cranesbills, ajugas or spreading rosettes of *Saxifraga × polita* 'Dentata'. This last plant is effective when the flowers have finished, with spoon-shaped, leathery leaves which look as if they had been cut round with pinking shears to create sharply toothed edges. Elsewhere, in a shady border, I have planted *Phlox paniculata* 'Harlequin', produced by Alan Bloom, to form a vertical behind the *Persicaria*. This Border Phlox needs some shade to protect its variegation – long, narrow leaves with a shadowed central zone surrounded by an irregular border of cream, which becomes wider and more conspicuous on leaves nearest the top of the stems. Heads of purple-violet flowers in August seem surprisingly good for a variegated plant.

Phlox paniculata, which grows wild in the woods of the eastern and central USA and is a parent of the well-known cultivars, the brightly coloured Border Phlox, is topped in late summer with cool, pale-mauve flowers. It looks well, and its willowy habit (over 1.2m/4ft) is supported when planted among *Euphorbia cornigera* which flowers at the same time. This Himalayan euphorbia

makes clumps of handsome foliage topped with large, loose heads of yellow-green flowers, which are guaranteed to freshen the scene in late summer when shady areas have become a little sombre.

The basal leaves of pulmonarias are particularly handsome in high summer, each plant forming large rosettes. Some are plain; others are variously marked with large or small spots, sometimes pale green on green, sometimes silvered, even silvered all over. All these stand out well among small-leaved carpeting plants. A recent introduction, making a flat, eye-catching, starfish-like shape is *Pulmonaria longifolia* 'Ankum', with long, narrow leaves, wavy-edged and heavily silvered. Its flowers are good too, deep gentian-blue, in spring.

Rodgersias are among the most sumptuous of foliage plants. They have astilbe-like, although heavier, plumes of pink or white flowers, but it is their leaves which contribute most to a design, throughout the season and until the frosts. Most of them grow wild in north-west China by stream-sides or in damp woods. Fortunately not all of my Wood Garden has starved gravel soil. Over many decades fine, silty soils have been washed down into the lower end, where, fed with compost, these handsome plants are making colonies by means of creeping rhizomes. Planted between shrubs where there is enough

moisture, they can take full sun, but in less favourable soil they need shade as well as shelter from winds to prevent the large leaves from scorching. Rodgersia leaves, unlike the simple outline of a hosta, have large, deeply veined leaflets held together on top of the leaf stem. The foliage of *Rodgersia aesculifolia* resembles, both in size and shape, that of a horse-chestnut, after which it is named. *R. pinnata* 'Superba' has been selected for its plumes of rich-raspberry-pink flowers followed by bronze seed heads. Another, *R. podophylla*, is a delight from early spring when the young, unfolding leaves are coffee-coloured, turning green as they expand, often changing to coppery-red tones in autumn. Each boldly handsome leaf is composed of five large leaflets, broadly triangular in shape with jagged tips. The heads of white, astilbe-like flowers are less remarkable.

LATE-SUMMER SHRUBS

The genus *Deutzia* is a lovely group of shrubs to add grace and lightness in both open and part shady places, associating well with hardy geraniums, tiarellas and polemoniums (Jacob's ladder). There are many to choose from, both species and hybrids. I wish I had spent more time visiting botanic gardens to become more aware of the range of trees and shrubs within individual families, but, as all gardeners say, the more we know, the more we realize how little we know. Deutzias make graceful bushes clothed in pointed, matt-green leaves, carrying racemes of small, white or pink flowers. All flowering shoots should be removed as soon after flowering as possible to make way for next year's, already rushing ahead. The well-known *Deutzia* × *kalmiiflora* has made a twiggy bush, transformed when small, cherry-red buds open white petals, giving an attractive, flushed-pink effect. I am miserable to have lost through carelessness (having allowed something else to smother it) the beautiful *D. longifolia* 'Veitchii'. Old slides show it in full glory, covered in clusters of lilac-pink flowers on long, arching boughs touching the ground. *D.* × *hybrida* 'Mont Rose', on the other hand, has made a tall (1.5m/5ft), upright-growing shrub, carrying pyramid-shaped clusters of lilac-pink flowers. It comes into bloom as *D.* × *rosea* begins to fade. There are numerous cultivars of this hybrid, which makes a medium-sized shrub, its arched branches making layers of blossom, the clusters of bell-shaped flowers opening pink and fading almost to white held along their entire length.

From a distance *Deutzia pulchra* (1.2 x 1.2m/4 x 4ft) appears palest cream, its arching habit showing off to perfection overlapping layers of branches clothed in small, pointed leaves faintly stippled green on a cream background. This unusual deciduous shrub is found wild in the Philippines and Taiwan,

Left: *Rodgersia podophylla* emerges from underground rhizomes with tightly folded clusters of leaflets poised on bare stems. At first they are an extraordinary dark bronze, deeply and intricately pleated. Slowly they unfold and spread wide like an open hand until green leaves with copper tints form a dramatic feature throughout summer. In some soils they turn amazing shades of red in autumn, but not in mine.

Overleaf: *Deutzia* × *hybrida* 'Mont Rose' forms an upright framework to support a cascade of lilac-pink blossom held in close panicles.

Deutzia pulchra 'Variegata' forms a graceful shape of many overlapping layers clothed in pale cream leaves and makes a luminous feature against a background of green.

thus not to be considered totally hardy, but it has flourished undamaged by cold over the last ten years in the Wood Garden. It was given to me many years ago by Brian Halliwell, then an assistant curator of Kew Gardens, where it was growing against a warm wall. In exposed situations it needs shelter. I value it greatly as a pale feature among more sombre shades of green. Holding a branch in my hand, or using it in a mixed foliage arrangement, I find its delicate colouring delightful, and know of nothing else like it. In early summer clusters of small, white flowers appear, but they are not noteworthy. In an attempt to introduce colour in spring, while it is still leafless, I have planted a blue *Clematis macropetala* to weave its way through the deutzia, but if the climber flourishes too well, to the detriment of the shrub, I may have to remove it.

A quiet shrub, the American native *Holodiscus discolor*, grown from seed I originally brought home from North Carolina, looks at its best this overcast Sunday afternoon. It has made a large shrub, about 2.4m/8ft tall and more across, its gracefully arching boughs hung with frothy, tapering bundles of tiny, cream flowers set off by scallop-edged, green leaves. It is not in the top flight of decorative shrubs, its drawback being in its dying-off period when the lacy panicles of flower turn a boring beige, but coming across it when fresh and in the right setting, a semi-wild informal area, I find it quietly charming. Many years ago I remember seeing it on a wet day in Scotland, draped like a lace shawl where it had grown through the branches of a fallen tree.

The unusual *Heptacodium miconioides*, a native of China, was brought to me from the Arnold Arboretum in Massachusetts. It has made a large shrub handsomely dressed in pairs of oval, pointed leaves, waiting till late summer to surprise me with wide panicles of small, white, star-shaped flowers, sweetly scented (if you retain a good sense of smell) on every terminal shoot and held on conspicuous calyces which turn red after the flowers have fallen.

I have already mentioned the yellow-leaved *Hypericum* × *inodorum* 'Ysella' associating well with yellow foxgloves. Elsewhere in the garden, in open situations, this shrub has been disfigured with rust, but so far it has remained healthy in part shade, fresh as new paint, a glowing pale yellow, tucked between *Amelanchier lamarckii* and *Corylopsis glabrescens* var. *gotoana*, both quiet now. Yellow-leaved shrubs become less bright in shade, but they start the season well before the shadows deepen, fading gradually to light green by late summer. I am thinking of the *Philadelphus coronarius* 'Aureus' (2 x 2m/6½ft x 6½ft) which I have already described with *Dipelta* in the Long Shady Walk. This mock orange means as much to me as a yellow-flowered azalea, its young foliage imitating sunlight in shadowy places in the Wood Garden. The vivid tones slowly fade as the leaves mature. The colour is not so intense in light shade, but neither is there unsightly scorching, as can occur in full sun. On humid days in early summer a thousand small, cream flowers distil a sweet scent for yards.

Two years ago I planted several other philadelphus in the Wood Garden, but I am beginning to think they need more light to flower well – another mistake to be rectified and to make a space through which to view what lies beyond. However, I feel bound to describe one I planted several years ago on the edge of the wood in a mixed shrub border. It is *P.* 'Sybille', a tall, elegantly arching shrub wreathed in large, rounded, creamy-white flowers, heavily scented. (I am disturbed, on checking out this shrub, to find it described as having almost square flowers with purple staining!) My plant came originally from the garden of Mrs Sybil Sherwood, which led me to think it had been chosen for her. Whatever its name, it is very distinctive. On checking this, we find it is a Lemoine hybrid of 1917.

Cornus mas 'Variegata' is one of the loveliest shrubs to illuminate a darkening background. It is not merely the light introduced by oval, pointed leaves with wide, cream margins, but the fact that each pair of leaves is spaced along the slender, spreading branches which creates this delicate effect. On the east-facing boundary of the Wood Garden several *C. alba* 'Aurea', hard-pruned in spring, catch the eye now, their large, oval, melon-yellow leaves held above a ground cover of dark-green *Symphytum ibericum* and blue-grey hostas, while the Golden Creeping Jenny forms rivulets along a narrow path's edge. I am grateful to my visitors who respect the garden, walking as they must in places in single file, otherwise these paths would have widened like carriageways, losing the sense of mystery and surprise that waits there. *Cornus alba* 'Elegantissima' has white variegation which repeats the snowy blossom of the 'Kiftsgate' rose tumbling to ground level from a Silver Birch nearby. It will continue to make a feature long after the rose has faded. Its greyish-green leaves have irregular, white margins, yet are not misshapen as are some forms of variegation. A few shoots, devoid of chlorophyll, remain entirely white. In poor conditions, too dry or too exposed to bright sun, I have seen this shrub looking miserable, with browned edges to the leaves, but in part shade and retentive soil it is a truly elegant feature throughout the growing season.

Fuchsia magellanica 'Versicolor' is a beautiful foliage plant which produces a long succession of elegant flowers.

In the Long Shady Walk many fuchsias make shrubby plants, up to 1.2m/4ft tall, in part shade, as long as the soil is well fed and not too dry, and provide both flower and leaf colour from June to the first frosts. *Fuchsia magellanica* var. *molinae* 'Sharpitor' (75cm/30in), with small, brightly variegated, oval leaves on green stems that set off the long, slender flowers in palest pink and lilac, is especially valuable for giving a fresh effect among darker shrubs. I describe other fuchsias on page 196.

Unless you can find shelter from drying winds, and are prepared to water regularly in summer, hydrangeas tend to suffer in many Essex gardens. They need well-nourished, moist but not waterlogged soil. I have tried and failed with the cultivated mopheaded varieties which make such magnificent late-summer displays in the West Country and other places where summer rainfall is reliable. Fortunately some of the lacecap varieties are more tolerant, particularly in light shade, and their delicate form is more sympathetic among the other plants in the Wood Garden. One of my favourites is *Hydrangea arborescens* subsp. *discolor* 'Sterilis'. Contrariwise, this is *not* a lacecap, but its character appeals to me, fitting perfectly into the woodland setting. On somewhat lax, woody stems it carries pale heads of small, green flowers which show up well against a dark background. They last well for several weeks, finally turning soft brown. Left unpruned, the slowly spreading colony of stems produces a more lavish display of smaller heads; pruning results in larger but fewer flower heads.

Hydrangea aspera 'Macrophylla' makes a rather leggy shrub, handsomely clothed in long, dark-green, hairy leaves, and in late summer carries large, flat heads of small, mauve flowers surrounded by large, white, sterile florets which slowly fade to pink. In Scotland I have seen great shrubs covered with heads the size of tea plates. We struggled initially with ours as late-spring frosts repeatedly cut back the new growth, but at last it has made a woody frame and flowers regularly. *H. a.* subsp. *sargentiana* makes a tall, leggy shrub with more rounded, velvet-textured, green leaves above which stand smaller heads of white flowers. They remain attractive for many weeks as they slowly fade to shades of green, still retaining good shape.

Hydrangea heteromalla 'Snowcap' is a huge, woody hydrangea, given to me by John Bond, who was Keeper of the Royal Windsor Gardens. It is well placed, so far, in a gap open to the sky, where it flaunts branches some 3m/10ft tall, bearing typical lacecap flowers – wide, flat heads of small, white, fertile flowers surrounded by large, cream, sterile flowers, fading to brown yet remaining attractive well into autumn.

The hydrangea I still admire in mid-winter, when its desiccated, pale-fawn flower heads float like lace doilies between the green-stained trunks of young oaks, is, I think, *H. macrophylla* 'Mariesii Perfecta' (syn. *H. m.* 'Bluewave'), although it might be 'Lilacina'. In late summer these heads have blue, sterile florets surrounding a deeper-blue centre. Wherever the soil is less acid the colour varies attractively to shades of pinky-lilac, lovely near to colonies of Japanese anemones. Another hydrangea I feel lucky to be able to grow is *H. m.* 'Veitchii'. This is one of the best white-flowered lacecaps. In favourable conditions it makes a medium-sized bush with exceptionally beautiful flowers. It has a centre of light-blue flowers, surrounded by extra-large, creamy-white, sterile florets. And, finally, I grow *H. m.* 'Ayesha'. I first saw this curiously attractive form in the garden of Norman Haddon in Porlock, Devon. The individual flowers have thick, curved petals, reminding me somehow of porcelain, shaped more like lilac flowers than normal hydrangea petals. They are a soft rose-pink opening from cream buds.

Hydrangea aspera subsp. *sargentiana* was first found in west Hupeh, China, by E. H. Wilson. Distinguished by its rich, velvet-green leaves, its flat, lace-like flower heads persist well into autumn.

Towards the end of the summer of 2001, I became concerned by the gloom in the Wood Garden where the overhead canopy, mainly of oaks, had expanded in ten years to shut out much of the light. So, while it was heavy with leaf, David, who has worked with me for eighteen years, and Gerard, who has been here since he was a boy and has an eye for the future of trees, studied the problem together, to plan what we could do in the months to come. Some oaks would have to be removed. We marked the less healthy or less shapely ones, looking up all the time to see where new corridors of light would fall and where those remaining would have light and space to develop more shapely crowns over the *next* ten years!

6 | Autumn's Sunlit Openings

OVERALL, EARLY AUTUMN IS QUIET in the Wood Garden, with few flowering plants, but still good combinations of foliage. Long shadows alternate with brilliant strips of light lying across dry pathways, bouncing blinding-white off the surface of shiny leaves like those of hostas, wild ginger (*Asarum europaeum*) and epimediums; the last, now dark green and leathery, will develop good autumn colour. Low sunlight catches both the top and undersides of the leaves of Solomon's Seal, dark shadows trapped between. Its gracefully arched stems – provided you have dealt with sawfly caterpillars in June – continue to look well until cold, misty mornings in October bring a sudden change. Then, almost overnight, together with hostas, they turn to honey and amber tints, catching the eye from far away.

Colour is limited at this time of year and thus all the more precious. *Viola cornuta* embroiders the path edge in improved soil and light shade. If I could have only one viola, it might be this, the Horned Violet, so called because of the long, curving spur which joins the back of the petals. Colour forms vary from white, through lavender-blue, to a really good violet-blue, the long-stemmed flowers standing well above carpets of small leaves. The main flush

Left: Suddenly, in early autumn, a carpet of colour appears beneath the Great Oak where the earth was bare all summer except for a protecting layer of leaf mould. The area receives very little moisture in high summer but with the onset of shorter days the resting bulbs and corms come to life. They include *Cyclamen hederifolium* in shades of pink and white, and the dark-stemmed *Colchicum speciosum* 'Atrorubens'.

of flower is in May, softening blue-leaved hostas, tangling with neighbours by means of scrambling shoots, but never a menace. Tidied up after flowering, this long-lived perennial promptly makes fresh growth, and now gives sprinklings of autumn colour. On the whole violas occur in damp situations in the wild, and I have seen *V. cornuta* weaving through dense herbage in sunlit meadows in the Pyrenees, where boiling clouds roll off the Atlantic to shower them most afternoons. We find that other small violas do best in the cool conditions of north- and east-facing borders.

Actaeas, some of which formerly we called *Cimicifuga*, contribute elegant verticals, their tall, branching stems topped with narrow, bottlebrush-like spires of fluffy cream or white flowers. They need cool soil that does not dry out and shelter from hot sun or strong wind which can damage the foliage.

In open glades the colchicums herald a change of scene and mood, as if the garden had suddenly put on a party dress and invited berrying shrubs to join in. Small-flowered cyclamen (*Cyclamen hederifolium*) make patterns of foliage and flowers across the green floor in the Little Grassy Wood and stand out like embroidered posies against the crushed-bark mulch in the Wood Garden, to be followed by robust bunches of marbled leaves. The pink and white flowers repeat the tones of Japanese anemones standing tall in sunlit openings and partial shade, sheltered by the understorey shrubs which create small microclimates. Trailing runners of Golden Creeping Jenny emerge from beneath dark-green, vine-shaped anemone leaves, looking like splashes of sunlight when the day is overcast.

Elsewhere a yellow pool of Creeping Jenny, with bold clumps of the bronze-tinted *Heuchera americana* and the small, maple-leaved *Tiarella cordifolia*, is surrounded by the narrow leaves of young forget-me-nots (*Myosotis sylvatica*). (These need some restraining, or thinning, but are easily removed.) The large-leaved *Weigela* 'Gustave Malet' forms a canopy over this mixed carpet, while a fine grass, *Calamagrostis arundinacea*, forms soft, graceful tussocks, with long, trailing flower heads like tresses of shining brown hair, followed by tiny, bronze-coloured seeds. In winter the foliage of this grass sometimes develops tints of red, orange and yellow.

Repetition is all, I sometimes think, as walking round a bend in the path I see *Kirengeshoma palmata* standing agreeably tall, after an unaccustomed cool and wet July. It needs humus-rich, lime-free soil in semi-shade among ferns and hostas. From late summer to autumn heavy clusters of fat, hazelnut-like buds open shuttlecock-shaped flowers about 5cm/2in long, butter-yellow, of a thick, wax-like texture. Irregularly cut, maple-like leaves clothe dark-purple stems which bow, like Chinese mandarins, under the weight of the flowers.

And since this digression began with the idea of repetition, I was pleased to find those strangely beautiful, yellow flowers further along the path, hanging above yet more trailing stems of the modest Golden Creeping Jenny.

It is a thrill to turn a shady corner in early September and be startled by the beauty of the Willow Gentian (*Gentiana asclepiadea*), so called on account of its narrow leaves on slender, arching stems. A native of the sub-alpine woods of Europe, it takes a while to establish, yet once suited, in leafy soil, it improves every year, creating a sheaf of stems bowed with the typical trumpet-shaped flowers, held in every leaf-joint on the upper half of the stems. The colour is breathtaking, a glorious dark blue, opening from long, pointed buds, with or without a white throat. There are variations. For many years we had a white gentian, but as can happen, it seems to have been overgrown. We have a strange lilac-pink form coming along, not yet proven in the garden. I like especially a pale-blue form, grown from seed sent to me by Graham Stuart Thomas, which now is bowed to the ground with a sheaf of flower-laden stems.

We originally obtained this plant, now called *Actaea simplex*, as *Cimicifuga ramosa* 'Prichard's Giant'. The flowering stems stand 1.8–2m/6–7ft tall, branching into secondary shoots which prolong the display well into autumn. In spite of their height they need no staking.

Drifts of large-flowered *Colchicum* 'Rosy Dawn' grow through carpets of periwinkle, *Vinca minor* 'La Grave', which support the goblet-shaped flowers and protect them from mud splashes.

Like the gentians, drifts of colchicums introduce an element of surprise and pleasure in early autumn. Since the end of August their pale noses have been pushing through carpets of *Ajuga reptans* 'Atropurpurea', the pale-lilac-pink chalices and white, naked stems making vivid contrast against the bugle's dark-purple-tinted leaf rosettes. Now visitors are greeted by hundreds of rosy-mauve goblets making waves of colour through a tapestry backcloth of vinca, Sweet Woodruff, *Geranium macrorrhizum* and *Tiarella cordifolia*, which help to support them and prevent mud splashes.

In the wild, colchicums grow in high mountain meadows; heavy shade does not suit them, so I have disobeyed the theory of planting according to Nature! However, by choosing glades where shafts of sunlight fall uninterrupted, my disobedience has been successful, so far. To make further drifts, we divide the cochicums after the leaves have died down, generally in June, and feed the soil to encourage large, shining, chestnut-coloured bulbs. Each bulb has increased to a cluster of ten or more, depending on how long they have been planted. One of the earliest to flower is *Colchicum parnassicum*. Its narrow, pale-lilac-mauve flowers on short, white stems open wide to produce a star-like effect. Following it comes *C.* 'Rosy Dawn', with extra-fine, goblet-shaped, rosy-mauve flowers which open 10cm/4in across in the sun to show a deep, white throat. Strong stems stand up well to wind and wet. Like little wineglasses on tall, slender stems is *C. autumnale* 'Album', while the darkest colchicum, and one of the latest I have, is *C. speciosum* 'Atrorubens' with deep-reddish-purple flowers on purple-stained stems. It is planted among the black, spider-like leaf clusters of *Ophiopogon planiscapus* 'Nigrescens', which mark their space when colchicum flowers and leaves have disappeared. Most lovely of all, perhaps, and certainly one of the latest, is *C. speciosum* 'Album', as fresh and pure in colour and form in autumn as the snowdrops are in spring.

WANDERING ANEMONES

Backlit and beautiful as low sunlight falls through their petals, wandering parties of Japanese anemones rise above ferns where snowdrops and aconites covered the space in January and February. The lovely, old variety *Anemone × hybrida* 'Honorine Jobert' (1.2m/4ft) is unsurpassed. Its saucer-shaped, white flowers, filled with yellow stamens, raise my spirits for weeks, well into November. Standing tall and pure against a leafy background, they pick up the white variegation in the eye-catching elder, *Sambucus nigra* 'Pulverulenta'. Unless well-grown this shrub can look a mess when bright sun scorches the delicate leaves, but in dappled shade and deep, rich soil it grows strongly, despite having little chlorophyll. To help maintain vigour I prune it every spring to a strong, basal framework, about chest-high, when it proceeds to throw up new, branching stems 1m/40in and more tall. Early in the season the leaves are predominantly green but now, as summer turns to autumn, they are so heavily speckled with white, especially the tip shoots, that the whole bush appears ghostly pale, surrounded by the plain greenery of ferns and hostas.

Both *Anemone hupehensis* 'Hadspen Abundance' and *A. × hybrida* 'September Charm' have alternate light- and dark-pink sepals and petals, but the flowers of the latter are larger and more upright-facing. Their stoloniferous roots appreciate my light, sandy soil. They have spread to form large colonies of flowering stems, a delight to walk through, almost head-high, planted either side of a path. In a quite different setting, but one I will always remember, pink Japanese anemones had been allowed to invade minute crevices at the edges of long, curving steps in the garden of Lord Aberconway, Bodnant Garden in Conwy, Wales. Flowers, leaves and stems peeping through the stone palisade softened this fine architectural feature. In the Wood Garden, I can see some restraint will be needed before my Japanese anemones wander too far.

Colchicum speciosum 'Album' grows through shining, evergreen mats of *Fragaria chiloensis* 'Chaval'.

Overleaf: Japanese anemones have spread their thin wandering roots to create colonies of pink and white blossoms dancing along an open, sunlit glade.

Anemone tomentosa, from open woodland and among shady rocks in northeast China, is very similar to the Japanese anemones, flowering a little earlier. It makes handsome stands of branching stems, clothed in large, healthy-looking leaves, producing sheaves of flowers, pale pink within, dark on the reverse. I think it one of the best.

As I have said before, during most summers in the past, after weeks without rain in July and August, we have had to irrigate the Wood Garden, otherwise the anemones would be drooping and sad.

GLOWING BERRIES

The pale-green flower spathes of *Arum italicum* 'Marmoratum' ('Pictum'), usually hiding among the leaves in early summer, have now been replaced by bright heads of scarlet fruits, packed into dense, juicy clusters on top of bare stems. They do not last long. Mallard ducks love them and so do blackbirds. I have seen them jumping up to snatch the berries when hard put to find something moist. Children must be warned not to treat these as fruits, since they are toxic to human beings.

The yellow-fruited Guelder Rose, *Viburnum opulus* 'Fructu Luteo', has been hung with bunches of transparent amber berries for several weeks. Most are gone now, having provided a feast, I suspect, for the blackbirds. How bleak the garden would be without these birds, their fussy bustling in the

Grape-like bunches of translucent fruits of *Viburnum opulus* 'Fructu Luteo' provide a feast for the eye until blackbirds develop a taste for them.

undergrowth, their clear song ringing across the garden, performed from the tops of the tallest trees. I enjoy the yellow-fruited viburnum for weeks throughout the summer. First the cream, flat, lacecap-like heads, made up of small, fertile flowers in the centre surrounded by a showy border of large sterile ones. Then follow weeks of change as the green bunches of berries slowly mature, through pale opaque-green to transparent-yellow and finally amber. Years ago my interest in flower arranging prompted me to grow this Guelder Rose, since when I have used the berries at all stages. I planted it in an east-facing mixed border of trees and shrubs dividing the Wood Garden from the nursery stock beds. After ten years' growth, it has made a huge bush, some 3m/10ft high and 4m/13ft across. It will benefit from winter pruning – thinning, reducing by a third, both height and width – to revitalize it and make room for neighbours.

Because I like to mix evergreen shrubs with deciduous shrubs, not far from the deciduous *Viburnum opulus* you will not be surprised to find a fine privet, the evergreen *Ligustrum* 'Vicaryi'. Both the viburnum and ligustrum need enough light to perform well, but that we have given them, fully exposed to the sun-drenched nursery beds opposite. Now, in November, the privet's arched branches are wreathed with clusters of purple-black berries, while the evergreen foliage provides shelter, and makes a good background for the intensely scarlet stems of *Cornus alba* 'Sibirica', known as the Westonbirt Dogwood. This is the finest of the red-stemmed dogwoods, breathtaking when caught in low winter sunlight, a graceful bamboo arching overhead and bleached stems of a grass completing the scene.

Sorbus hupehensis var. *obtusa* is a remarkable sight in autumn when hung with bunches of small, richly pink fruits.

A Chinese mountain ash, *Sorbus hupehensis* var. *obtusa*, has benefited from a cooler summer. In the mid-1990s when temperatures touched 33C/92°F, these trees suffered and their fruits shrivelled, but now their branches are bowed beneath great clusters of small, rose-pink berries. When I first saw this tree, leafless in autumn, at the Sunningdale Nurseries (not long after the war), run then by Graham Stuart Thomas and the late James Russell, from a distance I thought that it was full of pink blossom, so effective is it when the leaves have fallen. *S. hupehensis* itself (another plant from Hupeh in west China), rising tall above *Cornus sanguinea* 'Midwinter Fire', has similar bunches of fruit, but they are like white bonechina, faintly flushed pink as they mature.

Euonymus europaeus 'Red Cascade' is one of the best, free-fruiting forms of our native Spindle Tree. In this picture the wealth of berries has fallen, but I share the photographer's pleasure in this design of colour and form.

On the edge of the wood, where there is more light, are several forms of Spindle Tree, *Euonymus europaeus*. One we had long years ago from the Washfield Nursery, begun by Hilda Davenport Jones, to whom Elizabeth Strangman still proudly refers as 'Boss'. Its arching branches are hung with deep-raspberry-red fruits filled with orange seeds. I think it is *E. e.* 'Red Cascade'. Another variation appeared in the garden here. Unlike the native form which, with me, only occasionally sets good crops, this makes a twiggy bush, so laden with fruit, so colourful in effect, it shines out among its neighbours like the proverbial burning bush. The berries are not quite so large or deeply pink as the type, but you would scarcely notice that, so abundant are they.

Last February we were met just inside the wood by the mysterious scent of *Sarcococca hookeriana* var. *digyna*. Now, in November, those same bushes are studded with shining, black fruits, very like the edible blackcurrant, while the new shoot extensions above them are threaded with flower buds, an encouraging sight this overcast, damp day, to carry my thoughts forward to spring. Although there is a certain melancholy, the sky overcast, the ground

saturated and carpeted with sodden leaves – and more rain is threatened – there remains much to lift low spirits. Colonies of *Reineckea carnea* spread fresh-green foliage among rosettes of *Pachysandra terminalis* and curled fronds of Hart's Tongue Fern, *Asplenium scolopendrium*. For added drama the black-leaved *Ophiopogon planiscapus* 'Nigrescens' carries sprays of shining, black berries, large as blackcurrants. Bright, marbled leaves of arum contrast with the small, ladder-like fronds of the Hard Fern, *Blechnum spicant*, and further, surprisingly fresh, fronds of Hart's Tongue Fern. The wet autumn has encouraged these new leaves to push robustly through tired fronds that weathered the drought of August.

A shrub transformed by more generous rainfall is *Callicarpa bodinieri* var. *giraldii* 'Profusion'. For many years it had grown reluctantly, a small, stunted thing, making no effort to please, but suddenly, without realizing what has been happening, I find myself looking *up* into a graceful shrub 2m/6½ ft tall and 3m/10ft across, its bare branches festooned with clusters of tiny, pearl-like, violet berries. From a distance you are drawn to this haze of unexpected colour emerging out of a grey November mist. Earlier dark-green, pointed

Overleaf: *Callicarpa bodinieri* var. *giraldii* 'Profusion' is a most welcome surprise to come across in November when its bare branches are festooned with clusters of tiny, violet berries.

leaves almost hid the insignificant flowers, but as autumn approaches they too become tinged with purple before they fall, leaving the berries fully exposed. This shrub is found wild in north-east China, in woods and low scrub, but needs enough light and retentive soil to fruit well. Mine is planted on the north-facing corner at the end of the Long Shady Walk. If possible I like to repeat a colour, sometimes close by, sometimes further away to draw the eye into the distance. *Liriope muscari* (possibly from the same Chinese woods as the callicarpa) looks good nearby, with spikes of light-violet flowers. Liriope, with its bold tussocks of dark-green, strap-shaped leaves, provides good contrast of form throughout the year among carpeting plants. Although it can be grown in sun, I am glad to find it makes better-quality, taller spikes of its curious flowers in part shade. Standing 45–50cm/18–20in tall, well above the leaves, the stems are closely packed with small buds, which open reminiscent of Grape Hyacinths but with longer spires of flowers.

NOVEMBER HIGHLIGHTS

It is a Sunday morning in mid-November, a day of special beauty caught between grey moods after another week of rain and gales. I am standing beneath a Silver Birch, *Betula pendula*, which I planted about thirty years ago. At this moment it seems to me the loveliest thing in the garden, the bottom half in shadow, the lowest branches blown bare by recent gales; only a few locket-shaped leaves, outlined as dark shapes, flutter in the faintest breath of air. Much higher up, clear, cold sunlight illuminates the white-barked trunk and branches, and a shower of leaves not yet shattered by the wind – gilded leaves, white clouds and deep-blue sky creating a brilliant mosaic.

As usual I have measured the weekly rainfall, recording it on a sheet pinned inside a cupboard door in my utility room, where I occasionally skin pheasants (so much quicker than plucking them) and do the flowers, when I make time. We have had 22cm/9in of rain since 1 October; as I have already written, our entire average for the 'winter' six months is 25cm/10in. What is to come, I wonder? How will it affect the garden? Everywhere squelches with water underfoot. The wood floor is littered with green ash leaves ripped from the large tree on the south boundary. Unlike curling, brown oak leaves, which make an attractive carpet, the green leaves, with their long, pale stems, lie sodden and dishevelled, making a restless pattern over the dark pathways; a mute expression of the savage force which tore them from their tree before they had time to die gracefully in tints of lemon-yellow.

Once more I am sitting on the little plank bench in the Wood Garden, near the oak where *Hydrangea anomala* subsp. *petiolaris* now ascends to about

Right: *Liriope muscari* spends most of the year as an evergreen feature – a tussock of dark green, strap-shaped leaves. In late autumn narrow spires of curious flowers emerge, light violet in colour, hardly opening their close-set buds, reminiscent of the Grape Hyacinth, *Muscari armeniacum*.

Above: *Hydrangea anomala* subsp. *petiolaris* clothes the bole of a tall oak tree with pale yellow leaves before they fall.

Above right: The leaves of *Enkianthus campanulatus* turn to shades of red and amber, well presented on tiers of horizontal branches.

6m/20ft. The tree is still wreathed in pale, honey-coloured, oval leaves, attached to the main rope-like stems which encircle the trunk, while the lateral branches of the hydrangea, swept bare of leaves, extend a haze of copper-tinted twigs, presenting lacecap-like heads of bleached-brown flowers.

Pale, ghostly seed heads of *Actaea matsumurae* 'White Pearl' (*Cimicifuga*) float on slender, branching stems, almost invisible in the dusk of evening. They repeat the pale tones of the hydrangea. Earlier their snowy-white tapers echoed the white colchicums beneath them, continuing to make vertical accents while they developed lime-green seed heads and are even doing so now as desiccated, transparent, empty shells.

Every leaf on the horizontal branches of *Enkianthus campanulatus*, whose quiet charm and dangling flowers so delighted me in early summer (see page 88), has turned to amber, flushed with tints of red. With all this rich but ephemeral autumn colour and the ground below littered with signs of decay, it is heartening to see freshly emerging leaves of *Arum italicum* 'Marmoratum' and the large, round leaves of the Giant Celandine (*Ranunculus ficaria* subsp. *chrysocephalus*). There are ever-increasing patches of cyclamens and yards and yards of parasol-leaved cranesbills and frosted lamiums, while a million seedlings of forget-me-nots foretell the wash of blue which will flow through empty spaces in spring. Beneath all sleep snowdrops and little wild daffodils.

Once again I am drawn to write about *Amelanchier lamarckii* as I did in early spring. Now, beneath the Great Oak at the end of the Long Shady Walk,

a little group of three glows like live coals, every oval leaf flooded with rich crimson and orange tints. I planted them here where, backed by the shining-green, small-leaved laurel, *Prunus laurocerasus* 'Otto Luyken', I can see them from the house. Earlier the floor beneath was carpeted with pink and white cyclamen whose marbled leaves will continue to be attractive for the rest of the winter.

Even on the greyest November mornings three bushes of *Cornus sanguinea* 'Midwinter Fire' greet me at the entrance to the Wood Garden with a vivid display of melon-yellow leaves, not yet blown away by violent gusts of wind. Beneath the glowing colour is spread a living carpet of the evergreen *Epimedium × perralchicum*, every heart-shaped, pointed leaf on wire-thin stems presented in overlapping layers. Nearby *Ribes sanguineum* 'Albescens' is making an autumnal effect I do not remember noticing before. As the chlorophyll is withdrawn the lobed leaves are variously marbled in shades of red and yellow, with green still staining the veins and leaf-margins.

The large, oval leaves of various dogwoods (forms of *Cornus alba*) are turning clear yellow, making pale, bulky features against dark, shadowy evergreens and pillared trunks of the oaks. The leafless, branching stems of *Rubus cockburnianus* from China, which are plum-purple when young and become whitened with a waxy bloom as they mature, have arched and bowed to form a silvered cage. This Ghost Bramble needs to be pruned regularly to encourage bright, fresh growth, effective with lime-green- and red-stemmed

Above left: *Amelanchier lamarckii* glows in late autumn sunshine, its small oval leaves flecked with rich crimson and orange tints.

Above: *Cornus sanguinea* 'Midwinter Fire' stands out against a dark background when its leaves turn to shades of lemon and peach before a sharp frost finally shatters them. Then the stems form a haze of warm colour, glowing from a distance like the remains of a bonfire (illustrated on pages 180–1).

When the leaves have fallen from the Ghost Bramble (*Rubus cockburnianus*) a 'whitewashed' tangle of stems and branches is revealed, purple when young, becoming coated with white wax as they mature. This bramble will grow in heavy soil where there is room for it to make a thicket. Mine is most effective in winter, reflected in the black 'mirror' of a pond.

dogwoods. *R. c.* 'Goldenvale' grows less vigorously, 90–120cm/3–4ft, with bright-lemon-yellow leaves which turn pale green in shade, a delight in the right place (perhaps in a container, if you haven't yards of empty space).

The wood is alive, with accents provided by evergreens, including viburnum, skimmia, cotoneaster and hollies, while the large, elegant leaves of *Mahonia japonica*, carried on gaunt stems, create a different focal point. With the sky partially obscured by the oak canopy, late in turning this year, the scene could be gloomy, but the final autumnal display of deciduous trees and shrubs, as they prepare themselves for winter sleep, illuminates the garden – like lamps lit at dusk. But now it is one o'clock, lunch time. The sky is once more menacing, heavy with rain clouds. I am wet and cold. My bones ache. I shall walk home to the comfort and company of my wood-burning stove.

LETTING IN THE LIGHT

Over the past couple of years I have been concerned, and at times depressed, I admit, by inevitable signs of ageing, not only in myself but in the garden too. It is more than forty years since we began planting here. How many people find themselves, late in life, learning to deal with a new aspect to their gardening career? Posing this question to a group of visiting horticulturists, the only answer I received was that most people sell before that stage is reached. The rest of us face a new project, learning to maintain and revitalize an established garden.

There is not much we can do about ourselves, except possibly replace a few worn-out parts, rather like gingering up an old tractor, but we can do a lot more to invigorate the garden, even if it means making difficult and sometimes painful decisions. Somehow, in realizing those decisions, by opening up new aspects, our own enthusiasm and vitality is rekindled. In 2001 I was overwhelmed by the abundance of growth put on by trees and shrubs.

Previously the garden seemed under control, partly due to our efforts, but largely governed by our growing conditions – cold, damp winters and warm summers with guaranteed periods of drought. Since the mid-1990s winters have been much milder and, until 2000 and 2001, summers were equally dry but with unusually high temperatures. However, as a result of cooler and wetter summers ('Ideal weather for plants,' teases David, when visitors grouse, frustrated by arriving on a wet day), trees and shrubs which had barely made average extension growth have suddenly exploded, transforming my world. Even the ancient boundary oaks, which I had imagined would be fairly set in their ways, have surreptitiously advanced over the years to shade out flowering shrubs planted beneath them, where originally there had appeared to be endless empty space asking to be filled.

After four decades of watching the garden mature, it is ironic now to find it on its way to becoming overblown, oppressive in places, even, dare I say it, out of hand. In the beginning I visualized irregular patterns of shapes and textures painted across our huge, empty East Anglian sky, and eventually achieved these. Suddenly it seems the spaces between the shapes are closing in, I am losing too much of the sky, of wonderful cloudscapes. If nothing is done I will feel hemmed in, overwhelmed and depressed.

Part of the problem has been caused by our initial planting. In the main garden, where we have spring-fed soil and where the farm boundary of ancient oaks determined the scale of the planting, we felt that medium-sized flowering trees, such as crab apples and laburnum, needed dominant trees, such as the Tulip Tree (*Liriodendron tulipifera*) and the beautiful Indian Horse-chestnut (*Aesculus indica*), to relate to the overall scale of the garden-to-be. For vertical accents we planted both the American Swamp Cypress (*Taxodium distichum*) and the Chinese Dawn Redwood (*Metasequoia glyptostroboides*). As these amazing conifers have grown, we have already been obliged to remove several of them since, like most inexperienced gardeners, forty years ago we had no idea how much space such trees demand. Those that remain now add nobility to the overall planting, soaring like church spires above my 'village' of supporting trees and shrubs.

What next? How *did* we cope with the overgrown trees? I am lucky to have Gerard, who over twenty-five years has become expert in tree surgery, having attended courses on the use of suitable equipment and all that is imperative for health and safety, for himself and anyone who assists him. I am not the most mechanically minded gardener, so the details of the various sizes of hoist, methods of transportation, and cost of hiring per day are provided by Gerard on page 214, but the point I wish to make is that for a large garden or estate these machines enable tree surgery to be done more quickly and safely, whether by trained staff or a hired contractor.

For really tall trees, 9–12m/30–40ft tall, which we need to prune or prepare for removal, we hire a hoist from a horticultural supplier who specializes in equipment for parks and golf courses. The operator stands on a railed platform, to which he is strapped for safety, and the hoist lifts him high into the air by means of the telescopic arm. It was exciting to have this bird's-eye view of the garden lying like an oasis among the open fields. In 2001 we hired such a machine for one day at a time during September – before rain made the ground too soft and with the winter months ahead in which any damaged shrubs could heal and we could prepare the soil for new plants where there was fresh space and more light.

When removing large trees the other valuable tool to hire is a stump grinder. Previously we have laboured away digging out tree stumps, armed with mattocks and spades, risking pulled muscles, taking maybe two days or more. Faced with the stump of a *Pinus radiata*, thirty-five years old, 1m/40in across and with all its subsidiary roots, we found a local man who arrived with his machine and ground out the stump before I had finished breakfast, thus missing the chance to see how it worked. Impressed, we booked him to remove the stumps of nine more oaks. There still remained the tough job of digging out supporting roots with a mattock.

Of much more general use, and a boon for most gardeners contemplating tree surgery, is a long-arm pruner which does away with the dangerous practice of holding on to a tall metal ladder with one hand while balancing a heavy power saw in the other. Visitors are impressed (and so are we) with this adaptable tool. It has a reach from 2.2m/7ft to 4m/13ft, which means you can do much of your tree pruning from the ground. Both a saw and lopper can easily be attached to the head of the pole by a press-button, while another button extends the pole to the stage you require. The lopper is geared for cutting power (it works like secateurs), with an adjustable angled head for ease of cutting, and can take out branches about 2.5cm/1in in diameter. The saw will cut through whatever the operator can manage. It *is* hard work on the shoulders. To ease the weight and for safety's sake, it is important to take big boughs down in stages, remembering there is a sudden kick-back at the sawn edge when a heavy bough is suddenly released.

I have written about the need to maintain balance by cutting back some of the shrubs which form a windbreak and evergreen background for the mixed planting of shade-lovers which grow along the Long Shady Walk (see page 119). When we first contemplate a windswept site, we plant enough to create the required effect as soon as possible. As time goes by, perhaps unobserved, some of the weaker subjects are smothered out by more robust neighbours and the area needed for interesting perennials is reduced, possibly to a narrow strip along the front edge. A time comes when it is quite revelatory to get inside some of these woody plantations and find out just how much space has been lost. While winter is the ideal time to prune, when least damage is done to the floor cover of plants, we remembered last autumn's unusually heavy rains draining off the neighbouring farm which made this area of grass on silty soil too wet for us to cart off a lot of prunings. In 2001 we decided to

tackle the job in August when the ground was dry and firm. Some of the laurels and several *Viburnum tinus* were removed – the laurustinus do not flower well if too shaded. The rest we cut back to form woody frameworks, leaving enough foliage to check the west wind. Our neighbouring farmer should be pleased, since overhanging shrubs from my side can impede the progress of his tractor. On our side we have created several deep bays, which will form sheltered homes for new introductions.

A stony heart is sometimes needed to turf out an old friend. I have to tell myself I have had many years of pleasure from this or that plant, or tree, since my picture is not a static canvas, the views changing every year. Some will be obliterated if nothing is done to preserve them. My practice when contemplating the removal of a tree or shrub is to study the victim from all sides during different seasons, to ensure that a good view will be revealed, or that shelter will still be provided by something growing beyond. Once the deed is done there is a great sense of relief. Suddenly there is more light and air; the feeling of oppression lifts as bays or inlets are revealed where years of surreptitious growth had obliterated precious space needed for shade-loving perennials and bulbs.

While he was reducing the height and bulk of the shrubs which form a barrier between us and the worst wind, Gerard also removed a low horizontal bough on the Great Oak, opening up a long window of sky to the setting sun. Low, golden light floods once more across the garden to reach the sitting area outside my living room, illuminating at tea-time the pot gardens filled with a medley of half-hardy plants, gilding the trunks of *Magnolia* × *soulangeana* and piercing the wine-purple leaves of *Vitis vinifera* 'Purpurea' growing on the

We were obliged to cut down the Aspen (*Populus tremula*), since it tends to sucker, but to my dismay hundreds more appeared after the deed was done. Since we garden organically, only on rare occasions do we resort to using chemicals. In this instance, we bored holes in the top of the stump, poured in brushwood killer and 'corked' the holes. There was a risk of the chemical translocating to other shrubs and plants nearby, but nothing else was affected; only the aspen shoots growing from the underground root system were destroyed.

This view west across the Water Garden was exposed after removing low branches of an ancient holly, which hung to the ground like a crinoline. In the foreground on the right are five of the holly's seven trunks. In the centre is *Paulownia tomentosa* whose flowers, opening in late spring before the leaves, resemble large blue foxgloves. It is entwined with another *Hydrangea anomala* subsp. *petiolaris*, while beyond is the Himalayan Birch, *Betula utilis* var. *jacquemontii*, whose trunk and branches are white as writing paper. Beneath the tall oaks in the distance is part of the Long Shady Walk.

west-facing house wall. Indoors the low light reaches the whitewashed wall of the fireplace, painting it with a pattern of leaf silhouettes growing outside.

From time to time *Prunus lusitanica*, the Portugal Laurel, needs restricting unless you have endless space. We planted it almost forty years ago, about 3m/10ft away from the vast trunk of another ancient oak where it has thrived and formed a handsome, evergreen shape, especially important in winter. But it was pushing aside the Witch Hazel, *Hamamelis mollis*, burying bluebells and blue periwinkle growing beneath. If laurel is regularly pruned, as when planted as a hedge, there is no problem, but when it is left free to make a vast shrub, most of the foliage is on the outside. Look inside and you find much of the framework is almost bare. It is a painful decision to cut a densely leaved specimen to leave an almost bare structure looking like intertwined elephant trunks. But this is what Christopher, our ex-school teacher, did last January, confident it would refurnish itself. Within a comparatively short time, as the sap rose, minute embryo buds could be seen breaking through the bare bark. And now, in late autumn, the witch hazel seems to be smiling smugly, aglow with pale-honey-coloured leaves, having space enough to reshape itself, while in future we must trim the laurel just enough to keep it to its allotted space.

This same ancient oak has another lifelong companion, a huge holly; possibly both were planted or seeded hundreds of years ago as part of an ancient hedgerow. Our split-level house lies on the shallow bank between these two fine remnants on one side and, on the other, the vast, pollarded oak

growing at the entrance to the garden. When the site for the new garden was first cleared, these two great trees presented us with plenty of problems, with light, sandy soil, low rainfall and wind whistling away what little moisture there was. Compost was essential to give even tough plants a start, including epimediums, ivies, *Euphorbia amygdaloides* var. *robbiae* and periwinkles, but once these became established they helped to trap fallen leaves and create a microclimate. Viewed from the outside, the holly towered almost as tall as the oak, its lax branches falling to the ground like a great crinoline. Again I was beginning to feel threatened by this native whose territory I had invaded to make a garden. How could we curb it without losing its nobility? It was quite an experience to dive beneath the skirts of the crinoline and find a circle of seven trunks, each bowed away from the original base, each about 30cm/1ft in diameter, supporting the huge head, and to see that by working from the inside we could remove the lower branches from the trunks quite high up, rather than snipping away from the outside, and thus expose this magic circle of trunks which we had not seen for years. Neither were we aware of the view, seen now through the trunks to the lower garden, to the crimson tower of *Liquidambar styraciflua* and the pole-like structure of *Ginkgo biloba*, its branches forming a lace-like pattern of fan-shaped leaves against a blue sky, confetti-like leaves of yellow and green littering the grass below. Using the hoist, Gerard was able to reduce the height and width of the holly by about a third, without in any way spoiling its appearance.

7 | The Depths of Winter

I T IS AS FASCINATING TO MAKE PATTERNS with the structure and form of both deciduous and evergreen trees and shrubs in winter as it is to play with colour in summer. *Cotoneaster lacteus* is laden all along its arched boughs with clusters of red berries. Its mid-summer prune encouraged it to form new flowering shoots and now the combination of fruit and oval, evergreen leaves creates a welcoming effect in winter. For some reason birds leave them alone unless they are very hard pressed by bad weather. Even leaf-losing shrubs, such as *Stephanandra incisa* 'Crispa', which can look like bundles of wire-netting if they lack good structure, are transformed into gilded cages by early morning hoar-frost. I welcome snow when it comes, not only for the fairyland effect but because, rather than running quickly off the surface, an eiderdown of snow melts slowly into dry soil that is tightly interlaced with roots.

I feel invigorated by so much the Wood Garden can give me at this low point of the year. Beneath the trees there is always life, the soil almost totally covered with a fascinating mixture of shapes, sizes, textures and shades of green, yellow, bronze and purple leaves or just stems, each enhanced by

Left: Fallen leaves could inspire designs for tapestry work, captured here by Steven Wooster on a frosty morning. The collapsed fern is probably the Common Male Fern, *Dryopteris filix-mas*, while copper- and orange-toned oak leaves have drifted silently among them. The large, deeply cut leaves are from the Scarlet Oak, *Quercus coccinea*, which varies grown from seed, the best forms having glowing scarlet autumn colour. The smaller, round-lobed leaves are from common English Oak, *Quercus robur*.

contrast with its neighbour. You can count on *Hacquetia epipactis* to lift your spirits on a gloomy winter's day, even before the aconites and snowdrops have thought of waking up. Some time in January they open, at ground level, heads of tiny, yellow flowers surrounded by conspicuous, olive-green, petal-like bracts – a bit like those of an astrantia – gradually forming little bouquets of flower above clumps of palmate leaves. The plants need a moist, shady spot during the growing season, but a strong, deep root system enables them to tolerate dry conditions later in the year. I confess I am annoyed with myself for having lost this little plant, after many years of enjoying its company; possibly because I neglected to guard against other plants invading its territory after it dies down in mid-summer.

Many good foliage plants last well into winter, providing more interest and pleasure than the empty herbaceous border, which, by late autumn and winter, offers only bare soil and brittle skeletons. We have a remarkable example of this in a long border in an open situation just before you enter the Wood Garden. It is part of a collection of stock plants of late-summer and autumn perennials – asters, kniphofias, ornamental grasses and helianthus – needed for propagation, but grouped to make an inviting display. Now it is looking uncomfortably naked, especially when we have just emerged from the Wood Garden where 'there is always something to look at, no matter how much we cut down and tidy up,' says Winnie Dearsley, who has helped care for my gardens for over thirty years.

On a frosty, sunlit morning at the end of January I walked across to the Long Shady Walk to see what I had been missing. First to greet me were patches of primroses, already opening their first flowers close by the pagoda-shaped dogwood I wrote about earlier. That same pale tone is repeated in the broad, cream leaf-margins of *Pachysandra terminalis* 'Variegata', and again in the unusual Lenten Rose, *Helleborus* × *hybridus* Kochii Group. Its short, branching stems, 30–38 cm/12–15 in, carry quantities of pale, nodding buds, already opening primrose-yellow shallow saucers, most welcome in the winter garden. On a sloping clay bank *Salix nakamurana* var. *yezoalpina,* a prostrate willow from Japan, sprawls horizontally, a pattern of brown, rugged stems over the bare soil, which will be studded with pale catkins in early spring, followed by large, round leaves which make effective ground cover. Before they fall the leaves turn a beautiful shade of melon-yellow.

A cock pheasant squawks its warning, 'Chur, chur, churr-uck!!', as I pass, exploding at my feet, a whirling mass of indignation. Each of us almost jumps out of our skin as we patrol the boundary netting. It is a sound, and hazard, of winter.

BEAUTY IN LEAVES

In the Little Grassy Wood I take as much pleasure in the leaves of *Cyclamen hederifolium* in winter as I do in their posies of pink and white flowers in late summer and autumn. I like to walk slowly among them to observe the endless variation in leaf patterns. No two plants are identical. 'Hederifolium' means ivy-leaved – the leaves are roughly triangular, partially lobed, with wavy edges. They are exquisitely marbled in many shades of green, silver and grey, the patterns painted along the intricate vein systems or suffused into the spaces between. Leaf size and outline vary too, some having smooth edges, others finely serrated. It is always a thrill to spot a particularly distinctive form, perhaps much longer and narrower than most, with a dramatically dark heart outlined in silver.

Among the starved grass, mown close in late summer, cyclamens have established well. Throughout winter one of my treats is to walk among the patchwork quilt of cyclamen leaves to see if last year's youngsters (grown the previous three years from seed) have settled down. We should be able to rely

No two plants of the hardy cyclamen, *Cyclamen hederifolium*, have identical foliage. Each has leaves that differ in shape, outline and complicated patterns, creating marbled effects in shades of green, silver and grey. Throughout winter they contribute as much to the garden as do their pink and white flowers in autumn.

on self-sown seedlings, but grey squirrels have taken up residence and I suspect they discover those strange little draw-string-like bags, which are cyclamen seed pods, tucked beneath the leaves on tightly curled stems, and relish the sticky seeds inside. By careful searching we manage to find several hundred newborn seedlings among the leaves in early spring, often little clumps sitting on top of the flat corm where they have no chance of developing. These are collected and planted out in trays. After three years they are about the size of a hazelnut, large enough to pot individually. When they have produced strong roots and leaves, we plant them out, adding to the drifts already established. We have had as much pleasure from rescuing young seedlings and growing them on as we have, from autumn to spring, watching the pattern of foliage and flowers spreading across the green grass floor.

From the house I can look across to a curving border which lies beneath the umbrella-like head of one of our most ancient oaks. Because the soil remains dry here in summer and we do not irrigate, it is practically bare once bulbous plants have faded, except for a tidy blanket of composted leaf mould. *Cyclamen hederifolium* seem to be able to cope with very dry situations, building up woody corms (as much as 15cm/6in across) that enable them to store food and moisture for when they lie dormant in the dry summer

Cyclamen coum produces rounded leaves throughout winter; they may be pale green, partially silvered or entirely silvered except for a narrow green rim. The first flowers open in any mild spell, the main display appearing in late winter and early spring, with colours ranging from white through rose pink to a striking deep-pink form.

months. By September they provide hundreds of pink and white posies, followed by robust bunches of marbled leaves. At the end of January, looking across one of the ponds from the house, I can see drifts of snowdrops carpeting this large, shaded bed, like snowfall. (Not today I can't! Freezing fog has obliterated the garden all day.)

The first flowers of *Cyclamen coum* appear in winter, with more to follow, well into spring. Unlike *C. hederifolium* with pointed petals, *C. coum* has rounded petals twisting away from the ovary to make a pretty, fluted shape as I look down on them. After three or four years from germination, seedlings produce all shades from white through soft rose to deep cyclamen-pink. The leaves are rounded, not lobed. They may be plain green, partially silvered, or almost entirely silvered with a narrow, green rim. Cyclamen belong to the family *Primulaceae*. Perhaps you are as surprised as I was to discover this, especially since I have often (and still do) compared the way erythronium flare back their petals to resemble cyclamens, but erythroniums belong to the lily family.

Before finishing these notes I was driven indoors by a bitter north wind, so I picked a few cyclamen leaves to study their quiet beauty in comfort. Arranged simply in a small, shallow bowl standing on my table, they make a completely satisfying picture in the lamplight: nothing else is needed.

REGULAR WINTER MAINTENANCE

It is impossible to walk in the garden in winter without being aware of what needs to be done now, while assessing what can be left for another year. Ferns, which collapse into brown, feathery heaps, should be cut at ground level before they have buried aconites and snowdrops. Epimediums require attention, too. Lesley Hills (together with Winnie Dearsley) has tended the garden for twenty-five years, but is spending the winter in Australia with her family. She will return for her final year and retire in autumn 2002. Her concern before leaving was to remind Christina, who now is responsible for the care of the garden, to cut down the old epimedium foliage at the beginning of February, to avoid shearing off the flower stems.

Some years ago I almost lost *Salix* × *stipularis*, so am glad to see such a good, strong bush established again from a cutting rescued from a decrepit plant. Bush willows look best if they are regularly pruned during the dormant season to a stout framework rather than being cut to ground level. We remove about half of the two-year-old stems and any misshapen or weakly pieces, and tip the rest if height needs to be regulated. We use the same method with the dogwoods (*Cornus*). It ensures a rush of new, invigorated growth, and at the same time you are left with a shrub to look at, albeit reduced.

I am sorry to see the shabby leaves of *Iris foetidissima*, a plant which years ago I valued highly for the winter effect of rich green leaves and orange fruits. These irises still fruit, half-heartedly, but throughout summer pale lesions disfigure the fans of leaves until most of them wither. Seedlings begin life healthily enough, but soon develop the telltale symptoms. I suppose we should spray with something deadly, but I do not choose to do that.

Ambling along the Long Shady Walk, I find that the background planting of shrubs continues to need attention. Common Laurel (*Prunus laurocerasus*), *Viburnum tinus*, *Phillyrea angustifolia* with sweet-scented, white flowers, a few specimens of *Rhododendron ponticum* – all need tipping to encourage more compact shapes, to maintain a good wind-barrier, and leave space for the shade-lovers beneath. Various forms of holly, both plain-leaved and variegated, are pruned to form dense verticals, in contrast to other free-flowing shapes. It is useful to remember with leggy growers like holly that at each point you cut you will cause several shoots to grow instead of one. It may take two or three seasons of cutting back branches until you arrive at a compact framework furnished with plenty of short shoots.

Although *Mahonia × wagneri* 'Moseri', a lovely hybrid to which Graham Stuart Thomas introduced me, grows well enough along this border, it needs a more exposed position to show off its best. The new leaves in spring are the loveliest pale yellowy-green, slowly developing coral tints as they mature, intensifying to shades of red and becoming a deeper red by autumn, a colour which lasts throughout winter. I confess that I tried this mahonia in the Wood Garden, but it needs stronger light to achieve the best colour, with possibly hebes and berberis for companions, which would benefit from the contrast of larger leaves of the mahonia. Just one of my mistakes!

At the end of the Long Shady Walk is *Taxus baccata* 'Elegantissima', a golden-leaved yew. It is a fine sight when all the young foliage is bright golden-yellow. The cutting I was given more than forty years ago took *months* to root. I guarded it like a baby until it could stand alone, then the day came when it towered above me, with leggy laterals reaching out on all sides. It needed serious attention. We removed the lowest boughs, reduced both height and width and cut some branches to let in more light. This enabled the remaining almost-bare branches to break new shoots all along their length so that the following year we could reduce branches overall to encourage and retain a more compact shape.

Throughout winter I am drawn to my group of *Cornus sanguinea* 'Midwinter Fire' at the entrance to the Wood Garden. Against a background of bare, black trees and shrubs shrouded in grey mist it makes an indefinite

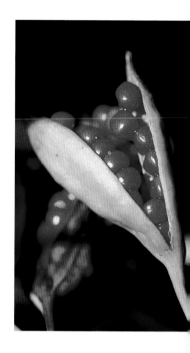

Above: The seed capsule of *Iris foetidissima*.

Left: *Mahonia aquifolium* touched with frost. During the two-year period of writing this book, we have had scarcely enough ice on the ponds to bear a duck. In earlier times we could walk across the ponds, and on rare occasions we had magical snowfalls when everything disappeared beneath an undulating blanket of white.

Overleaf: *Cornus sanguinea* 'Midwinter Fire' is enchanting for most months of the year: in spring and autumn its leaves are delicately tinted pale coral and cream, and in winter the bare bones glow like living coals. It has one fault, however: it spreads slowly by suckering shoots.

Skimmia japonica, native of Japan and far-eastern Asia, prefers well-fed, slightly acid soil, but it is tolerant of shady sites in town gardens, where its neat habit and proportion are welcome. There are numerous forms available. Male and female are needed to produce good crops of berries. Neglected shrubs can be restored to order by judicious pruning over a period of time, rather than hacking back all at once, which can shock some shrubs to death.

haze of warm colour, glowing from a distance like the remains of a bonfire. The colour is brightest in the heart of the bush where the stems are pale yellow, while the terminal shoots are vivid coral-red. They are underplanted with *Vinca minor* 'La Grave' for foliage ground cover all year and for posies of blue periwinkle flowers in spring. Now that the dogwoods have well-established, sturdy frameworks, we prune them in late winter to encourage plenty of new growth at all levels, which ensures good winter colour. Every cut you make encourages buds to break, whether at ground level, mid-way or at the tips, thus producing bright new stems throughout the bush. My enthusiasm for this shrub must not inhibit me from warning you that, once established, it does spread by suckering shoots.

The yellow-leaved dogwood, *Cornus alba* 'Aurea', makes much more vigorous, whippy stems of polished mahogany. They too need pruning to encourage young, well-coloured wood and large, lemon-yellow leaves. The ground beneath is carpeted with *Symphytum* ' Hidcote Pink', fallen leaves and drifts of snowdrops in late winter.

As I have written, over the years the Long Shady Walk has become a cool, green refuge for people and shade-loving plants; but nowhere remains perfect, nothing is static in the garden. In solving one problem we sometimes create others. In this case the grass path had become the problem, or rather the difficulty of maintaining good turf when it was suffering from too much shade and too many feet. Regular patching of the worn and ragged carpet became impractical, so in early winter 2000 I made the decision to remove all the grass, bring in some of our gravelly soil from elsewhere to make a firmer, yet free-draining base and then cover it all with crushed bark. Immediately two jobs were eliminated, both mowing the grass and trimming two long edges. Almost at once we liked the look of the new path, and could see how plants would be able to flow more naturally, unrestricted by clipped turf edging. And as the warmth of the sun brings out the resinous smell of the fresh bark I am transported back to holidays in the Alps when Andrew and I enjoyed botanizing and picnicking in the mountain woods, sitting where the woodsmen had felled and stacked the scented spruce.

Although we try to remember to cut well-berried branches of holly well before Christmas, keeping them fresh in large buckets of water hidden from predatory birds, flocks of pigeons sometimes strip the trees before we have had time to notice. I rarely use holly berries, preferring the larger, showier, red berries of *Skimmia japonica*, which, stripped of its leaves, can easily be tucked among prickly holly to create a brighter, bolder effect. Writing this towards the end of January 2001, I am reminded how on the shortest day I made a large arrangement of mixed evergreens and coloured stems to stand on an ancient church chest in my entrance hall. I used upright branched stems of shining holly (without berries), feathery dark yew, trails of the beautifully marbled leaves of *Hedera colchica* 'Sulphur Heart' ('Paddy's Pride'), large leaves of Spotted Laurel (*Aucuba japonica* 'Crotonifolia'), topped with tall tapers of red- and green-stemmed dogwoods and lit with pale-green heads of hydrangea, all shades of green, enlivened by the rouged leaves of *Mahonia* × *wagneri* 'Moseri' and clusters of rose-pink sorbus berries. Dare I admit it is still there, the dogwoods sprouting tiny, green leaves! Time I changed it for bare branches of Twisted Willow, *Salix babylonica* 'Crispa' ('Annularis'). They will be transformed with little, twisted, ribbon-like leaves, bringing April into the house in February before the garden is fully awake, although beneath the trees and ground cover it has never truly slept.

8 | Shade-Tolerant Plants

PUT SIMPLY, MY PRINCIPLES OF GARDENING ARE to provide plants with the kind of conditions for which Nature has fitted them, to arrange them in planned groups, covering the ground with foliage for as long as possible and providing interest with bold plants. The list on page 186 of trees, shrubs and climbers that provide shelter and microclimates in the Wood Garden includes shrubs for shade or partial shade that provide seasonal interest. There follows a selection of garden-worthy perennials, bulbs, ferns and grasses that could be termed shade-tolerant. I include some treasures suitable for small, shady areas and for north- or east-facing borders, some of which would be lost in my Wood Garden. These are marked with the symbol ★. Each plant is given a hardiness zone rating which suggests the approximate minimum temperature it will tolerate in winter. However, this can be only a rough guide, since hardiness depends on a great many factors, including the depth of a plant's roots, the structure of the soil in which it is planted, its water content at the onset of frost and the amount of sunlight to which it is exposed. Further factors affecting hardiness include the duration of cold weather (especially of early-morning temperatures), the force of the wind, and the length and heat of the preceding summer.

Left: The longest-lasting designs are based on foliage alone. Here the heart-shaped leaves of *Epimedium × versicolor* 'Sulphureum' are just losing their reddish tint of spring. Bowles' Golden Grass, *Milium effusum* 'Aureum', will retain its colour for some time to come, while the silver-leaved *Lamium maculatum* 'White Nancy' will reclothe itself with fresh leaves after flowering.

Trees, shrubs and climbers

Amelanchier lamarckii Zone 5
Buxus sempervirens Zone 6
Callicarpa bodinieri var. giraldii 'Profusion' Zone 6
Camellia × williamsii 'Donation' Zone 7
Clematis montana var. sericea Zone 6
Cornus alba 'Aurea' Zone 2
Cornus alba 'Elegantissima' Zone 2
Cornus alba 'Sibirica' Zone 2
Cornus mas Zone 5
Cornus mas 'Variegata' Zone 5
Cornus sanguinea 'Midwinter Fire' Zone 5
Corylopsis glabrescens var. gotoana Zone 6
Corylopsis sinensis f. veitchiana Zone 7
Cotoneaster conspicuus 'Red Alert' Zone 6
Cotoneaster lacteus Zone 6
Daphne laureola Zone 7
Decaisnea fargesii Zone 7
Deutzia × hybrida 'Mont Rose' Zone 6
Deutzia × kalmiiflora Zone 6
Deutzia longifolia 'Veitchii' Zone 7
Deutzia pulchra Zone 7
Deutzia × rosea Zone 7
Diervilla × splendens Zone 5
Enkianthus campanulatus Zone 5
Eucryphia cordifolia × lucida Zone 9
Eucryphia × nymansensis 'Nymansay' Zone 8
Euonymus europaeus 'Red Cascade' Zone 4
Exochorda × macrantha 'The Bride' Zone 5
Exochorda × macrantha 'The Pearl' Zone 5
Hamamelis mollis Zone 6
Hedera canariensis 'Gloire de Marengo' Zone 7
Hedera helix f. poetarum 'Poetica Arborea' Zone 6
Heptacodium miconiodes Zone 5
Holodiscus discolor Zone 6
Hydrangea anomala subsp. petiolaris Zone 5
Hydrangea arborescens subsp. discolor 'Sterilis' Zone 4
Hydrangea aspera 'Macrophylla' Zone 7
Hydrangea aspera subsp. sargentiana Zone 7
Hydrangea heteromalla 'Snowcap' Zone 7
Hydrangea macrophylla 'Ayesha' Zone 6
Hydrangea macrophylla 'Mariesii Perfecta' Zone 6
Hydrangea macrophylla 'Veitchii' Zone 6
Hypericum × inodorum 'Ysella' Zone 7

Ilex aquifolium 'Bacciflava' Zone 7
Ilex aquifolium 'Handsworth New Silver' Zone 7
Kolkwitzia amabilis Zone 5
Ligustrum 'Vicaryi' Zone 6
Lonicera periclymenum Zone 5
Lonicera periclymenum 'Graham Thomas' Zone 5
Lonicera periclymenum 'Serotina' Zone 5
Lonicera pileata Zone 6
Magnolia × loebneri 'Leonard Messel' Zone 5
Magnolia stellata Zone 5
Mahonia aquifolium Zone 5

Betula pendula

Mahonia × media 'Charity' Zone 7
Mahonia × media 'Lionel Fortescue' Zone 7
Mahonia × media 'Winter Sun' Zone 7
Physocarpus opulifolius 'Dart's Gold' Zone 3
Pieris japonica 'Rosea' Zone 5
Pieris japonica 'Tilford' Zone 5
Philadelphus coronarius 'Aureus' Zone 5
Philadelphus 'Sybille' Zone 6
Pileostegia viburnoides Zone 7
Prunus laurocerasus Zone 6
Rhododenron ponticum Zone 5
Ribes laurifolium Zone 8
Ribes sanguineum 'Albescens' Zone 6
Ribes sanguineum 'Brocklebankii' Zone 6
Ribes sanguineum 'White Icicle' Zone 6
Rosa 'Bobbie James' Zone 5
Rosa filipes 'Kiftsgate' Zone 5
Rosa 'Hidcote Gold' Zone 5
Rosa 'Paul's Himalayan Musk' Zone 5
Rubus 'Benenden' Zone 5
Rubus cockburnianus 'Goldenvale' Zone 6
Rubus idaeus 'Aureus' Zone 4
Salix × stipularis Zone 6
Sambucus nigra 'Pulverulenta' Zone 5
Sarcococca confusa Zone 6
Sarcococca hookeriana var. digyna Zone 6
Skimmia × confusa 'Kew Green' Zone 7
Skimmia japonica 'Bowles' Dwarf Female' Zone 7
Skimmia japonica 'Bowles' Dwarf Male' Zone 7
Skimmia japonica 'Rubella' Zone 7
Sorbus hupehensis Zone 6
Sorbus hupehensis var. obtusa Zone 6
Spiraea japonica 'Goldflame' Zone 4
Staphylea × elegans Zone 6
Staphylea trifolia Zone 4
Stephanandra incisa 'Crispa' Zone 4
Viburnum × bodnantense 'Dawn' Zone 7
Viburnum farreri (syn. V. fragrans) Zone 6
Viburnum opulus 'Fructu Luteo' Zone 4
Viburnum tinus 'Eve Price' Zone 8
Weigela 'Florida Variegata' Zone 5
Weigela 'Gustave Malet' Zone 5
Weigela 'Looymansii Aurea' Zone 5
Weigela middendorffiana Zone 5
Weigela 'Mont Blanc' Zone 5

Deutzia × rosea

Euonymus europaeus 'Red Cascade'

Rubus idaeus 'Aureus'

Staphylea trifolia

Weigela 'Florida Variegata'

HARDINESS ZONES

Zone	Average Minimum Winter Temperature	
	C	°F
I	BELOW −46	BELOW −50°
2	−46 TO −40	−50° TO −40°
3	−40 TO −34	−40° TO −30°
4	−34 TO −29	−30° TO −20°
5	−29 TO −23	−20° TO −10°
6	−23 TO −18	−10° TO 0°
7	−18 TO −12	0° TO 10°
8	−12 TO −7	10° TO 20°
9	−7 TO −1	20° TO 30°
IO	−1 TO 4	30° TO 40°

Actaea pachypoda

Actaea rubra

Ajuga (with forget-me-nots)

PERENNIALS AND BULBS

The symbol ★ indicates plants for small, shady areas.

Actaea
This genus now includes plants we knew as cimicifuga. All need cool shade, not dry.
A. matsumurae 'White Pearl' (syn. *Cimicifuga simplex* var. *matsumurae* 'White Pearl'). This is a most elegant plant in autumn when branching stems carry snowy-white bottle brushes 13cm/5in long. These develop into a desirable, lime-green seed head. 90cm–120cm/3–4ft.
A. m. 'Frau Herms' has dark stems and larger tapers of creamy-white, fluffy flowers that open a week or so in advance of both 'White Pearl' and *A. m.* 'Elstead', which is taller (1.3m/4¼ft) and has purplish stems and buds opening creamy-white with pink stamens. All flower October – November. Zone 4
A. pachypoda. The White Baneberry makes elegant clumps of stiff, slender stems, furnished with light-green, divided leaves. Spires of fluffy, white flowers become spikes of pea-sized, white berries in late summer, each carrying a black dot and fastened by a short, red, swollen stem. 75cm/30in. Zone 4
A. rubra. A choice feature plant for cool shade, this forms a clump of soft-green, divided foliage from which emerge

several stems of small, white flowers followed by handsome trusses of glistening red berries. 60cm/2ft. Zone 4
A. simplex Atropurpurea Group (syn. *Cimicifuga simplex* var. *simplex* Atropurpurea Group). Deeply cut leaves and stems are dark purple, topped in early autumn with slender spires of small, sweetly scented, cream flowers. 1.8m/6ft. Zone 3

Adonis amurensis 'Fukujukai' ★
Semi-double, golden, buttercup-like flowers open from bronze buds nestling in a ruff of feathery, bronze leaves. These change to green, dying down by mid-summer. 25cm/10in. Zone 4

Aegopodium podagraria 'Variegatum' (See page 127.) 60cm/2ft. Zone 3

Ajuga
Bugles make eye-catching carpets of flower in May and June when their densely packed flowers emerge from overwintered leaf rosettes. After flowering, new trailing stems flow to make ground cover, the forms with good, coloured foliage creating another colour harmony among surrounding plants. They will not tolerate very dry soil. Watch for attack by aphids and mildew, both of which can spoil the clean foliage effect.

A. pyramidalis. ★ Good, glossy green ground cover, with pyramids of intensely blue flowers, rivalling gentians. 23cm/9in. Zone 5
A. reptans 'Burgundy Glow'. Beautiful foliage suffused rose and magenta, regularly edged with cream, makes a vivid carpet all winter, with spires of blue flowers in spring. 15cm/6in.
A. r. 'Catlin's Giant' is larger in every respect (see page 95); both
A. r. 'Atropurpurea', with burnished, purple foliage, and *A. r.* 'Purple Brocade', with deeply veined, purple leaves with ruffled edges, make a contrast in texture as well as colour. 20cm/8in. Zone 3

Alchemilla conjuncta ★
For those who look closely, this is a charming plant, with small, exquisitely cut leaves backed with shining silk, which forms a silver edge on the top side. 10cm/4in. Zone 5
A. erythropoda. ★ Small, scalloped leaves of soft blue-green are set off by sprays of tiny, lime-green stars in mid-summer. 15cm/6in. Zone 3
A. mollis. The invaluable Lady's Mantle forms a mound of velvety rounded leaves. When their serrated edges are full of dewdrops, each leaf looks like a beaded shawl. 45cm/18in. Zone 4

Anemone apennina var. *albiflora*

Anemone nemorosa 'Allenii'

Anemone ranunculoides 'Pleniflora'

Androsace geraniifolia ★
From northern India and Tibet, this has rounded, scallop-edged leaves that form rosettes, each carrying long-stemmed clusters of small, primula-like, white flowers in mid-summer. New leaf rosettes on long stems arch over to touch the soil and make new plants. This would be lost in real woodland, but is ideal for a shady rock garden or raised bed. 13cm/5in. Zone 6

Anemone – Dwarf Forms
A. apennina. Tuberous rhizomes produce deep-blue, starry flowers, similar to those of *A. blanda* but with narrower petals. It will succeed in the grassy floor of light woodland; flowering March to April (see page 60). 20cm/8in. *A. a.* var. *albiflora* produces crowds of palest-blue, daisy-shaped flowers, open to the sun, showing hearts filled with white stamens around a green ovary. 23–30cm/9–12in. Zone 5
A. × lipsiensis (syn. *A. × seemannii*). Pale, sulphur yellow flowers emerge in April from thin, horizontal rootstocks (see page 60). 15cm/6in. Zone 4
A. nemorosa. (See pages 59–60.)
A. n. 'Allenii' and *A. n.* 'Robinsoniana' (both 20cm/8in) have lavender-blue flowers *A. n.* 'Royal Blue' (15cm–6in) is a lovely blue form; white forms include *A. n.* 'Lady Doneraile' (15–18cm/6–7in) and the double *A. n.* 'Vestal'; the green flowers of *A. n.* 'Virescens' (15–18cm/6–7in) are

curiously attractive. Zone 4
A. ranunculoides 'Pleniflora'. (See page 60.) 10cm/4in. Zone 4
A. trifolia. From woods and upper slopes of the southern Alps, this is a firmer-leaved version of *A. nemorosa*, forming cushions covered with flat, white, starry flowers whose purity is emphasized with white stamens around a green ovary. 15cm/6in. Zone 6

Anemone – Border Forms
A. hupehensis 'Hadspen Abundance'. (See page 153.) From Hupeh in west China, this is a good edge-of-border plant, free-flowering *A. h.* var. *japonica* 'Prinz Heinrich' has a seemingly double layer of petals, narrow, slightly twisted and quilled, in a deep-pink shade. 60–75 cm/24–30in. Zone 5
A. × hybrida 'Honorine Jobert' and 'September Charm'. (See page 153.)
A. × h. 'Königin Charlotte' is also a fine plant, with large blooms of rich-rose-pink with well-formed, rounded petals. 1.2m/4ft. Zone 5
A. sylvestris. Dangles delicate, white flowers (like over-large snowdrops), which turn into bundles of cream fluff containing seeds. It colonizes well in light soil, but is more restricted in heavy soil. Flowering begins in spring, continuing intermittently throughout summer. 30–46cm/12–18in. Zone 4
A. tomentosa. (See page 156.) 1.2–1.5m/4–5ft. Zone 5

Anthriscus sylvestris 'Ravenswing' (See page 134.) Zone 4

Aquilegia
A beautiful genus (see page 90). Unless otherwise stated, Zone 2
A. flabellata var. *pumila.* ★ This has exceptional, bold, bluish foliage, while the large, soft-blue-and-white flowers are irresistible in early summer. 15cm/6in.
A. f. alba has creamy-white flowers shadowed with green. 20cm/8in. Zone 4
A. vulgaris var. *flore-pleno* 'Adelaide Addison'. (See page 90.) *A. v.* 'Nivea' (Munstead White) has light-green leaves that set off creamy-white flowers, true from seed, lovely in small colonies.
A. v. var. *stellata* 'Nora Barlow'. (See page 90.) 75cm/30in.

Anemone × hybrida 'Honorine Jobert'

A. v. **Vervaeneana Group**. The leaves, marbled in shades of gold, white and russet, appear cream from a distance. The flowers are pink. 60cm/2ft. Zone 4

Arisaema candidissimum
(See page 129.) Zone 7
A. ciliatum (See page 127.) Zone 7
A. tortuosum (See page 129.) Zone 7
A. triphyllum (See page 127.) Zone 4

Arisarum proboscideum ★
(See page 95.) 10cm/4in. Zone 6

Arthropodium candidum ★
Above low clumps of pale-coffee-coloured, grass-like foliage, stand wiry, branching stems starred with tiny, white flowers in mid-summer, still worth looking at in October when full of minute, black seeds. Good with *Cyclamen* or as contrast with *Ophiopogon planiscapus* 'Nigrescens'. 23cm/9in. Zone 8

Arum italicum 'Marmoratum' ('Pictum')
(See page 3.) Exotic leaves unroll in late autumn, continuing to grow throughout the winter, bowing beneath bitter frost, but standing undamaged immediately it thaws. By April they are full height, dark, glossy-green, spear-shaped and veined with ivory. In September, above bare earth, appear stems of red berries. 38cm/15in. Zone 6

Aruncus aethusifolius ★
This produces low clumps of fresh-green leaves as finely cut as chervil but with more substance. A forest of wiry flower stems arise 30cm/1ft, carrying tiny, astilbe-like heads of small, creamy-white flowers in June. By September they are still attractive, with barren heads tinted light chestnut, while seed-bearing heads are dark, shining brown, and foliage develops pink and reddish autumn tints. Zone 4
A. dioicus (See page 122.) A superb plant that needs rich soil. 1.2–1.8m/4–6ft.
A. d. 'Kneiffii' has leaves finely divided as though eaten to the veins by caterpillars, but such a lacy effect is charming beneath smaller plumes of creamy-white flowers. 90cm/3ft. Zone 2

Arisaema candidissimum

Asarum europaeum
(See page 101.) 13cm/5in. Zone 6

Astrantia
(See page 107.) Prefers retentive soil improved with leaf mould in partial shade. Deadheading will extend the flowering season into autumn and prevent unwanted seedlings, which are unlikely to come true from selected forms. Zone 4
A. 'Buckland'. White outer 'ray' petals, green-tipped, filled with a posy of quivering, tiny, pink flowers, give the overall effect of pale pink. It is very free-flowering for weeks in summer. 75cm/30in.
A. major subsp. *involucrata* 'Shaggy' (See page 107).
A. m. 'Rubra' (See page 108.) This is a wine-coloured form, others of which include *A. m.* 'Hadspen Blood', *A. m.* 'Claret' and *A. m.* 'Ruby Wedding'. Irresistible for garden design or flower arranging is *A. m.* 'Sunningdale Variegated', possibly the most beautiful variegated foliage plant in spring: large, hand-shaped and pointed leaves are

elegantly marked with yellow and cream; branching stems of white, flushed-pink posy flowers are an added bonus from summer to autumn. 75cm/30in.
A. maxima. Graceful, branching stems are topped in mid- to late summer with strawberry-pink, broad-petalled flowers, filled with quivering masses of pink stamens, each flower resembling a Victorian posy. 75cm/30in.

Bergenia
The species are among the most valuable evergreen ground cover, and for flower arranging. In part shade as well as sun, well-placed groups are as important in dry areas as hostas in damper, cooler conditions. Many hybrid forms are available.
B. cordifolia 'Purpurea'. A superb plant, ideal for ground cover and contrast, this has large, rounded, wavy leaves. Occasionally in summer one turns bright red or yellow, while winter frost burnishes them all to a purplish-red. Tall rhubarb-red stalks carry vivid, magenta flowers intermittently throughout summer. 45cm/18in. Zone 3
B. crassifolia 'Autumn Red'. Smaller leaves than *B. cordifolia*, flat and spoon-shaped, turn vividly red in winter. Soft, pink flowers appear in early summer. 30cm/1ft. Zone 3
B. stracheyi. ★ A tiny species from Afghanistan and the west Himalayas in which short-stemmed clusters of rose-pink flowers huddle among small, rounded leaves. 15cm/6in. Zone 6
B. 'Ballawley'. Largest of all hybrids, this has shining, fresh-green leaves all summer that are bronzed and reddened by frost. Branching heads of rose-red flowers on tall stems appear in spring and a few in autumn. 60cm/2ft. Zone 6
B. 'Beethoven'. An Eric Smith hybrid, this has large, dense clusters of white flowers held in coral-red calyces from May to June. 30cm/1ft. Zone 4
B. 'Morgenröte' (Morning Red). Large rosettes of rounded leaves produce dense heads of cherry-pink flowers in spring followed by an impressive second flowering in June. 45cm/18in. Zone 4

Arum italicum 'Marmoratum' ('Pictum')

Aruncus diocus

Astrantia 'Buckland'

Bergenia cordifolia 'Purpurea'

Brunnera macrophylla 'Dawson's White'

Cardamine pentaphylla

Corydalis flexuosa 'Père David'

B. 'Schneekönigin' (Snow Queen). An interesting German hybrid, this has extra-large flowers, palest shell-pink, almost white. 38cm/15in. Zone 4

Brunnera macrophylla
(See page 74.) 45cm/18in.
B. m. 'Hadspen Cream' and **B. m. 'Langtrees'** (See page 74.) 45cm/18in.
B. m. 'Dawson's White' (See page 74.) 30cm/12in. Zone 3

Buglossoides purpurocaerulea
(See page 127.) This needs sun and well-drained soil and will tolerate chalk. It thrives in open spaces in the poor sand of my Wood Garden. 38cm/15in. Zone 5

Cardamine
(See pages 76–7.) There are numerous cardamines for light shade; all flower in April or May and are 25–30cm/ 10–12in unless otherwise stated.
C. bulbifera (See page 77.) Zone 3
C. kitaibelii. Above low clusters of light-green, palmate leaves stand trusses of chalk-white cruciferous flowers. Zone 5
C. pentaphylla. ★ (See page 76.) Zone 5
C. quinquefolia. (See page 76.) Zone 4
C. trifolia. ★ This makes neat, attractive edging in part shade: close-packed, trifoliate leaves, evergreen tinged purple in winter, are covered with heads of tiny, white, cress-like flowers. 18cm/9in. Zone 5

Cenolophium denudatum
(See page 136.) 90cm–1.2m/3–4ft. Zone 3

Chaerophyllum hirsutum 'Roseum'
(See page 136.) 60–75cm/2–2½ft. Zone 5

Chrysosplenium davidianum ★
At first glance this looks as if it is a bright carpet of tiny euphorbias (see page 61). Round, flat heads (5cm/2in across), on 5cm/2in stems, consist of small, cup-shaped, bright-yellow saxifrage flowers surrounded by round, scallop-edged bracts. Hairy, reddish stems carry soft, furry leaves spreading horizontally to form low carpeting plants. Best in part shade and moist soil. March to April. Zone 5

Cimicifuga
See *Actaea*

Colchicum
(See pages 152–3.) Meadow saffrons are from high mountain meadows so do not belong to a woodland association of plants, but where there is ample light, along a path in an open glade, they flourish and bring a wash of welcome colour in early autumn. Unless otherwise stated Zone 6
C. autumnale 'Album'. (See page 153.) Zone 5
C. 'Glory of Heemstede'. Narrowish 'petals' create an upright chalice shape,

rich mauve with faint chequering, on pale stems. 15cm/6in.
C. 'Lilac Wonder'. Similar to *C. parnassicum* but a deeper shade of lilac-mauve. 10cm/4in.
C. parnassicum. (See page 152.) 10cm/4in.
C. 'Rosy Dawn'. (See page 152.) Increases freely. 15cm/6in.
C. speciosum 'Album'. (See page 153.) Superb, white flowers, rounded, like large wine goblets, on pale-green stems, to be treasured. *C. s.* 'Atrorubens' is a rarely offered wine-purple form with purple-stained stems. 15cm/6in.

Convallaria majalis
When conditions are right in humus-rich soil, among shrubs perhaps, where there is room for wandering rhizomes, why not plant a bed of Lily-of-the-Valley to scent the air in late spring and perhaps have handfuls to pick for the house? The variegated form *C. m.* 'Albostriata' 13–15cm/5–6in has attractive, cream stripes. *C. m.* 'Hardwick Hall' is taller 30cm/1ft with large, pointed oval leaves outlined with an irregular yellow edge, and big flowers. Zone 4

Corydalis cava
(See page 78.) 15–20cm/6–8in.
C. c. albiflora is taller. 20–30cm/8–12in. Zone 6
C. cheilanthifolia. ★ Fine-cut, fern-like leaves form a handsome base for a long

Dactylorhiza × braunii

Dicentra formosa alba

Dicentra spectabilis

succession of greenish-yellow, spurred flowers in early summer. Good in part shade with small ajugas, mitellas or Creeping Jenny. 30cm/1ft. Zone 5
C. flexuosa **'China Blue'**. ★ This extraordinary plant shows fresh flowers from spring until late July, when it is still three-parts covered with clusters of glacier-blue flowers, looking like shoals of little fishes swimming through a sea of finely cut, blue-grey leaves, 30cm/1ft.
C. f. **'Père David'** has light-green, divided leaves and sky-blue flowers, 30cm/1ft.
C. f. **'Purple Leaf'** makes low mounds, 25cm/10in, of finely cut leaves, stained and stroked with patches of reddish-tan, smothered for weeks in spring and early summer with clusters of tiny, blue, tubular flowers warmed with red. For humus-rich, loose soil and part shade. Zone 5

Cyclamen hederifolium ★
(See pages 175-7.) The earliest and showiest cyclamen for naturalizing under trees. 10cm/4in. Zone 5
C. coum. (See page 177.) Zone 6

Dactylorhiza × braunii ★
One of the most handsome of the terrestrial orchids for sun or semi-shade and good, leaf-mould soil, slender stems, clothed in spotted, pointed, green leaves, carry pyramid-shaped heads (25cm/10in long) of crimson-purple flowers. Early summer. 60cm/2ft. Zone 5

Dicentra **'Bacchanal'**
(See page 89.) Similar in habit to *D. formosa*, this has clustered heads of glowing, wine-red flowers above pale-green, finely cut leaves. 30–38cm/12–15in. Zone 4
D. formosa. From soft, ferny hummocks of deeply divided leaves on juicy, pink-tinted stems, dangle little, mauvish-pink lockets in spring and early summer. Easily grown in cool conditions. Beautiful contrast with hostas and tiarellas.
D. f. alba has much paler-green leaves on glassy-green stems and fragile, white flowers. 30–45cm/12–18in. Zone 4
D. **'Langtrees'**. ★ Small, cream-and-pink flowers are followed by new basal leaves of an outstanding colour, almost blue, finely cut. For cool soil. 30cm/1ft. Zone 4
D. macrantha. ★ A rare treasure for those who can suit it, the branching stems set with finely cut, bronzed-green leaves carry pale-greenish-yellow flowers, long and narrow, about 7.5cm/3in, dangling like elegant earrings. It needs cool, damp shady conditions, protected from drying wind and early frosts. 45cm/18in. Zone 4
D. spectabilis and *D. s.* **'Alba'**. (See page 79.) Needs rich, deep soil. 60cm/2ft. Zone 3

Digitalis ferruginea
A gem of a foxglove: tall flower stems bear close-set, rounded buds which open to smallish, short trumpets of coppery-

yellow, veined brown. 90cm/3ft. Zone 6
D. grandiflora (ambigua). From velvety green foliage come branching stems of soft, yellow foxgloves. Sound perennial. 60cm/2ft. Zone 2
D. lutea. (See page 123.) Zone 4
D. × *mertonensis* (*D. purpurea* × *D. grandiflora*). Large flowers in lovely shades of deep old-rose have a hint of copper. Fairly perennial if divided after flowering, it comes true from seed. Likes part shade. 60cm/2ft. Zone 4
D. parviflora. ★ Close-packed, cylindrical heads of narrow, bronze-brown flowers on stiff, upright stems are most intriguing in July above bold clumps of narrow, dark-green leaves. 60cm/2ft. Zone 5
D. purpurea f. *albiflora*. Let this lovely white form of our native biennial foxglove seed: most seedlings come true but if any have purple leaf stalks they will have purple flowers. Remove these to keep the strain pure. 1.2m/4ft plus. Zone 5

Diphylleia cymosa
The Umbrella Leaf is an eye-catching foliage plant for cool shade and retentive soil. Large, rounded leaves, deeply cut, almost divided in half, present a flat tabletop, red-stained when young, maturing rich green. Above them, in early summer, appear clusters of small, white flowers succeeded by sloe-coloured berries attached to brilliant-red, enamelled stalks. 60cm/2ft. Zone 5

Epimedium davidii

Epimedium × versicolor 'Versicolor'

Disporum sessile 'Variegatum' ★
Like a small but daintier Solomon's Seal,
from a wandering, starfish-shaped
rootstock rise slender stems that bear
pretty leaves, fresh green, broadly striped
cream. Creamy-white, bell-shaped
flowers dangle beneath the leaves in
spring. 30–38cm/12–15in. Zone 4

Dodecatheon meadia ★
This forms a basal clump of smooth,
broad-bladed leaves, rather like those of a
primrose. Heads of down-turned, dart-
like flowers, in shades of pinky-mauve
with reflexed petals, are poised on bare
stems. It needs damp soil laced with
humus, preferably in part shade.
25cm/10in. Zone 3

Doronicum pardalianches
(See page 90.) The Great Leopard's Bane.
1.2m/4ft. Zone 4

Epimedium
Most valued and beautiful of foliage
plants, it will put up with dry shade, but
makes superb ground cover more quickly
in rich, damp leaf mould. The less
vigorous forms are ideal in small areas.
E. davidii. ★ Above small, pointed,
leathery leaves, stained bronze in spring,
stand wire-thin, dark stems carrying
flights of lemon-yellow, long-spurred
flowers, backed with dark-red calyces.
30–38cm/12–15in. Zone 6

E. 'Enchantress'. ★ Low mounds of long,
leathery, pointed leaves are bright green
in spring, when it carries sprays of pale-
pink flowers, and purple-stained in
winter. 25cm/10in. Zone 5
E. grandiflorum 'Crimson Beauty'. ★
Deep-rose flowers, long calyces and
spurred petals in deep rose-pink create a
semi-double effect. 30cm/1ft.
E. g. subsp. *koreanum* ★ makes sprays of
creamy-yellow, columbine-like flowers;
long, shimmering spurs dangle among the
clumps of emerging leaf stems, above
light-green leaves, tinted bronze in
spring. 30–45cm/12–18in.
E. g. 'Lilafee' ★ has narrow, oval leaves,
softly bronzed when young; from dark-
purple buds open long sprays of light-
purple flowers fading to white-tipped
spurs. 30cm/1ft. Zone 5
E. × perralchicum 'Frohnleiten'. ★ This
excellent plant forms neat clumps of
evergreen foliage beautifully marbled
with warm reds and bronze in spring, and
colours again in autumn. Sprays of
bright-yellow flowers are held above the
foliage. 38cm/15in. Zone 5
E. pubigerum. This has handsome foliage
with many small creamy flowers on tall
stems, up to 38cm/15in. Zone 5
E. × rubrum. A splendid ground-cover
plant in shade and among shrubs: elegant,
heart-shaped leaves on wiry stems
emerge in soft tints of bronze-red, fading
to light green, assuming vivid coral-red

shades in autumn. Rose flowers appear in
spring. 23cm/9in. Zone 4
E. setosum. ★ Distinctive, narrow, pointed,
heart-shaped leaves in bright pea-green
carry flights of creamy-white flowers on
thread-thin stems. Enchanting.
15–38cm/6–15in. Zone 6
E. × versicolor 'Sulphureum'. More
vigorous than *E. × rubrum*, the leaves
combine delicate shades of bronze in
early spring, ideal for picking. The
delicate, sulphur-yellow flowers are borne
on wiry stems, half-buried among the
leaves for protection. In autumn the
green summer foliage again becomes
marbled with bronze, remaining all
winter. 30cm/1ft. *E. × v.* 'Versicolor'
makes overlapping layers of pea-green
leaves, marbled reddish-bronze, above
which stand showers of stems smothered
in tight, ruby buds which open flowers
with faded-pink petals and yellow
mouths. The overall effect is of soft,
bronze-orange. 30cm/1ft. Zone 5
E. × youngianum 'Merlin'. ★ Above the
new spring foliage suffused with shades of
brown, wiry stems carry spurless, chubby
flowers opening soft purple and white
from wine-purple, pointed buds.
30–38cm/12–15in. *E. × y.* 'Niveum' ★
is a gem, making neat clumps of smaller
foliage in soft shades of milk chocolate in
spring, above which float clouds of pure-
white, starry flowers. 25cm/10in. Zone 5

Erythronium dens-canis

Erythronium dens-canis 'Snowflake'

Erythronium 'Sundisc'

Epipactis gigantea ★

The Marsh Helleborine from North America is a rather misleading common name for this attractive plant for a cool, damp place. It has many stiff stems, clothed in simple, pointed, upturned leaves, carrying spires of small, green-and-copper-coloured, orchid-like flowers in mid-summer. 25cm/10in. Zone 4

Eranthis hyemalis

(See page 33.) Naturalized in Britain; wild in parts of Europe. 10–15cm/4–6in. Zone 4

Erythronium californicum 'White Beauty' ★

Pale-cream, lily-shaped flowers reflex to show cream stamens with a ring of reddish stain at their base. The leaves are strongly mottled with brown. April. 25cm/10in. Zone 5

E. dens-canis. (See page 59.) The Dog's Tooth Violet. 15cm/6in.

E. d. 'Snowflake' has larger flowers on 12cm/5in stems. The long, pointed petals are faintly touched pink, with brown feathering on the backs. Bronze is repeated in the marbled leaves, the flower stems and the bronze zone at the base of the petals where they flare back to expose greyish-mauve stamens and a white stigma. Zone 3

E. 'Pagoda'. (See page 81.) 30–40cm/12–16in. Zone 5

E. revolutum. (See page 81.) Zone 5

E. 'Sundisc'. (See page 81.) Huge, tongue-shaped leaves 12cm/5in across, 25cm/10in long, are boldly marbled with brown, looking like snakeskin. Well above, on bare stems 38–45cm/15–18in, dangle bright-lemon lily-flowers with recurved petals; tip them up to see the reddish-brown disc surrounding stamens and ovary. Zone 5

Euphorbia

Most spurges need an open, sunny situation, but the following do well in shade or part shade.

E. amygdaloides 'Purpurea'. This superb

Euphorbia jacquemontii

Wood Spurge has maroon stems carrying dark evergreen leaves; new spring shoots are vividly tinted beetroot-red, followed by bright-yellow-green flower bracts. 75cm/30in. Zone 6 *E. a.* var. *robbiae* (See page 67.) 60cm/2ft. Zone 8

E. cornigera. (See page 138.) 90cm/3ft. Zone 6

E. jacquemontii. This Himalayan species flowers for weeks in mid-summer.

E. sikkimensis. Ruby-red leaf rosettes appear in early spring; by mid-summer willowy stems are topped with yellow-green flowers. By August blue-green seed pods contrast with vivid-lime collars. Needs retentive soil. 1.2m/4ft. Zone 6

Euphorbia amygdaloides 'Purpurea'

Fritillaria camschatcensis

Fritillaria meleagris

Fuchsia 'Riccartonii'

Fragaria chiloensis 'Chaval'
Although its pink leaf stalks are 15cm/6in long, this plant appears to hug the soil, forming close-knit, wide-spreading carpets of small, polished, evergreen leaves. It makes quick and handsome ground cover beneath trees and shrubs (in sun too), and is ideal to set off bulbs, from snowdrops to late-summer lilies. Zone 4

Fritillaria camschatcensis ★
At the end of May several open bells, unbelievably black – smooth outside, heavily corrugated inside – dangle from the top of fleshy stems clothed in whorls of green, glossy leaves. Needs rich leaf-mould soil in sun or part shade. 51cm/20in. Zone 4
F. meleagris. Snake's Head Fritillary. (See page 56 & 58.) Zone 4

Fuchsia
Hardy fuchsias provide flower and leaf colour from June to the frosts. In well-fed, retentive soil in sun or part shade, the following will make large, shrubby plants, but can be pruned hard in spring where space is limited.
F. 'Genii'. This is valued for its beautiful, golden foliage set off by red stems, and red-and-purple flowers. Mulch well the first winter and cut back top growth each spring. 60cm/2ft. Zone 7
F. 'Hawkshead'. This enchanting hybrid of *F. magellanica* has long, narrow, ivory-

white flowers, the tip of each pointed petal, stained green, like elegant, painted fingernails. It will make a shrub 1m/40in plus, depending on conditions; prefers a cool site and retentive soil. Zone 7
F. magellanica 'Versicolor' (See page 146.) A beautiful foliage plants, this has tall, arching stems bearing dainty foliage suffused grey, rose and cream, and a long succession of slim, cherry-coloured flowers with violet 'petticoats'. 1.2m/4ft. Zone 8.
F. 'Pumila'. Makes a compact, bushy plant clothed in small, green, pointed leaves, with arching branches fringed with dark-red buds which open long, slender, scarlet flowers revealing purple 'petticoats' and tassels of long stamens. 38cm/15in. Zone 7
F. 'Riccartonii'. A vigorous, branching plant with small, crimson buds and flowers similar to *F.* 'Pumila' 1.2m/4ft. Zone 8
F. 'Whiteknights Pearl'. Decked with slender, uniformly rose-pink flowers, this is an irresistible sight for weeks from late summer. 90cm/3ft. Zone 7

Galanthus ★
(See pages 36–41.) Here are a very few of the many variants of snowdrop chosen for good form and vigour, all of which are suitable for small gardens. Divide clumps after flowering, every three to four years.

Single Forms
G. 'Atkinsii'. (See page 39.) 30cm/1ft. Zone 5
G. 'Brenda Troyle'. A large, elegant snowdrop; when open wide the petals measure 5cm/2in across, held well on 25cm/10in stalks. Zone 5
G. elwesii 'Cedric's Prolific'. (See page 40.) The inner segments are marked with a broad 'V' at the tips. Sometimes the outer segments are marked with fine, short, green lines. The grey-green leaves, up to 2.5cm/1in across, form an effective feature. *G. e.* 'Comet' is even larger, with 'petals' 7.5cm/3in across when opened wide, nodding on long pedicels.
G. e. var. *monostictus* (syn. *G. caucasicus*) has large, single flowers held on stems up to 40cm/16in long, supported by broad, grey-green leaves 2.5cm/1in across. A vigorous grower, it quickly makes generous clumps of bulbs.
G. e. var. *m.* Hiemalis Group (See page 38.) *G. e.* 'Three Leaves' (See page 40.) Zone 6
G. e. 'Washfield Colesbourne' (See page 40.) Zone 4
G. ikariae. (See page 40.) Zone 6
G. 'Mrs Thompson'. (See page 39.) 25–30cm/10–1ft stems. Zone 5
G. nivalis. The Common Snowdrop has many variants, both single and double. They include such familiar names as
G. n. Scharlockii Group which has two long spathes projecting well above the

flower, rather like a hare's ears; also
G. n. **'Viridapicis'** (See page 36.)
G. *plicatus* **'Beth Chatto'** (See page 42.)
Zone 6
G. *p.* **'Washfield Warham'** ('Finale').
(See pages 39 and 55.) Zone 6
G. *reginae-olgae* subsp. *reginae-olgae*
(See page 38.) Zone 6
G. **'S. Arnott'** (See page 36.) This is
one of the best, increasing well and
flowering freely. In winter sun large,
cupped sepals 5cm/2in across flare wide-
open to show the strong, green arch at
the top of the inner petals. The narrow
petals are twice as long as the inner
segments. Established clumps make
conspicuous 'snow patches'. 25cm/10in.
Zone 5
G. **'Wisley Magnet'**. Outer petals are
3.5cm/1½in long, while the central
segments have an extra broad 'V', very
effective when seen swaying from the
long, thread-like pedicels. Zone 5

Double Forms
G. **'Desdemona'** (See page 40). Zone 5
G. **'Hippolyta'** (See page 40). Zone 5
G. **'Dionysus'** (See page 40). Zone 5
G. **'Ophelia'**. This has slightly smaller
flowers than G. 'Hippolyta' on
25cm/10in stems with less closely packed
segments, but flares back her outer 'petals'
till they curl upwards to expose fully her
underwear. Zone 5
G. **'Lady Beatrix Stanley'** (See page 39.)
Zone 5
G. *nivalis* **'Blewbury Tart'** (See page 39.)
The double form of **G. n. 'Flore Pleno'**
has six long, individually curved outer
'petals' embracing loosely gathered layers
of light-green-and-white-striped inner
segments. The nodding heads, almost
5cm/2in across, generously produced,
make some of the best 'snow patches' in
the garden. **G. n. 'Lady Elphinstone'**
(See page 39.) Zone 4

Galium odoratum
(See page 67.) 12cm/5in. Zone 5

Gentiana asclepiadea ★ (See page 151.)
90cm/3ft. Zone 5

Galanthus 'Atkinsii'

Galanthus elwesii 'Cedric's Prolific'

Galanthus 'Wisley Magnet'

Galanthus 'Dionysus'

Geranium
(See pages 123–6.) The cranesbills are
bettered by none for attractive and weed-
proof ground cover. The parasol-shaped
foliage, more or less deeply cut, is always
beautiful and often scented. The flowers
are jewel-like in intensity of colour and
produced over a long period in great
profusion. All are easy to grow, most of
them in ordinary soil; the following
perform well in part shade.

G. × *cantabrigiense* **'Cambridge'**.
Luminous soft-mauve flowers smother
low cushions of parasol-shaped leaves,
which have good autumn colour.
38cm/15in. Zone 4
G. *endressii*. Rose-pink flowers appear
from summer to autumn over pretty,
pale-green foliage; excellent spreading
ground cover, in sun or part shade.
38cm/15in. Zone 4
G. *macrorrhizum*. (See page 126.) This

Geranium 'Nimbus'

Geranium nodosum

group includes several forms that flower May to June: **G. m. 'Album'**, **G. m. 'Bevan's Variety'** (vivid magenta-pink flowers), **G. m. 'Ingwersen's Variety'** (green, fragrant foliage, soft-lilac-pink flowers, some autumn colour), and **G. m. 'Variegatum'** (slightly felted leaves splashed with cream, primrose-yellow and a dash of red around the scalloped edges, magenta-pink flowers). Zone 4

G. maculatum. Neither blue nor pink, the flowers are an in-between shade of cool lilac with paler centres which bleach into the edge of the petals as they fade, creating a delicate effect. Lovely with *Aquilegia vulgaris* var. *flore-pleno* 'Adelaide Addison'. 60cm/2ft. Zone 5

G. × magnificum. Strong clumps of handsome, dark-green foliage colour well in autumn. The flowers are rich-violet-blue, heavily veined, on 60cm/2ft stalks in mid-summer. Zone 4

G. 'Nimbus'. (*G. clarkei* 'Kashmir Purple' × *G. collinum*). This forms a lacy mound, 60–90cm/2–3ft across, of finely cut leaves smothered in high summer with starry, bluish-purple flowers. Zone 4

G. nodosum. Myriad light-purple flowers whose pale centres are enlivened by thin, crimson veins and pale-blue stamens, flutter on thin, dark stems above smooth, maple-shaped leaves. Good in shade or sun. 38cm/15in. Zone 5

G. × oxonianum 'Claridge Druce'. (See page 123.) 45cm/18in.

G. × o. 'Wargrave Pink' is similar to *G. endressii* but with flowers of salmon-pink. 38cm/15in. Zone 5

G. phaeum. The Mourning Widow is a strong grower in shade, with small flowers of sombre purple, silk-textured in early summer. 75–90cm/30–36in.

G. p. 'Album' creates contrast and a light, delicate effect in dim places. 60cm/2ft.

G. p. 'Samobor' (See page 91.) I value for its large leaves, strikingly marked with a central brown blotch. 60–75cm/24–30in. Zone 4

G. procurrens. Prostrate stems, well-branched and covered with pretty, cut leaves, make ideal ground cover quickly covering yards. Zone 6

Geranium phaeum

G. 'Spinners'. Over finely cut leaves, this produces a shower of exquisite flowers in mid-summer of a colour which glows under thunderous skies – a luminous light purple that pales towards the centre where translucent, red veins thread through a blue base. 60–75cm/24–30in. Zone 5

Gillenia trifoliata
(See pages 120 & 123.) 1.2m/4ft. Zone 4

Hacquetia epipactis
(See page 174.) 6cm/2½in. Zone 5

Hedera
Ivies are perfect ground cover in dark places and are invaluable for covering unsightly walls or fences, the variegated forms providing bright contrast, especially in winter. Zone 5

H. helix 'Ivalace'. This has small, incurved leaves, dark green with pale-green veins. **H. h. 'Melanie'** is an unusual and very attractive variant of *H.* 'Cristata' in which every round and crimpled leaf is bordered with plum-red.

H. h. f. poetarum 'Poetica Arborea' (See page 23.) Another rarely seen ivy, a mature, fruiting form that slowly makes a dome-shaped bush and is covered throughout the winter with clusters of fruit which, by spring, have become not black, but orange. 1.2m/4ft.

Helleborus

(See pages 49–53 and our *Handbook* for further descriptions.) Plants of long-lasting beauty, hellebores have handsome, evergreen foliage, many making bold ground cover and bearing flowers of sculptured form. They are easily grown when drainage is good and humus abundant.

H. argutifolius (*H. corsicus*). The Corsican Hellebore has many stiff stems bearing handsome, claw-like foliage of cool jade-green. In winter these tend to fall out like the spokes of a wheel to make way for new shoots. By January every stem is topped with clusters of apple-green cups which continue to June. 60cm/2ft. Zone 7

H. foetidus. From neater and smaller clumps of holly-green, divided, fan-shaped leaves fall clusters of palest-green bells, thimble-sized, edged with maroon. The Stinking Hellebore is a true winter flower. 60cm/2ft. Zone 6

H. × hybridus (*H. orientalis* of gardens) (See page 49.) We cut the leaves off in winter before the flowers appear to prevent the spread of botrytis, which sometimes damages the flowering stems. Flowers February to April. 46cm/18in. Zones 5. *H. × h.* **Kochii Group** (See pages 51 & 174.) Flowers at the same time as *H. niger*, from mid-January to early March. 30cm/1ft. Zone 5

H. niger. The well-known flowers of the Christmas Rose stand just above dark-green, leathery leaves – white, wide-open blooms, sometimes tinged pink. This needs retentive but well-drained soil, in sun or part shade, top dressed with old manure or compost. 25 cm/10in. Zone 4

Helleborus × nigercors. (See page 52.) 30cm/1ft.

H. × sternii **'Boughton Beauty'** (*H. argutifolius × H. lividus*). Stout maroon stems clothed in dark-green, leathery leaves, sometimes laced with silver, carry branched heads of old-rose buds opening pale-green centres, filled with cream stamens, making overall an exciting combination. It needs shelter from icy winds. Flowers January to June. 75–90cm/30–36in. Zone 7

H. viridis. ★ An established clump of fresh, leafy stems, crowded with buds and shallow, apple-green saucers filled with cream stamens, is a pleasure for weeks from early February until late spring. 30cm/1ft. Zone 6

Helleborus × hybridus 'Apple Blossom'

Helleborus × hybridus spotted

Helleborus × hybridus purple

Helleborus × hybridus veined

Helleborus × nigercors

Helleborus × sternii 'Boughton Beauty'

Heuchera 'Chocolate Ruffles'

Heuchera 'Persian Carpet'

Hepatica nobilis 'Rubra Plena' ⋆
In early spring double, pink flowers
appear above rounded leaves on the plant
we used to call *Anemone hepatica*; it needs
damp, leaf-mould soil in partial shade.
10cm/4in. Zone 5

H. transsilvanica. ⋆ I am uncertain of the
name for this fine form I found in an old
garden. In early spring many petals of rich
blue make flowers 2cm/¾in across,
smothering the overwintered leaves; the
new ones continue to make handsome
ground cover for the rest of the year.
H. t. 'Lilacina' has pale-lilac flowers,
almost as large as the type, freely produced
in early spring. 10cm/4in. Zone 5

Heuchera ⋆
This does not like to be scorched or dried
out, so a cool situation in partial shade
suits it best. Replant in fresh soil every
few years.
H. americana. Mounds of rounded, ivy-
shaped leaves with silky top sides appear
in spring in soft shades of tan, finally
becoming dark green. New leaves
continue to appear, if conditions are
good, maintaining an interesting colour
effect. Thin, bare stems carry broad spires
of tiny, brown-and-green flowers in early
to mid-summer. 45cm/18in. Zone 4
H. 'Chocolate Ruffles'. (See page 89.)
38cm/16½in. Zone 5
H. cylindrica 'Greenfinch'. Lovely for
picking, this has tall, well-formed spikes

of olive-green bells in midsummer.
75cm/30in. Zone 4
H. micrantha var. **diversifolia 'Palace
Purple'.** (See page 129.) 45cm/18in.
Zone 4
H. 'Persian Carpet'. (See page 129.)
This is one of the best dark-leaved
heucheras. 45cm/18in. Zone 5
H. villosa. Above a mound of fresh-green,
maple-shaped leaves stand long-lasting
spires of tiny, greenish-white flowers,
creating a spring-like effect for weeks in
mid- to late summer. 60cm/2ft.
H. v. 'Royal Red' (See page 129.)
45cm/18in. Zone 6

× Heucherella alba 'Bridget Bloom' ⋆
From marbled foliage, interesting all year
round, appears a mass of light-pink flower
spikes in late spring to early summer. It
likes a little shade and humus-fed, light
soil. **× H. a. 'Rosalie'** has fluffy heads of

× *Heucherella alba* 'Bridget Bloom'

shrimp-pink flowers standing above
light-green, lobed leaves, prettily marbled
tan. 45cm/18in. Zone 4
× Heucherella 'Viking Ship' ⋆. Above
attractive leaves appear many spires of
brownish-pink buds on olive stems,
opening pale pink tiny flowers that form
a low haze of colour. 45cm/18in. Zone 4

Hosta
There are countless variations of hosta.
The following are a few basic types. They
will survive almost anywhere, but look
best, and do better, in partial shade, in
cool, well-fed soil, where, once
established, many will produce immense
leaves, totally weed-proof. Trumpet-
shaped flowers add interest from late
summer to autumn. Most yellow-leaved
forms need shade or partial shade to
prevent scorching.
H. fortunei var. **albopicta.** (See page 137.)

× *Heucherella* 'Viking Ship'

Hosta fortunei 'Marginata Alba'

Hosta sieboldiana 'Frances Williams'

Hosta sieboldiana var. *elegens*

45cm/18in. *H. f. f. aurea* has young leaves of soft buttercup-yellow, slowly ageing to green. 38cm/16½in. *H. f.* **var.** *aureomarginata* has rich-green leaves with broad, creamy-yellow borders, retaining the colour well into autumn. 75cm/30in. *H. f.* **'Marginata Alba'** has large, sage-green leaves, grey beneath, broadly edged with white; some, buried beneath the top layers, may be half-white. Given time to establish, and shade to produce good variegation, it is one of the best white-edged hostas. 75cm/30in. *H. f.* **'Spinners'** makes large, robust clumps of overlapping, sage-green leaves, boldly edged with cream, that remain fresh, creating a strong focal point all summer. 60cm/2ft. Zone 3

H. 'Gold Standard'. Medium-sized leaves, strongly veined, are a lovely shade of yellow, thinly rimmed with green, becoming rich yellow as the leaves mature. Pale lavender flowers appear in mid-summer. 60cm/2ft. Zone 3

H. (Tardiana Group) **'Halcyon'.** Raised by Eric Smith, this is possibly the best blue-leaved hosta. Heart-shaped leaves are so coated with a fine wax film that they appear blue. Handsome heads of lilac-blue flowers on purplish stems are produced in late summer. 30cm/1ft. Zone 3

H. 'Honeybells'. This has good, fresh-green leaves and makes a fine show of fragrant, lilac flowers in late summer.

90cm/36in. Zone 3

H. 'Krossa Regal'. Handsome, glaucous leaves on tall stems are lightly corrugated with parallel veins. Because each tip is tilted upwards, the wavy edges show a glimpse of pale-grey-blue bloom on the underside. Spires of lilac flowers appear mid- to late summer. 1.2m/4ft. Zone 3

H. lancifolia. (See page 137.) Spires of deep-lilac flowers make a long display in late summer. 60cm/2ft. Zone 3

H. 'Royal Standard'. This has the good looks of one of its parents, *H. plantaginea*, but is more robust and flowers much more generously. The broad, heart-shaped foliage is light green, above which stand tall, strong stems of flowers which are a joy in late summer, being large, pure white and scented. 75cm/30in. Zone 3

H. sieboldiana **and** *H. s.* **var.** *elegans.*(See page 137.) As well as the foliage, palest-lilac flowers command admiration, and finally the seed pods, which, having burst and scattered their black seeds, split into tiny, straw-coloured segments like starry flowers. *H. s.* **'Frances Williams'** (See page 121.) 75cm/30in. Zone 3

H. 'Tall Boy'. This makes an impressive clump of rich-green, heart-shaped, long, pointed leaves. Large, rounded, violet-mauve flowers dangle from tall stems over a long period in mid-summer. 1.2m/4ft. Zone 3

H. 'Thumb Nail'. ★ Standing only 15–20cm/6–8in tall in full flower in early

July, this tiny hosta is well named, making dense clusters of pointed, oval leaves scarcely 2.5cm/1in long, yet freely produces dainty spires of lilac flowers. It looks well on a shady raised bed with dwarf ferns and mossy saxifrages. Zone 3

Kirengeshoma palmata

(See page 150.) *K. p.* **Koreana Group** is a shorter, more upright plant with the same drooping clusters of pale-butter-yellow, shuttlecock-shaped flowers in autumn. 60–75cm/24–30in. Zone 5

Kirengeshoma palmata

Lamium galeobdolon subsp. *montanum* 'Silberteppich'

Leucojum vernum var. *vagneri*

Lilium hansonii

Lilium martagon var. *album*

Lamium

With varying degrees of variegation and vigour, the dead nettles provide both ground cover and colour contrast, adding to the tapestry effect of the woodland carpet. *L. galeobdolon* is the only one to be wary of as it travels far and wide.

L. galeobdolon subsp. *montanum* '**Florentinum**'. Ideal for smothering untidy hedge bottoms or as ground cover in shady places, long, trailing stems are clothed in dark, nettle-like leaves, brilliantly frosted with white. Yellow flowers appear in spring. 30cm/1ft.

L. g. subsp. *m.* '**Silberteppich**' (Silver Carpet) is not invasive, forming clusters of silver leaves netted with green veins. Pretty sprays of yellow nettle flowers appear in spring. 25cm/10in. Zone 5

L. maculatum '**Aureum**' (syn. *L. m.* 'Gold Nuggets'). The leaves become a strong yellow-ochre as they mature, marked with a narrow, white zone down the centre. *L. m.* '**Beacon Silver**' makes very good cover in cool soil in part shade, with leaves totally silvered apart from a narrow, green edging. 10cm/4in.

L. m. '**Cannon's Gold**' has larger, bolder leaves than *L. m.* 'Aureum', of a uniform yellowish-green tone, with lilac-pink, lipped flowers tucked between the leaves. 20cm/8in. *L. m.* '**Pink Pewter**' has totally silvered leaves with crinkly, green margins, and pale-pink flowers. 20cm/8in.

L. m. '**White Nancy**' is silver-leaved with white flowers. Zone 3

L. orvala. 60cm/2ft stems carry pairs of dark, pointed, strongly veined leaves. Beneath each pair is a whorl of rich-strawberry-pink, lipped flowers. Zone 4

Leucojum aestivum '**Gravetye Giant**' (See page 72.) The Summer Snowflake flowers here in April and into May. It differs from *L. vernum* in having smaller flowers, but more of them, from three to five dangling from the top of tall bare stems 60cm/2ft. Zone 4

L. vernum var. *vagneri*. This Spring Snowflake makes strong clumps of bulbs, often mistaken for a snowdrop, since it flowers at much the same time, but it has lampshade-like bells, made up of six pointed petals held open wide, showing green tips. It carries two flowers per stem, above lush, strap-shaped leaves. It differs from *L. vernum* in being larger and more robust. Zone 4

Lilium hansonii

(See page 94.) 1m/3½ft. Zone 4

L. martagon. The Turk's Cap Lily of the Swiss mountain meadows has tall, slender stems carrying several pink- or purplish-and-white flowers in June/July. It does best in light soil with added compost, among shrubs, or in open spaces in woodland. 1.2m/4ft. Zone 4

L. m var. *album*. is the white form. Zone 4

Narcissus cyclamineus

Narcissus 'Eystettensis'

Narcissus pallidiflorus

Liriope muscari ★
(See page 162.) *L. m.* 'Monroe White'
has shorter spikes of white flowers
opening from greenish-cream buds.
38cm/15in. Zone 6
L. 'Samantha'. This has spikes of lilac-
pink flowers. 38cm/15in. Zone 6

Lunaria rediviva
(See page 89.) The perennial honesty has
heads of pale-lilac-white, sweetly scented
flowers in early spring. The white, papery
seed-cases which follow in autumn are
elliptical, not round as has the biennial
honesty. 75cm/30in. Zone 6
L. annua 'Variegata'. (See page 94.)
Zone 7

Lysimachia nummularia 'Aurea'
Golden Creeping Jenny. (See pages 74,
145 and 150.) 5cm/2in. Zone 4

Mitella breweri ★
In spring forests of pale, slender stems
carry wands of minute, green flowers
above scallop-edged, dark-green leaves.
17cm/7in. Zone 5
M. caulescens. ★ Thread-like stems run
over the soil, forming carpets or edgings
of pea-green, heart-shaped leaves, with
tiny, palest-green, frilly flowers in spring.
8cm/3in. Zone 5

Myrrhis odorata
(See page 134.) 1m/40in. Zone 4

Narcissus
N. 'Beersheba'. (See page 72.) Zone 4
N. 'Cedric Morris'. (See pages 34-6.)
15–25cm/6–10in. Zone 5
N. cyclamineus. (See page 69.) Zone 5
N. 'Eystettensis' (Queen Anne's Double
Daffodil). (See page 69.) About
20cm/8in. Zone 4
N. 'February Gold'. (See page 68.) Zone 5
N. 'Jenny'. (See page 72.) Zone 5
N. minor. (See page 69.) Zone 5
N. pallidiflorus. (See page 69.) Zone 4
Narcissus pseudonarcissus subsp.

pseudonarcissus. (See page 68.)
N. 'Rip van Winkle'. (See page 69.) Zone 4
N. Tête-à-tête. (See page 69.) Zone 4
N. 'Thalia'. (See page 72.) Zone 5
N. 'Tresamble'. (See page 72.) Zone 4

Omphalodes cappadocica ★
(See page 74.) 23cm/9in. *O. c.* 'Cherry
Ingram' has gentian-blue, forget-me-
not-like flowers larger than the type, free-
flowering. 25cm/10in. *O. c.* 'Starry Eyes'
20cm/8in. Zone 6
O. verna. Blue-eyed Mary makes creeping

Omphalodes cappadocica

Ornithogalum nutans

Oxalis oregana

Pachysandra terminalis 'Variegata'

mats of rich green, broadly oval leaves, forming good ground cover in deep or part shade, embroidered with little, forget-me-not-like flowers in spring. *O. v.* '**Alba**' has sprays of pure-white, starry flowers. 10cm/4in. Zone 5

Ophiopogon planiscapus '**Nigrescens**' ★
Arching, strap-shaped leaves make spidery clusters against soil, making a feature all year round and remarkable because they are black, literally black. I have laid a leaf along a black-painted door-latch to find little, if any, difference. If you look carefully among the leaves in summer you will find short sprays of tiny, mauve bells which mature to become shiny, black berries lasting well into winter. It creeps slowly in well-drained but retentive soil, in sun or part shade. 25cm/10in. Zone 6

Ornithogalum nutans ★
The Drooping Star of Bethlehem produces slender, hyacinth-like spikes of silvery-white flowers marked with green stripes. Like bluebells, it seeds freely, and so naturalizes beneath deciduous shrubs where its bundles of leaves can collapse later in summer. 15cm/6in. Zone 6

Oxalis oregana
Wood Sorrel makes a green carpet, spangled with pink flowers in the form I know (ex Mount Stewart). Zone 7

Pachyphragma macrophyllum
(See page 73.) 30–45cm/12–18in. Zone 5

Pachysandra terminalis
Evergreen rosettes of toothed, glossy, rich-green leaves make this a highly valued carpeter for covering bare earth beneath trees or shrubs; insignificant, white flowers, scented, appear in spring. 30cm/12in. *P. t.* '**Variegata**' (See page 174.) With leaves edged cream, this is not quite so vigorous. 23cm/9in. Zone 5

Paeonia
The following peonies need a cool situation, sheltered from wind. Being single, the blooms are short-lived but so lovely they linger forever in the mind.

P. '**Avant Garde**'. (See page 109.) Zone 3
P. '**Late Windflower**'. (See page 108.) 75cm/30in. Zone 3
P. mascula **subsp.** *arietina*. Round, fat buds open large, bowl-shaped flowers sheltering the boss of yellow stamens. One established plant is a joy; a group, with flowers floating above finely cut leaves like cherry-red balloons, is enchanting from May to June. 75–90cm/60–36in. Zone 5
P. mlokosewitschii. (See pages 55 and 109.) 60cm/2ft. Zone 5

Persicaria polymorpha
A tall, columnar plant, composed of strong stems clothed in large, pointed, green leaves, topped in mid-summer with

Persicaria polymorpha

Persicaria virginiana Variegata Group

Phlox paniculata 'Norah Leigh'

Polygonatum × hybridum 'Betberg'

Polygonatum × hybridum 'Striatum'

widely branched heads of small, creamy-white flowers. By September the flowers are stained bronze-pink and green. For deep rich soil, sun or part shade, sheltered from wind. 1.8m/6ft. Zone 4

P. virginiana **Variegata Group** (syn. *Tovara filiformis*). (See page 138.) Low, branching plants are covered with large, oval leaves marbled in shades of cream and green, faintly brushed with pink. In *P. v.* **Variegata Group 'Painter's Palette'** the centre of each leaf is marked with a strong 'V' sign, which is brick-red when fresh but darkens to blackish-brown. Tiny, rat-tail wisps of little, brown flowers appear in late summer. Both plants need shelter from sun-scorch and wind. 61cm/2ft. Zone 5

Phlox

From North America come many different forms of phlox, both tall and mat forming, adapted to a wide range of conditions. Those needing semi-shade and medium to acid soil enriched with humus include the following. The prostrate forms are a delight, both for their weed-suppressing habit, and for their flowers, beautiful individually or in the mass.

P. divaricata **'Blue Dreams'**. ★ (See page 100.) Zone 4

P. maculata **'Alpha'**. Border phlox with narrow, cylindrical heads of cool-lilac-rose, sweetly scented flowers, produced in long succession from late summer well

into autumn. Needs no staking. 60–75cm/24–30in. Zone 4

P. paniculata **'Mount Fuji'**. Beautiful balanced heads of ivory-white, scented flowers. 90cm/3ft.

P. p. **'Norah Leigh'** and **'Harlequin'** (See page 138.) These variegated forms of border phlox, have violet-purple flowers, more intense in the latter. The leaves of 'Norah Leigh' are dramatically variegated, often more cream than green. Both need well-fed, retentive soil and some shade. 76cm/30in. Zone 4

P. pilosa. ★ (See page 100.) 38cm/15in. Zone 5

P. stolonifera. (See page 99.) Zone 3

Polemonium

The following are for retentive soil in light shade.

P. caeruleum. (See page 90.)

P. c. **subsp.** *caeruleum* **f.** *album* is a good, white form, in flower for weeks from late spring to late summer. 60cm/2ft. Zone 4

P. carneum. (See page 90.) 45cm/18in. Zone 4

P. **'Lambrook Mauve'**. (See page 90.) 38cm/15in. Zone 4

Polygonatum curvistylum

Slender, arching stems clothed in narrow, purple-tinted leaves carry clusters of little, mauve, bell-like flowers in June. 60cm/2ft. Zone 5

P. falcatum **'Variegatum'**. (See page 122.) Zone 4

P. × hybridum. This is the usual Solomon's Seal. Close-set, spreading rhizomes send up tall, arching stems with shining, dark-green leaves. In May they bear on the lower side of the leafy shoots white bells flushed green. 75cm/30in. Zone 4

P. × h. **'Betberg'** (See page 122.) 75–90cm/30–36in. Zone 4

P. × h. **'Striatum'** has leaves boldly striped and edged creamy-white. 60cm/2ft. Zone 4

P. multiflorum. Distinct from *P. × hybridum*, this has shorter, slightly arched stems holding closely set leaves that stand upright on the upper side to show wax-blue undersides. Beneath hang small, cream bells followed by berries, at first dark, bloom-coated green, finally almost black. 60cm/2ft. Zone 3

P. odoratum **'Silver Wings'**. (See page 122.) This selected cultivar of Solomon's Seal is distinguished by its habit of growth, having short stems set at an angle, the better to display a fringe of green-tipped, scented flowers. 45cm/18in. Zone 4

P. verticillatum. This slowly forms a slender column 90cm/3ft tall of primly erect stems, clothed at intervals with whorls of very narrow, pointed leaves. In spring clusters of small flowers hang along the upper ends, followed by small, red berries. By autumn the whole plant glows like a lamp in shades of honey and amber. Zone 4

Primula vulgaris

Primula vulgaris subsp. *sibthorpii*

Pulmonaria 'Beth's Blue'

Pratia angulata ' Treadwellii'

In cool soil this quickly spreads prostrate, creeping stems, smothered all summer with stalkless, starry, white flowers which by autumn have formed small, rose-madder berries. 5cm/2in. Zone 7

P. pedunculata. ★ Prostrate stems of tiny, green leaves hug cool, moist soil, quickly forming dense mats, sprinkled in summer with small, pale-blue, stemless flowers. *P. p.* 'County Park' has dark-gentian-blue, starry flowers. For sun or part shade, not dry soil. Zone 7

Primula ★

The following need soil that does not dry out easily.

P. denticulata. The Drumstick Primula has a large, round head of soft-lavender flowers. *P. d.* var. *alba* has yellow-eyed, white flowers and luscious, pale-green leaves. Spring. 30cm/1ft. Zone 6

P. 'Guinevere'. Pale-lilac flowers contrast with bronze-purple foliage. Spring. 15cm/6in. Zone 6

P. polyneura. Flowers are in shades of pink to wine-red over pretty, deeply crinkled leaves, scallop-edged and woolly-backed. It likes cool shade. 20cm/8in. Zone 5

P. vialii. Looking not unlike a dwarf kniphofia, the long, tapering heads of closely packed, red buds open lilac-purple-primrose-yellow flowers, making a dramatic colour combination in mid-summer. 30–45cm/12–18in. Zone 6

P. vulgaris. The common yellow primrose. *P.v.* subsp. *sibthorpii* is a pretty, pink form. Zone 5

Pulmonaria

In groups, the lungworts make excellent ground cover in moisture-retaining soil, preferring full or partial shade. Individual plants are suitable for small areas. Included here is a small selection; there is considerable variation, both from interbred seedlings and varying clones.

P. angustifolia 'Munstead Blue'. Making pools of clear, true blue, this is the shortest and the earliest to flower, with unspotted, dark-green, smallish leaves. 20cm/8in. Zone 3

P. 'Beth's Blue'. Fresh-green leaves, slightly spotted, contrast with rich-blue flowers. 25cm/10in. Zone 4

P. 'Beth's Pink'. Broad leaves, heavily spotted, and coral-red flowers. 25cm/10in. Zone 4

P. 'Blauer Hügel'. Very handsome, producing quantities of vivid, gentian-blue flowers of good size, opening wide. 45–60cm/18–24in. Zone 4

P. 'Blue Crown'. Dark reddish buds quickly change, first to purple and then intense violet-blue, held above dark-green leaves indefinitely mottled. 45cm/18in. Zone 4

P. 'Blue Ensign'. This opens wide-eyed, gentian-blue flowers. 38cm/15in. Zone 4

P. 'Glacier'. Barely pink buds open pure-white flowers. 25cm/10in. Zone 4

P. 'Little Star'. A compact plant with narrow, slightly spotted leaves and short stems of rich-blue flowers. Zone 4

P. longifolia. The flat basal rosettes form an eye-catching star shape against the soil, each dark-green, white-spotted leaf being long and narrow, tapering to a point. The latest to flower – rich blue in dense terminal clusters – last into summer. Cultivars include *P. l.* 'Ankum' (see page 139) and 'Mado' (light-blue flowers, much-spotted leaves). 30cm/1ft. Zone 4

P. 'Mawson's Blue'. Striking, dark-green leaves with taller sprays of gentian-blue flowers, flowering after *P. angustifolia* 'Munstead Blue'. 38cm/15in. Zone 4

P. 'Netta Statham'. The narrow-leaved form has spaced, pale-green spots on deeper green. Exceptionally good gentian-blue flowers are held well upright over a long period. Stems 30–40cm/12–16in. Zone 4

P. officinalis 'Blue Mist'. From Amy Doncaster, this has lavender-tinted buds that open pale-sky-blue flowers to create a soft haze of colour in early March. 15–20cm/6–8in. Zone 4

P. Opal ('Ocupol'). This forms a bouquet packed with flowering stems carrying terminal clusters of palest-blue flowers held above neat foliage, so heavily spotted it contributes to the cool, greyish tone overall. 45cm/18in. Zone 4

P. rubra. Weed-smothering clumps of

Pulmonaria 'Beth's Pink'

Pulmonaria Opal ('Ocupol')

large, light-green leaves, unspotted, are preceded in very early spring by clustered heads of coral-red, tubular flowers. 30cm/1ft. *P. r.* **'Redstart'** has coral-red flowers, without a hint of blue.

P. r. **'David Ward'** (See page 56.) This must have shade and soil that does not dry out: if exposed to sun or wind the delicate margins scorch and the leaves curl. Zone 5

P. saccharata. Leaves up to 30cm/1ft long, rough-textured, dark green, are variously marbled in silver and grey-green. Masses of blue-and-rose flowers appear in March. Other fine forms (also 30cm/1ft) include: *P. s.* **'Alba'** Large, snow-white flowers, followed by rosettes of well-marked leaves; *P. s.* **Argentea Group** Frosted-silver leaves; and *P. s.* **'Reginald Kaye'** Large, silvered spots in leaf centres, while broad borders are picked out in smaller spots. *P. s.* **'Frühlingshimmel'** (Spring Sky) is smaller, with open, bell, clear-blue flowers, maturing from pale-pink buds which contrast with reddish-brown calyces. 20–25cm/8–10in. Zone 4

P. **'Smoky Blue'** Good-sized flowers open salmon-pink changing to blue, giving overall an amethyst effect of pink sliding into blue. Still making a show in early May. Zone 4

P. **'Tim's Silver'.** The silver surface coating gives a satin sheen to the leaves, almost entirely covered, except for a fine, green rim. Flowers a good mid-blue in April to May. 30cm/1ft. Zone 4

Ranunculus ficaria 'Brazen Hussy'

Ranunculus ficaria **var.** *aurantiacus*
This single celandine has orange flowers from March to April. 7cm/3in.

R. f. **'Brazen Hussy'** (See page 44.) Has dark-brown, polished leaves. *R. f.* **subsp.** *chrysocephalus* (See page 44.) This is the largest of the celandines. 20cm/8in.

R. f. **'Coppernob'** has dark-brown leaves, similar to those of *R. f.* **'Brazen Hussy'**, set off by shining-orange flowers. 7cm/3in.

R. f. *flore-pleno* is a double, very attractive with tightly packed petals of glistening yellow, green-centred when young in April. 9cm/3½in. Zone 5

Rodgersia podophylla

Reineckea carnea
(See page 159.) 30cm/1ft. Zone 4

Rodgersia
These are among the finest foliage plants for marshy land, waterside and damp soil in woodland. They make slowly spreading rhizomes.

R. aesculifolia. (See page 141.) 1.2m/4ft. Zone 5

R. pinnata **'Superba'**.(See page 141.) 90cm/3ft. Zone 5

R. podophylla. (See page 141.) 60cm/2ft. Zone 5

Saxifraga fortunei 'Rubrifolia'

Saxifraga × *polita* 'Dentata'

Smilacina racemosa

Rubus idaeus 'Aureus'
(See page 64.) 61–76cm/24–30in. Zone 4

Saxifraga
S. exarata subsp. *moschata* 'Cloth of
Gold'. ★ Small rosettes of delicate,
golden, mossy leaves must be protected
from direct sunlight. 8cm/3in. Zone 5
S. fortunei 'Rubrifolia'. ★ A choice and
rare plant for cool soil in a sheltered
corner, this has round, varnished leaves,
bronze-red above, carmine beneath, that
form a succulent-looking clump. In
October wide sprays of white, starry
flowers stand well above on rose-pink
stems. 30cm/12in. Zone 6
S. × *geum* Dixter form. ★ (See page 95.)
38cm/15in. Zone 5
S. 'Ingeborg'. ★ This low, mossy, cushion
saxifrage, is smothered in May with
bright-ruby flowers that fade to a striped
pink, creating a pretty, two-tone effect.
15cm/6in. Zone 5
S. × *polita* 'Dentata'. ★ (See page 138.)
Evergreen rosettes of dark-green, spoon-
shaped leaves have edges that look as if
they had been cut with pinking shears.
Sprays of small, almost-white flowers
appear in May. 23cm/9in. Zone 4
S. × *urbium* 'Aureopunctata'. ★ This
variegated version of London Pride
makes attractive ground cover all year
with spreading rosettes of leathery leaves
speckled with gold. It carries sprays of
little pink flowers on 38cm/15in stems in
May. Zone 5

Symphytum 'Goldsmith'

Symphytum × *uplandicum* 'Variegatum'

Scilla bithynica ★
(See page 59.) Zone 5
S. siberica. ★ Of all the desirable forms of
scilla and chionodoxa I value the Siberian
Squill for its striking, deep-blue colour,
distinct from any other. It prefers a rich,
sandy soil where it seeds true, creating
welcome contrast of colour among
dicentras and tiarellas, sky-blue flowers
happily increasing the effect with self-
sown seedlings which colonize in thin
grass as well as in borders. Zone 5

Smilacina racemosa
(See page 89.) 75cm/30in. Zone 4

Symphytum asperum
(See page 100.) 90cm/36in. Zone 4
S. caucasicum (See page 100.) 60cm/2ft.
Zone 4
S. 'Goldsmith' (*S. grandiflorum*
'Variegatum'). Selected by that observant
plantsman Eric Smith, this cultivar makes
low mounds of dark-green leaves,
handsomely suffused with cream and
yellow. 15cm/6in. Zone 5
S. 'Hidcote Blue'. (See page 100.)
I value this comfrey and *S.* 'Hidcote
Pink' as ground cover between shrubs.
45cm/18in. Zone 4
S. ibericum. This is a most useful and
handsome plant, spreading by underground shoots to make impenetrable
weed cover in shade among shrubs. In
spring, before the new leaves are fully
developed, the fiddle-neck clusters of

Tellima grandiflora 'Purpurteppich'

Teucrium scorodonia 'Crispum Marginatum'

Thalictrum aquilegiifolium var. *album*

flowers change from burnt-orange buds to creamy-yellow bells. 30cm/12in.

S. i. **'All Gold'** has large, dock-shaped leaves, 45cm/18in long, suffused yellow when young, gradually maturing to a big, green mound. Branched stems carry lilac, tubular flowers in early to mid-summer.

S. i. **'Blaueglocken'** from Herr Pagels in north Germany, forms spreading clumps of fresh-green, heavily veined leaves. Upright, branching stems tipped with crosiers of coral-red buds open narrow, tubular flowers of light Cambridge blue. 38cm/16½in. Zone 4

S. x *uplandicum* **'Variegatum'**. Greyish green leaves are broadly margined with cream. Zone 4

Tanacetum parthenium 'Aureum' ★
Lime-yellow, finely divided foliage throughout the year is charming to grow and to pick. The sprays of tiny white daisies are produced all summer. 30cm/1ft. Zone 6

Tellima ★
All need humus-rich soil in part shade.
T. grandiflora. (See page 100.)
T. g. **Odorata Group** has scented flowers.
T. g. **'Purpurteppich'** has green bells slightly larger than *T. g.* **Rubra Group**, which is an all-the-year-round foliage plant with tall spikes of pink-fringed, green bells in early summer. 60cm/2ft. Zone 4

Thalictrum delavayi

Thalictrum kiusianum

Teucrium scorodonia 'Crispum Marginatum'
(See page 127.) 30cm/1ft. Zone 5

Thalictrum aquilegiifolium
From a basal clump of grey-green leaves, finely divided, ascend slender, purple stems, carrying pretty fans of leaves, topped with large heads of fluffy, rosy-lilac flowers in early to mid-summer. Seed heads are good, green or dried.
T. a. var. *album* is the white-flowered variety. 1.2m/4ft. Zone 5
T. delavayi. This very elegant plant needs a cool place sheltered from wind, among shrubs, for example. Small, deep-lilac flowers enclosing tufts of cream stamens dangle in airy-fairy fashion from wide, branching heads; exquisite in late summer. 1.5m/5ft. Zone 5
T. kiusianum. ★ This little, woodland plant from Japan makes sprays of tiny, rounded leaves and heads of fluffy, rosy-mauve flowers. It will thread itself through light, leaf-mould soil, or a peat bed in part shade. We grow the improved Kew form. 12–15cm/5–6in. Zone 7

Tiarella cordifolia
(See page 88.) 30cm/1ft.
T. c. **'Slick Rock'** has tiny, green, heart-shaped leaves with serrated edges that form a ground-covering carpet beneath ferns and woodland grasses. Short spires of pink buds open white, starry flowers in spring. 5cm/2in. Zone 3

Tiarella 'Ninja'

Tiarella 'Pinwheel'

Tiarella 'Tiger Stripe'

T. 'Ninja'. ★ (See page 101.)
30–38cm/12–15in. Zone 5
T. 'Pinwheel'. ★ The marked, lobed
leaves have veins lightly picked out in
dark brown. Clump-forming.
38cm/15in. Zone 5
T. 'Tiger Stripe'. ★ (See page 101.)
Clump-forming. 38cm/15in. Zone 5
T. wherryi. ★ This is a very variable plant
in the wild, and in gardens hybrid
seedlings may have occurred so a certain
amount of confusion has arisen.
T. w. 'Bronze Beauty' has maple-shaped
leaves with serrated edges showing both
pale-green and deep-reddish-bronze
colouring. Dusty-pink buds on dark
stems open palest-pink, starry flowers.
Not invasive like *T. cordifolia*, this plant
and *T.w.* **'Green Velvet'** (starry, white
flowers, but with leaves like green
shadowed velvet) make slowly spreading
clumps, flowering from May to June.
25cm/10in. Zone 6

Tolmiea menziesii
For ground cover among shrubs, this has
tiarella-like foliage and spires of small,
coppery-brown flowers. New, little plants
are formed on top of the old leaves,
which root when pressed into the soil. In
T.m. 'Taff's Gold' each leaf is lightened
by irregular freckling of green and
primrose. 30cm/1ft. Zone 7

Trachystemon orientalis
(See page 66.) Superb ground cover in
dense shade with curious, blue, borage-
like flowers on pink, naked stems in
spring, before the leaves take over.
61cm/2ft. Zone 5

Tricyrtis formosana
A fascinating plant for shady places, its
stems are clothed with corrugated, oval
leaves, topped in autumn with sprays of
small, lily-like flowers, pale purple,
freckled with dark-purple spots.

76cm/30in. A selection that is darker and
taller (90cm–1m/3–3¼ft) than the type,
produces open, branched heads closely set
with dark-stained buds and flowers,
creating in October a handsome haze of
mauve and purple tones, each upturned,
lily-like flower heavily freckled with
purple. Zone 5
T. ohsumiensis. An exotic-looking plant
for cool, shady conditions and damp, leaf-
mould soil: pairs of rich-green, pointed

Trillium chloropetalum white

Trillium cuneatum

leaves facing opposite ways are wrapped round the stem, each forming a cradle for butter-yellow, lily-like flowers 5cm/2in across, faintly peppered with red. It is lovely with the low-growing fern, *Adiantum aleuticum* 'Imbricatum'. 60cm/2ft. Zone 6

T. **'Shimone'**. Many stems clothed in deeply veined, pointed leaves carry a profusion of upturned, white flowers lightly speckled with purple, creating a lilac effect, remaining good in mid-November. 90cm/3ft. Zone 5

T. **'Tojen'**. Branched, arching, purple stems, clothed in rich-green, deeply veined leaves, in September carry multitudes of unspotted flowers which open wide, mauve-tipped petals to show a white centre marked with yellow dots. Up to 1m/40in. Zone 5

T. **'White Towers'**. Green, felted leaves are set alternately along 75cm/30in stems. Each leaf base holds short-stemmed buds, opening unspotted creamy-white flowers with a yellow ring at the base of the petals. Zone 5

Trillium ★

These choice plants are suitable as feature plants in small shady areas in soil that does not dry out.

T. chloropetalum. (See page 82.) 38cm/15in. Zone 5

T. cuneatum. Making effective contrast above mat-forming plants, large, triangular leaves variously marbled in shades of green are centred with short, narrow, purple-stained calyces and stemless, wine-coloured petals fiercely upright. Seedlings vary considerably in size, leaf colour and flower quality. 30–38cm/12–15in. Zone 5

T. grandiflorum. (See page 82.) The White Wake Robin. 38cm/15in. Zone 4

T. rivale. (See page 84.) Zone 6

T. sessile. (See page 82.) 15cm/6in. Zone 4

Uvularia grandiflora ★

(See page 85.) 38–46cm/15–18in.

U. g. **var.** *pallida* is a choice treasure. 46cm/18in. Zone 5

U. perfoliata. ★ This comes into flower as *U. grandiflora* is fading. 30cm/1ft. Zone 5

Vancouveria chrysantha ★

(See page 99.) 30cm/1ft. Zone 6

V. hexandra. (See page 99.) 45cm/18in. Zone 5

Vinca

The periwinkles make excellent evergreen ground cover in shade. Mulch with peat or crushed bark to check weeds until ground cover is formed.

V. major **'Variegata'**. This beautiful, variegated form, boldly splashed with cream and gold, spreads by runners. 46cm/18in. Zone 6

V. minor **f.** *alba*. Small leaves marbled light and dark green set off white flowers in spring and early summer. 20cm/8in.

V. m. **'Argenteovariegata'** has small leaves variegated green and white on dwarfed plants, and pale-blue flowers. 15cm/6in.

V. m. **'Atropurpurea'** has plum-purple, single flowers. 20cm/8in.

V. m. **'La Grave'** (See page 66.) 20cm/8in. Zone 4

Viola ★

Violas do not like being scorched; the

following thrive in cool but not too shady conditions. They do best in retentive soil enriched with a little humus.

V. cornuta. (See page 149.)

V. c. **Alba Group** has a long succession of chalk-white flowers in spring and early summer with a late flush in autumn.

V. c. **Lilacina Group** makes moundy mats of fresh-green foliage covered with lilac flowers on very long stalks.

V. c. **Purpurea Group** has dark-purple-blue or violet-coloured flowers. 15cm/6in. Zone 5

V. gracilis. Above tidy mounds of foliage float a profusion of pansy-violets of deep-purple velvet in early summer. 15cm/6in. Zone 5

V. riviniana **Purpurea Group**. This makes a running mass of small, dark-purple leaves which set off the quantities of light-coloured, scentless flowers. Beautiful with Bowles' Golden Grass and snowdrops. 15cm/6in. Zone 5

V. septentrionalis. (See page 61.) 15cm/6in. Zone 4

V. sororia **'Freckles'**. Pale-blue ground freckled with purple spots in early spring. 13cm/5in. Zone 4

Uvularia grandiflora var. *pallida*

Vinca minor 'La Grave'

Asplenium scolopendrium Undulatum Group

Polypodium interjectum 'Cornubiense'

Blechnum penna-marina subsp. *alpinum*

Polystichum setiferum Plumosodivisilobum Group

FERNS

Shady places make the best sites for ferns, many of which I describe on pages 102–7.

***Adiantum aleuticum* 'Imbricatum'** ★
Black, wiry stems carry five or seven fronds threaded with tiny pinnae arranged like the fingers of a hand. 7–15cm/3–6in. Zone 3
A. pedatum. ★ (See page 106.) 38cm/15in. Zone 3
A. venustum. (See page 106.) Zone 4

Asplenium scolopendrium ★
The Hart's Tongue Fern has broad, undulating, strap-shaped leaves that provide contrast to the feathery ferns or rounded leaves of hostas.
***A. s.* Undulatum Group** has crimped margins to the leaves. 30cm/1ft. Zone 4

Athyrium filix-femina
The Lady Fern has a lace-like delicacy, preferring moist soil but will make do with less. Can grow to 1m/3¼ft plus according to conditions.
***A. f.-f.* 'Minutissimum'** ★ forms slowly increasing, dense clumps of small, lacy, typical fern leaves, attractive for edges of shady borders with a blue-leaved hosta and Golden Creeping Jenny. Zone 4

***A. niponicum* var. *pictum*.** (See page 107.) 30cm/1ft. Zone 7

Blechnum penna-marina* subsp. *alpinum ★
Creeping rhizomes produce crowds of small, ladder-shaped fronds. 25cm/10in. Zone 6

Cystopteris fragilis ★
Low, dense clumps of wiry stems carry dainty, lace-like foliage. It makes a compact edging plant, producing a succession of new growth when the weather turns cooler or damper. 25cm/10in. Zone 2

Dryopteris affinis (*D. pseudomas*)
(See page 102.) Although vigorous, this fern varies in height according to conditions. 60cm–1.5m/2–5ft. Zone 4
D. dilatata. A robust fern for naturalizing in woodland, this has dark-green, broad-based fronds on bright-green stalks. 1m/40in. Zone 3
D. erythrosora. (See page 103.) 45cm/18in. Zone 5
D. filix-mas. (See page 102.) 90cm/36in. Zone 3
D. wallichiana. (See page 104.) 1–1.5m/3–5ft. Zone 6

Matteuccia struthiopteris
(See page 104.) 90cm/3ft. Zone 2

Polypodium interjectum 'Cornubiense'
(See page 102.) 30cm/1ft. Zone 5

Polystichum aculeatum
In spring the unfurling fronds of the Hard Shield Fern curl over backwards like reversed crosiers, then form a perfect shuttlecock shape of fresh, glossy, daintily cut plumes from the centre of the previous year's ruff of overwintered, leathery fronds. 75cm/30in. Zone 4
P. setiferum Acutilobum Group. This variant of the Soft Shield Fern has narrow, daintily set fronds of great elegance. It grows almost anywhere not too dry, but luxuriates in cool, semi-shade. Usually 60cm/2ft, it grows taller in damp climates.
P. s. (Divisilobum Group) 'Dahlem' Individual upright, elegant fronds may exceed 90cm/3ft.
P. s. (Divisilobum Group) 'Herrenhausen' has more finely cut fronds that lie more horizontally, creating a large rosette of exquisite, lacy design that is perfect by the edge of a shady walk. Up to 75cm/30in.
P. s. Plumosodivisilobum Group is one of the very feathery forms, with each overlapping segment so frilled and fluted that the frond has a parsley-like effect in bright green. The back shows the strong mid-rib, heavily 'furred' with pale, chestnut-brown scales. 60cm/2ft. Zone 5

GRASSES AND GRASS-LIKE PLANTS

It is important not to divide grasses in autumn. The golden rule is to divide and replant in spring. The following grow in part shade.

Calamagrostis arundinacea
(See page 150.) 45cm/18in. Zone 5

Hakonechloa macra 'Aureola' ★
This makes soft clumps of foliage about 30cm/2ft high, each ribbon-like leaf vividly variegated gold and buff with touches of bronze. In good soil the leaves can be 60cm/2ft long but they arch over into overlapping mounds, about 45cm/18in wide. Zone 4

Holcus mollis 'Albovariegatus'
Creeping rhizomes carry tufts of soft leaves with broad, white margins centred by a narrow, green strip, giving the effect of a white carpet in spring, and again when new growth appears in autumn. Although invasive, it is easily dislodged. 15cm/6in. Zone 5

Luzula nivea ★
This graceful woodrush has wide sprays of tiny, parchment-coloured flowers in mid-summer, providing pretty contrast with ferns and violets. 45cm/18in. Zone 5
L. sylvatica 'Aurea'. Broad-bladed leaves of overall golden-yellow form arching clumps that command attention, especially in winter. Easy in any soil, but

best in retentive soil, in the open or part shade. 30cm/1ft. *L. s.* 'Marginata' forms dense tufts of rich-green leaves edged with white, and produces drooping sprays of gold-and-brown spikelets in early summer. 45cm/18in. Zone 6

Melica uniflora f. *albida* ★
(See page 95.) 45–60cm/18–24in.
M. u. 'Variegata' makes tuffets of narrow, ribbon-like leaves, striped cream and green, with a dainty, curving habit that contrasts with the green rosettes of *Saxifraga* × *polita* 'Dentata'. 30cm/1ft. Zone 5

Milium effusum 'Aureum' ★
(See page 69.) 38cm/15in. Zone 5

Phalaris arundinacea var. *picta* 'Feesey'
Clumps of white or green stems carry ribbon-shaped leaves beautifully striped, more white than green, faintly flushed pink when young. This is less invasive as the usual form of Gardener's Garters. 75cm/30in. Zone 4

Pleioblastus auricomus
The loveliest dwarf bamboo has fluttering, ribbon-shaped leaves, rich yellow, sometimes lightly pencilled with green. It looks freshest and best on new canes: cut the old ones to the ground each spring and dress with well-rotted compost. Up to 1.2m/4ft. Zone 7

Hakonechloa macra 'Aureola'

MECHANICAL EQUIPMENT FOR TREE SURGERY

Two people undertake the technical work in my garden. Gerard is in charge. He has passed his certificate of competence in chainsaw operations; his assistant Ben has been on a course on operating chainsaws. We all inspect the trees needing attention, then Gerard works in the cage, with Ben on the ground to give advice, if required, and to load the branches on to the tractor or Gator, a small four-wheeled track. Gerard wears all the right clothing for safety – including saw-proof trousers and helmet – and a harness to attach himself to the cage bars.

Taken at the time of writing (2002), the figures below give some idea of the basic cost of hiring equipment plus operators. In gardens or estates with staff trained in the use of power-operated machines, it is more economical to operate the equipment oneself. However one goes about it, Health and Safety recommendations must be followed.

NIFTYLIFT 120

From a small platform-base, a battery-powered hoist lifts a metal cage 12m/42ft into the air. It has two wheels and five jack legs, which must be fixed securely at level ground or there is a risk of tipping. It needs to be moved around by a tractor with turf tyres. Hire cost per day: £52.00 plus VAT and delivery charge.

NIFTYLIFT 170

A larger machine than the 120, this has an alarm system which prevents the machine from working if it is not level and stabilized. Working height 17m/56ft; will reach 18m/59ft. Hire cost per day: £140.00 plus VAT and delivery charge.

PEGASUS AT46

Similar to Niftylift 120 but this machine is self-propelled by a diesel engine, using dumper truck mechanics. Hire cost per day: £100.00 plus VAT and delivery charge.

WOLF MULTI STAR PRUNER ZM-V4

Adjustable reach, 2.2–4m/7–13ft. Includes RE-PRU, a 35cm/14in pruning saw, and RC-VM, an adjustable lopper-head, both locked in place with a push-button device.

FURTHER READING

Bishop, Matt, Aaron Davis and John Grimshaw *Snowdrops*, The Griffin Press 2002

Booth, Michael Haworth *The Hydrangeas*, Constable 1950

Chatto, Beth 'A Painter's Palette' (on Cedric Morris) in *Gardens of Inspiration* (ed. Erica Hunningher), BBC Worldwide and Dorling Kindersley (USA) 2001

Beth Chatto's Gravel Garden, Frances Lincoln and Viking (USA) 2000

Hansen, Richard, and Friedrich Stahl *Perennials and their Garden Habits*, Cambridge University Press, English translation 1993

Hillier's Manual of Trees and Shrubs (5th ed., 1981), David and Charles

The RHS Plant Finder 2001-2002 (2001), Dorling Kindersley

Lloyd, Christopher *The Well-Tempered Garden*, Cassell 2001

Mathew, Brian *Dwarf Bulbs*, Batsford 1973

Phillips, Roger, and Martyn Rix *Shrubs*, Pan 1989
Bulbs, Pan 1981

Thomas, Graham Stuart *Ornamental Shrubs, Climbers and Bamboos*, John Murray 1992
Perennial Garden Plants, Dent 1993
Plants for Ground-Cover, Dent 1977

RAINFALL FIGURES

Year	Winter (Oct–Mar)		Summer (April–Sept)		Totals	
	CM	IN	CM	IN	CM	IN
1970/71	32.99	12.99	21.29	8.38	54.28	21.37
1971/72	34.77	13.69	13.94	5.49	48.72	19.18
1972/73	10.41	4.1	27.36	10.77	37.77	14.87
1973/74	13.87	5.46	21.79	8.58	35.66	14.04
1974/75	37.77	14.87	24.51	9.65	62.28	24.52
1975/76	19.89	7.83	20.85	8.21	40.74	16.04
1976/77	31.42	12.37	21.72	8.55	53.14	20.92
1977/78	27.71	10.91	29.51	11.62	57.23	22.53
1978/79	35.36	13.92	23.50	9.25	58.85	23.17
1979/80	31.27	12.31	28.52	11.23	59.79	23.54
1980/81	30.20	11.89	28.22	11.11	58.45	23.01
1981/82	38.18	15.03	20.52	8.08	58.70	23.11
1982/83	37.16	14.63	27.71	10.91	64.87	25.54
1983/84	23.98	9.44	23.34	9.19	47.32	18.63
1984/85	28.80	11.34	28.07	11.05	56.87	22.39
1985/86	25.25	9.94	24.38	9.6	49.63	19.54
1986/87	25.96	10.22	41.94	16.51	67.89	26.73
1987/88	39.24	15.45	23.37	9.2	62.61	24.65
1988/89	22.30	8.78	21.06	8.29	43.36	17.07
1989/90	27.03	10.64	18.36	7.23	45.39	17.87
1990/91	26.49	10.43	24.79	9.76	51.28	20.19
1991/92	16.69	6.57	35.26	13.88	51.94	20.45
1992/93	27.20	10.71	29.92	11.78	57.12	22.49
1993/94	40.11	15.79	28.30	11.14	68.40	26.93
1994/95	39.47	15.54	16.59	6.53	56.06	22.07
1995/96	20.14	7.93	16.31	6.42	36.45	14.35
1996/97	23.98	9.44	26.75	10.53	50.72	19.97
1997/98	28.04	11.04	33.99	13.38	62.03	24.42
1998/99	34.80	13.7	29.77	11.72	64.57	25.42
1999/00	23.47	9.24	31.90	12.56	55.40	21.81
2000/01	59.49	23.42	37.26	14.67	96.75	38.09
Average	28.27	11.13	26.41	10.40	55.30	21.77

Index

Page numbers in *italic* refer to the illustrations and captions

Author's acknowledgements

This book is the result of good teamwork. First I would like to acknowledge the contribution of my Staff. Without their devoted care the gardens and nursery could not exist. Every member, whether in the garden, nursery, office or tea-room is important. We rely on each other, as links in a chain, whether producing plants, grooming the garden, dealing with enquiries or offering refreshment, for body and mind. Everyone is involved in a very personal way in helping maintain a way of life, which we share with our visitors whose appreciation and support provides the final, vital link.

Much unseen work is involved in preparing a gardening book for publication. Writing it seems to me, is only the beginning. I am most fortunate to have Erica Hunningher as my sensitive editor. Like a skilled midwife she takes on the task of delivering her author's work, with the clear-sighted ability to prune and reshape where there is too much clutter, thus letting in the light on my intentions.

Tricia Brett, my secretary, business manager and PA, typed the copy from my handwritten script and zealously checked the latest Latin names, while Tony Lord, editor of *The Plantfinder*, gave us his final decision on plant nomenclature. Chrissy McDonald drew and painted the garden plan on pages 12 to 13.

I would like to express my appreciation of the way Nigel Soper has designed my book, achieving a comfortable balance between text and pictures.

Steven Wooster brings the eye of an artist to the camera lens, finding beauty in the unexpected as well as capturing fleeting moments that come only once. Every year the garden develops and changes, nothing is repeated exactly.

More than fifty years ago I began gardening as an amateur, unaware of the endless interest and possibilities that lay ahead. At that time reading was the entrance into other peoples' gardens, and I read hungrily the writings of Margery Fish and E. A. Bowles, and later, as I found them, books by Gertrude Jekyll and William Robinson. There were few illustrations, all in black and white, allowing the imagination of the reader to paint the words in colour. As my vocabulary of garden plants grew, I think I read these books as a conductor reads the pages of a music score, sitting in a silent room, hearing the symphony in his head. Much as I value and admire the high standard of garden photography today, I am grateful for those years when I read, and re-read, without distractions, the experiences of the great gardeners of the past, realizing how much that we do today has been done and written in great detail before us. But as my old friend Cedric Morris said when we were discussing this fact, 'We may all have similar palettes but we all paint different pictures.' We all have freedom of choice.

Some of my best-used books of today are included in 'Further Reading' on page 214.

Photographer's note

Beth's woodland garden was looking great when I started taking pictures in April 1999 but Beth wanted a month-by-month record so I was anxious about how it would be looking in July and August, which are difficult months for any garden photography, when many of the plants have 'done-their-stuff' and are starting to look tired and lifeless. On my first few visits I concentrated on getting 'scene setters' of the garden as a whole. This was helped greatly by a fantastic display of forget-me-nots in 1999 (obviously a vintage year as they have never quite reached this pinnacle since). Over the course of the following three years I visited the gardens between thirty and forty times. I would walk with Beth around the gardens and she would show me the plants that she wanted photographed (generally a list of Latin names in spidery writing on a piece of cardboard!). It did prove invaluable, though, as it made me focus on plants that I would otherwise have overlooked, as I seem to be drawn to the obvious rather than the 'enchanting horticultural delight'. There was always something to photograph, no matter what time of year. As the woodland gardens are fairly sheltered there was never much frost to speak of, which is sad, as this is always a photogenic treat.

I found in general that the garden looked best through the camera in golden evening light as opposed to the very blue morning light that is difficult to correct, even with filtering. For the technophiles, in general the landscape and scenic pictures were taken on medium format and the plant details and close-ups on 35mm with a macro lens. Panoramic pictures were taken with a Hasselblad XPan – great for creating a different look and for making me think differently about the pictures I am trying to achieve. A colour meter also proved invaluable.